GOING POSTAL

An Immersive Narrative as a Mailman

Tom Spallone

Publisher's Cataloging-In-Publication Data
(Prepared by The Donohue Group, Inc.)

Names: Spallone, Tom, author.
Title: Going postal : an immersive narrative as a mailman / Tom Spallone.
Description: [First edition]. | [Boca Raton, Florida] : Manticore Press LLC, 2021. | Includes bibliographical references.
Identifiers: ISBN 9781736291832 (paperback) | ISBN 9781736291863 (ebook)
Subjects: LCSH: Spallone, Tom. | Letter carriers--United States--Biography. | Postal service--United States. | Epidemics--History--21st century. | COVID-19 (Disease)--Social aspects. | LCGFT: Creative nonfiction. | Autobiographies.
Classification: LCC HE6385.S63 A3 2021 (print) | LCC HE6385.S63 (ebook) | DDC 383.4973--dc23

This is a work of creative non-fiction. No incidents described in these pages were fictionalized, although embellishments have been made in certain circumstances in the interest of creative license. Every name mentioned are creations of the author's imagination.

Every effort has been made to trace or contact all copyright holders when necessary. The publisher will be pleased to make good any omissions or rectify any mistakes brought to their attention at the earliest opportunity.

First paperback edition February 2021

Book cover design by Milan Jovanovic
Chameleonstudio74 via 99Designs

Published by Manticore Press LLC
Info@manticorepressllc.com

For
Frank & Marie
Spallone

Contents

Chapter 1 – Some Imagination

I stared in disbelief at the blood pulsating from what used to be my right arm just below the elbow. I could clearly see bone, tenons, gristle, muscle and,..Blood…lots of blood. How could I still be standing? Surely I've lost enough blood to take down even the most determined of us. It must be shock.

The monster either finished with, or was bored of, mashing my detached right hand and forearm and was about to charge. I turned to run back to the truck but, it was on me. I had no chance. Heavy on my back, breath filled with hot moisture, nails digging-in at whatever it could, I went down. Being right handed, of course I tried to break my fall with my right…stump. That didn't go well. My face hit the pavement hard. The beast was prone for the kill. I heard a final snort before his fanged, gaping mouth lurched toward my throat. I pictured Quint just before the shark made his final bite at mid torso and ended his struggle as they both slipped off the boat, quietly into the deep.

This is what I imagined as I stood in the street with my black shoes and whites socks and bubble-padded Amazon package in my hand, staring at the largest dog ever known to exist. It stood in the neighbor's yard, stoic and still and stared at me questioningly.

All I had to do was cross the street and the front yard (which I surmised was the distance of about fifteen feet), scan the parcel and drop it at the front door. That's it. Nothing more. But, could I make it? The dog stood guard even though it was a neighbor dog. Still, something about the Postal uniform, or more specifically, the hat, that set dogs off. The mongrel's owner was useless as he struggled with something under a jacked-up car in the front yard of what can only respectfully be referred to as a slum. I can't count on him to act as interference to the potential attack. He'd probably encourage it.

No, I'm on my own. Que Ennio Morricone soundtrack with visions of a dusty western town where two stood in duel, waiting for each other to twitch so the other can draw; we stared at each other. I'm still safe, I thought. I can surely beat the thing to the other side of the truck and get in and that's that. Unless he eats the truck but, that's not very likely. I figured, let me take just one careful step and see what happens. On the other hand, I've heard it said, when it concerns dogs, that one should show no fear and just bound toward your destination like you own the place.

Nahh, the one careful step sounds like a better plan. If he reacts, I can beat it back to the safety of the truck. I took a step. Nothing. No movement, no sound. Hmm, there goes THAT plan. Another step? I guess so. I can't stand here all day. There's a clock. My god there's always that clock, relentlessly and unforgivingly ticking. Tick, tick, tick....each second that I stand here makes the rest of the day (should I survive it) harder. It's not about it being a hard day though. It's not about what kind of morning you had or afternoon or, a tough customer giving you a hard time; it's about each second! Tick, tick, tick. Each one clicks off in the head with a heavy beat. Each one a reminder that,…you've fallen behind! And if I've learned one thing, it's that you can NEVER get back time. Once it's gone, it's gone forever. Another second goes by; (tick), gone! Another one (tick), gone!

I take another step while eyeing the beast. Wait, should I be looking at him or should I ignore him? What's the proper protocol when dealing with wild animals? Wild animal, domestic pet…what's the difference?! I took yet another step and the canine didn't budge. It made me worry even more. What kind of dumb animal doesn't even react to a human walking semi-toward its territory? Is it insane? It makes me even more concerned.

Ok, I'm reaching the point of no return now. If I go any further and he charges, I may not be able to get back to the truck. Dog spray. That's it, I've got dog spray. What did they tell me in training? Use your mail bag to block the attack and spray the pepper spray right in the dog's face. Well, I don't have a mail bag. I guess they forgot to give me one and the spray…oops, it's in the truck. Brilliant! Another step. Nothing. Ok, plan C. I'll scan the package now, here in the street, to save time (even though, I'm not supposed to do that), I'll get close to the door and fling the parcel. Ok, sounds good. BUT, what if "flinging" it causes the dog to react like most do to the action of throwing something? Hmm, well, perhaps if it goes for the package, it won't go for me. That's the plan, let go.

Scanned - beep, delivered – beep, location – front door – beep. I marched toward the door and for a second, I started nervous whistling like this is no big deal and then thought, "Asshole, you're whistling and you're trying to be invisible to a dog?!" I put my pucker away. I got about 6 feet from the door and frisbeed it. Not being as aerodynamic as a Frisbee, it landed about three feet from the door. "Close enough for government work", I thought, and I turned and marched back toward the truck. Surprisingly, I didn't hear the nails of the animal scraping on pavement in full charge. I gave a casual glance back over my shoulder and saw that it stood in the same place as when I first encountered it. Not moving. I'm good. I can get back to the truck, no problem. I get in and slide the heavy metal door closed and assess the situation. The dog lost interest (if he had any) and walked slowly toward the a sun-bathed area of the yard and clumsily dropped to a napping position.

Look at ya, worried about being mauled by THAT thing! Why, he's just a big, lazy puppy dog. Don't you feel silly, with your throat torn out and you trying to cram your upper intestines back into the gaping hole that he was about to make? Pfft, no problem. I started the truck and put it in drive, slowly moving down the desolated road to my next destination as I reach for the dog spray and attach it to my belt. Just in case.

Chapter 2 – Ten Points

It began simply enough. Always looking for the next thing, Maria (my life partner) said, "why don't you apply to the post office?". The audio/visual and music gigs had dried up during the holiday season and, why not?, I thought, it's a part-time gig (allowing me to pursue my interests in music and writing) and, it doesn't seem too intense. And, it certainly satisfies one of my reasons for eschewing the surly bonds of corporate life in New York and starting over in south Florida where I can get out from behind a desk and get some sun in my face and a little sweat on my skin and maybe shed a few pounds and really start to get some things done.

"I just applied myself, yesterday." she said, "I'll send you the link." And so, the journey began. I found the link in my phone and followed it to the job description. Part-time letter carrier assistant in Deerfield Beach, Fl, it read. Hmm, not bad, right down the road. My main concern over the job description was that I certainly didn't want to be one of those counter people. I'm not standing there behind a counter, weighing packages and asking if you need stamps. Not that there's anything wrong with the job itself mind you, it's just not for me. Dealing with the public on a one-to-one basis like that is not my forte'. Being left completely alone to complete a job, now THAT'S in my wheelhouse. Walking from house to house and shoving some envelopes into a mailbox sounds pretty good at this point. I figure that I'd do it for a while and, always looking for a good subject matter to write about, I'd put pen to paper, as it were, and document the daily activities of a mailman. I was assuming the daily antics would be varied and amusing.

What I was not prepared for, however, was that the daily antics would take a back-seat to the jobs existence itself. It quickly became apparent to me that all is not what it appears with the United States Postal Service. The process it follows, the working environment, the varied people it hires and the reasons they stay on the job, the history, the reason for the job itself, became the muse and the desire to document it.

I'll do an insider view, I thought; an immersive journalistic account of the life of a mail carrier. Get in, write about it, and get out. I mentioned the idea of this project to a friend of mine and he said, "I've dealt with the Post Service for over twenty years and trust me, there's no book it!". He may be right but, my creative personality dictates the need to have another purpose to what might be considered a boring existence. And furthermore, playing devil's advocate, "You're going to write a book about putting envelopes into mail boxes?". Well, just about anything can be minimized down to an uninteresting and useless endeavor. There are no small parts, only small actors, it's been said. I certainly can attest to seeing many books in existence where the first thought was, "Somebody wrote a book about this?" And yet, there it is, on the shelf in Barnes & Noble or, available in multiple formats from Amazon. I confess to reading and enjoying a book written about a single truck, long distance moving business. You know, you put the heavy stuff into the truck first and make sure you wrap the delicate stuff properly so as to avoid breakage. And don't forget to do proper maintenance on your truck. That sort of thing. So, if THAT exists…

And true enough, should I actually have what I suspect is a mild case of attention deficit disorder, keeping a journal may just fill the void of excruciating boredom on an operation like this. But first, I have to get the job. No easy task really. I do remember once applying for a position as a letter carrier shortly after leaving my stint in the Navy. I never heard back from them. That was about thirty five years ago. Would it be easier now? I can't imagine it would be. There IS the age thing. But, there isn't supposed to be any age (or other) discrimination happening in this, and all workplaces these days so, let's see what happens. I'm physically fit enough, I thought. But let's face it, what does it really take to shove an envelope into a mail box? The requirements are such that I certainly can fulfil the occupational requirements.

I started filling out the application online. The job description did say that the application would only be considered if it was processed along with test results from the specific postal test. But, also in the job posting it had stated that all vacancies to take the test were already filled. I suppose that, should the candidates who actually took and passed the test and satisfy all other requirements, and were either dismissed or left of their own accord, would create a void, and then other applicants would then be allowed to take the test. Who's to say at this point? I'll just go with the application process and see what happens.

I completed the application and submitted it. Almost instantly I received an email verification that they have received my application and an additional email explaining what I needed to do in order to take the test. Hmm, that's odd; Maria applied the day before and only received verification that her application was received, but, no further information concerning a test. The only thing that we could figure was that I was a veteran and perhaps was automatically directed to the test taking area because of it. On the application there was an area where one could, if applicable, indicate that one was of a veteran's status. Of course I did that. It looks like veterans get an additional tens points added to the test results. They get even more if you're a disabled veteran. Sweet deal, I thought. Not the best test taker, I could use all the help I could get. Because I was claiming "veteran's status" I needed to provide proof, of course, of that status and needed to provide my DD-214.

U.S. Form DD-214, Certificate of Release or Discharge from Active Duty, is a report of separation and generally issued when a service member performs active duty in the United States Military service and contains such information as: Date and place of entry into active duty, home address at time of entry, date and place of release from active duty, home address after separation, last duty assignment and rank, military job specialty, military education, decorations, medals, badges, citations and campaign awards received, total creditable service, foreign service credited, separations information (date and type of separation, character of service, authority and reason for separation and separation and reenlistment eligibility codes). Basically, it's a military transcript, a resume and proof of service. Any veteran knows the importance of this document. I have a copy of mine laminated and stowed with all other important documentation as well as scanned as a pdf and is always at the ready should anyone ask for it. I attached it with my application and, as I've said, I assume that it was the driving force in determining who goes to the next step and who doesn't.

I took a cursory look at the test email and decided that I would put it off a day and take the test the next morning as, I work best in the morning. The test consisted of basic psychological probes consisting of, "What would you do in this situation?" or, "Give the best answer to the following question.", where the situation in question simulated life experiences. Oddly, the test didn't contain aptitude driven queries. Nothing like, "A package that you need to deliver is ticking. What would you do?", or perhaps a quick dyslexia check like, "There needs to be a pickup at 1800 S. 18st at 1300 and you go to 1300 N. 13st at 1800. What do you do?" Nothing like that. So, what is this test for, comprehension? Is it a test for possible aggressive tendencies which one can psychologically analyze by a pattern of answers?

"Nope, this guy answered "A" too many times. Clearly he has antigovernment tendencies and should be placed on a watch list?"

I completed the exam and saw that I received a score of 100. I figured, with my additional 10 point veterans bonus points, I'm looking at a final score of 110! Doing a quick analyses of the situation and in trying to determine who might be chosen for the job, I assess myself and consider; White, Male, Veteran, English speaking, Physically capable, 110 score! Who can be a more attractive candidate? Perhaps the disabled veteran who gets the extra points could be but, I wonder if the disability (depending on what it is we're talking about) doesn't satisfy the physical demands of the job, then I'm an apparent front runner, in my mind. And I only mention the White and Male part because, those two things supposedly garnish a preference or privilege, or so I'm told. Let's hope so in this case.

I quickly received notification that the test was accepted and that I'd be hearing from them soon as to what actions to take next. This seemed too easy. Especially considering that Maria, who is bi-lingual, and in my opinion, more qualified to do the job as, being in south Florida, being able to speak Spanish is not only a plus, but almost a necessity. Still, it did seem to be moving a bit unencumbered. And when things go too smoothly, I tend to become suspicious.

I began to forecast a starting point. It was mid-December. Surely nothing is happening until the new year. Just as well. Who starts a job the last week of the year? I put it out of my head and went about my business.

About a week later I receive notification from someone at a central location (I'm assuming what can be considered a Human Resource contact) that, while I've claimed Veterans Preference on my application, I don't actually qualify. I've been semi-aware of this situation previously but, as I've said, the application simply asked me if I was a veteran and the answer is, yes, yes I am. I've got the DD-214 to prove it. Turns out that it isn't that simple and there needs to be more in the way of qualification to garnish that sweet 10 points.

I read the list of qualifying attributes in order to receive those 10 points and, the take-away is that, unless I was at Pearl Harbor or single handedly arrested and killed Osama Bin Laden, I ain't gettin' no 10 points! I can get 10% off at Lowes and Home Depot but, no thank you for any additional benefit when applying for a government job. So much for that malarkey that the recruiter spouted, oh, so many years ago. Ok, I thought, I still have the 100. But, I tried to at least have it on record that, while I wasn't claiming a veterans preference, I still am a veteran! I mean, it's on the resume. And, frankly, for a government job such as Postal worker, don't you think it should have SOME merit? Not a stranger to bullshitting my way into a variety of jobs, I feel that it's incumbent on the potential candidate to use as much leverage as they've got to gain attention. And that's what I tried to do. In any case, I continued the process without the extra 10 points. In my fantastical mind I sort of felt that, because of my veterans status, they might give me preference with some sort of sweet route and leave the harder ones to those of less....privilege. Yet another ridiculous assertion on my part I found out later.

Waited another week before I hear anything else. When I did, it was an email directing me to go to a lab for a drug test. So as to not delay any further, I went and had the blood drawn the next day. And then I waited some more. About a week later, I received a call from someone at the actual post office where the job description indicated. He said I should come in to finish up some paperwork. I had been out driving around and running errands and not dressed appropriately but I said I could come in, in about an hour. I went home and prettied myself up.

I had been given the address on the phone and told where to go when I arrived. I parked and walked up to the Post Office loading dock where I saw a sign that read, "Postal Employees only. No trespassing". I rang the bell and waited for what seemed like a long time. A man came to the door an pushed it open. "I'm here to see Bill Wegman." No response. He just turned and retreated back into the building. No, "You must be Tom Spallone, nice to meet you! No greeting, no verbal acknowledgment whatsoever. Great, I thought, here we go again with the social hiccups. Bill turned out to be a nice guy however. He was acting Postmaster for the Deerfield Beach district, which operated two locations, one on either side of Rt. 95. We were at the annex location. The east side location was more of a standard Post Office that most people are familiar with.

Bill told me that there were just some things we needed to go over before the processing could be complete. Complete, I thought? Did I get the job? I wasn't really sure what was going on. Of course, I'd been in the private, corporate sector for so long that, I sort of got used to a certain way that a hiring and onboarding process took place. This was none of that. That surprised me because I figured that the Postal Service was in alignment with a military type of execution. For all the military's false, it does run on a previously determined schedule to the minute. Ask any veteran what time it is and they could probably tell you without looking at a clock and be within ten minutes at any time of the day. Just like they instruct police and fire personnel to know the compass rose and to know your positioning within it while in a building and to know the closest egress; veterans always know what time it. Because, whatever time it is, that's the scheduled time to be doing, what you're doing.

I sat in Bill's office and he said that he's waiting for Joe to come in. A dual interview. Everybody loves that. Joe came in and introduced himself to me with a firm handshake. We sat and it occurred to me that there are three bald, white guys sitting in the room. Is that why I'm being hired, I thought. Did they need another bald guy for the team?

Bill talked to me while referring to his computer screen. He rattled off questions that I know I've answered at least twice previously during the application process. Am I a citizen of the United States? What's my address, my social security number, etc.? Am I willing to work overtime?

Overtime, I thought, for a part-time job? I asked about it. I was told, "Oh, this is no part-time job. Actually you'll be looking for days off!". Hmm, what's THAT all about? Ok, I thought, let's continue. Are you able to work some weekends? "Sure", I said. I got a real bad feeling as I uttered that simple four letter word. But, I figured, working on weekends must be the overtime thing he was referring to. I'm sure that the Post Office needs occasional extra help at times and, I'm sure that they need extra help to come in on the odd Saturday to catch up during busy times. That's what I figured. Bill mentioned "Amazon Sunday" and that there'd be the need to work a Sunday every four weeks or so. Ok, I suppose. And, I thought, a Sunday, that's got to be time and a half pay, at least. Sweet!

The questioning continued with more standard questions like, if I'm able to stand and walk for long periods of time without the need of mechanical means. Again, my thoughts of the disabled veteran comes mind. If you're disabled, you get extra points on the test BUT, if you're disabled, you won't be physically able to perform the duties of the job. Catch-22.

I interjected with my own questions. You know, the way you're supposed to during an interview, if that's what this is. I asked both of them how long they've been on the job. Both in excess of 30 years. Joe said he used to work at the Manhattan office on 34th street. I mentioned that I was from New York as well and

Bill interjected, “Everyone here is from New York!”. Bill, himself, hailing from Long Island. Joe, a real straight shooter and very nice guy said, “People don’t really understand what a mail carrier job is”. As if reading my mind he said, “It isn’t just shoving envelopes into metal boxes.” I expressed sympathy that, I was sure there was more to it than that. Truer words were never spoken.

In conclusion, Bill asked if I had any further questions. Going back to the fact that apparently this is no longer a part-time position, I asked about if health benefits were provided. Frankly, in my simple mind, even at a part-time level, I figured that an employee of the United States Government, who goes on private citizen’s private property in rain, snow, heat and ice,…dogs, would be covered to the teeth with no or little cost health care. Yet another naïve assumption on my part. Bill said that it is, and it isn’t, offered. Once a carrier makes “career”, they are offered health insurance options at a cost to the employee. Making career might take one to three years! Before that, a carrier has the option to participate in another program which, basically is a “COBRA” type insurance, making it all but unaffordable on the $17.29 per hour salary for the starting mail carrier. One to three YEARS!? Do they really expect people to do this job with NO health coverage whatsoever for that amount of time? Who’d be dumb enough to do such a thing? Turns out, plenty.

I asked about timeline of hire and when I could expect to start should all the pieces fall into place. Bill said that this position is fast-tracked because they lost six people in one month recently and they are very shorthanded. Red flag! Six people in one month!? Surely some retired. And that would explain the extra fast timeline for making “career” within this office as, they seem to be aging out fast, making room for younger people, present company excluded. He said I should receive further instruction in a few days.

We bid goodbye and on my way out I gave a quick detective's glance around the inner workings of a post office. All quiet. Nice. All appears quiet and calm. Beautiful.

About a week later I hear from Bill. He said that, apparently there's a problem with my selective service registration. No problem really, I keep immaculate records. I've got my selective service notice in my "military" file in my file cabinet. I'll just get it and bring it to him. I dug it out and actually read it for the first time since receiving it in 1985. Yea, there might be a problem. On the form, it showed my address as that of my parent's home in 1985 (where I had landed for a few months after being discharged). Turns out, you must update your selective service record with your present address every time you move. Who knew this? How many times must I have moved since then, 12, 13 times!? Thinking about it, it makes sense. Beyond the absurd idea that a Good Conduct discharged veteran from the military, after serving a combined 4 years active/2 years inactive tour, actually needs to register for the draft, I supposed that, if they need you, they need to know how to find you. But, I also supposed that, if the government wants to find you, how hard would it be, really?

But, it turns out that, the address listed was a minor dilemma. The real problem was that my registration wasn't synched to my social security number. In the "modern" military, your social security number is your identifier. Why bother coming up with a different number? I looked at the form and sure enough, nowhere does it list my social security number? Thinking back 35 years earlier, I think I MAY have chosen to exclude this information in a minor, civil disobedient defiance. A middle finger to the government if they think they're going to draft me after serving, I guess. But here it is, 35 years later and it's an issue. So, we rectified the situation but, because of that little hiccup, it pushed back scheduling me for orientation classes. Two more weeks go by and, after passing a written, background, drug and selective service test, I receive an email with directions to report for orientation for employment with the United States Postal Service in West Palm Beach, Fl.

Chapter 3 - Orientation

Day 1

I was given directions to the Palm Beach County's central processing office of the Postal Service. It was across the street from yet another Trump golf course. I was directed to go through the electronic gates and park in the back and then walk to the side entrance where the turnstiles were. There was a choice of two gated entrances into the facility. I chose one and pushed the call button and waited. I pushed again, and waited. Meanwhile, people reporting for work were using the other gated entrance and using their electronic badges to trigger the gate to open. I pushed the button again, waited and then decided that this wasn't going anywhere and I backed-up and pulled into the other (working) gated entrance. Of course, as I did, a stream of cars pull into the gated entrance where I just was and waved their passes and the gate's arm activated with no problem. I pushed the call button and waited. I finally hear a muted squawk of a response coming from the tiny speaker. I explain that I'm there for orientation. No response, but the gate lifted. I drive through and start to look for the area of where I should park. In the back, I was told. If you've ever seen a postal facility annex, it's hard to determine front from back from side but, I followed the road. Seeing cars parked in an area, I pulled in. Something didn't seem right so, I turned around and exited that area and was stopped by an incoming white pickup. We mutually put our windows down and the driver asked, "Do you know where to go for orientation?". Clearly, both of us lost, I jokingly said that I was following HIM. I didn't know it then but I had met a good friend, and Tim and I would try to keep each other sane during the next months as, it turns out he'd be working out of the same Deerfield Beach office.

As we parked, I checked out Tim's license plate as I am want to do. Florida, yes but, a Chicago Bears frame surrounded the plate. We walked to the "side" of the building where the turnstiles were and other candidates stood. We were told to be there no later than 7:30am. They seem to make a big deal out of the fact that we should be parking at a certain time and that the walk to the turnstiles takes a few minutes and to be at the turnstiles at 7:20am as the instructor will come out at 7:25am and let everyone into the building.

I rather like this type of specific time reference. Something about it that compartmentalizes things. It reminds me of my lifelong friend, Mike Lambert where, in high school he'd say things like, "I'll be in front of your house to pick you up in seven minutes!" or, "I'll be there in three minutes." Ok Mike, a 5 or 10 minute increment indication would probably be good enough.

But, there we stood, new recruits, sizing each other up as we waited for the instructor to come and get us and take us into the bowels of a United States Postal Processing center.

An instructor came out of the building and opened a side door next to the turnstiles for us to enter. "Follow me", he said. We entered one by one into a building which can only be described as a Federal Building. That's just what it looked like. No frills. Looked like nothing had been renovated in 50 years. Bland on Bland. No slick glass and marble with a four inch heel clad receptionist here! But, I figured, that's the way it should be. Let's stop with the surface gloss-over (I'd had enough of that) and let's get down to business. We walk through the Norma Rae looking type of processing warehouse, being careful to not cross-over any of the yellow lines painted on the floor so as to not lose a limb in the sorting machinery.

We enter a classroom and take a seat and were told where the restrooms were located if needed and then to get comfortable as the instructor readied the presentation. I get myself situated in an area of the classroom and then make my way to the restroom. I couldn't help but notice the many signs as reminders of safety. Safety this, safety that. It's a good sign, I thought. The most valuable asset to a company is its employees after all. Ha! I'd have my mind changed about this soon enough.

We all settle in and Alan, our instructor starts his presentation. He jumps right in with time and how to get paid, knowing that, let's face it, that's why everyone is here. Until we are issued our electronic time cards at the station where we're to be working, one must fill out PS Form 1260, Nontransactor Card. The postal service operates on a pseudo-military time. Not sure what that meant at first but, I figured it shouldn't be a problem, I know and am comfortable with military time. Like the metric system, it actually makes much more sense than the standard way of measurement and time. But, like most things within the Postal Service, nothing is as it appears on the surface. Most people can appreciate the differences between standard and military time when referring to morning hours. It doesn't take much brain power to differentiate that 7:00am is the same thing as 0700. But when we cross the 12:59pm line, that's when it's interesting. Most people can accept that 1:00pm equals 1300 as it converts to military time. Surely,

1pm is the thirteenth hour of the day. Likewise, 2:00pm is equal to 1400 and 8:00pm is equal to 2000 as 8pm is the twentieth hour of the day. And so, 1:30pm, or, thirty minutes past the thirteenth hour of day, equals to 1330 in military time. But, in postal time, the hours behave like military time but, the minutes are treated differently. 1:00pm in standard time equals 1300 in military time which equals to 1300 in postal time. However, 01:30pm in standard time equals 1330 in military time which equals 1350 in postal time. It took me a minute to wrap my head around this concept. In postal world, and much like metric, the hour is based on a hundred increments, not sixty minutes. And so, if you divided the hour up by a hundred, you'd see that half past the hour would not equal thirty minutes but fifty minutes. Hang in there, you're doing fine.

Let's push in a little further. What time is it in postal time if, the rest of the world thinks it's 6:45pm? 1875 of course. What else could it be? Now let's go crazy. What time would it be in postal speak if the standard time was 9:10pm? Answer, 2117! Of course that's what it would be! So, is mail ever delayed? Depends on what time system you use.

So, as a first order of business, Alan had us begin to fill out our PS Form 1260 so that we may get paid for this orientation and use it as a training session as well. So, enter the date. Uh oh, don't tell me that the postal service does THAT differently too. No, we're safe with the MM/DD/YYYY deal. Then enter Ring Type. Hold on a second; Ring type? What's this? Your choices are, BT, OL, IL, MV, ET. Ok, what does all this mean? Alan says, enter BT for ring type because, that's when you are beginning your tour. Oh, so, like you mean, "starting"? Ok, BT it is. What time did I start today? Hah! I got this; 0730!!! Wrong! 0750!!! What are ya, stupid?

Having entered this information in pen and slightly agitated, Alan mumbled, “I guess you’ll be needing a new form huh?”

It reminded me of when, in Navy basic training, when we were issued our uniforms, we spent an entire day stenciling our names on everything that was issued to each individual. The only time while in basic training that I was called-out and reprimanded was during this time. Take your pants, put the stencil on the inner waist band one inch to the left of the center line of the rear waistband, apply the white stencil to the waist band. Take one white t-shirt, apply the stencil to the rear inside of the shirt at the center point, apply the black stencil pen to the stencil. Take one tidy whitey and…I couldn’t take it anymore. I got the gist of what was supposed to happen here. I just took all my underwear and blew out all the stenciling in one push rather than the fits and starts method from the company commander. I got caught. “Did someone go ahead and stencil all of their underwear when I clearly said to only do as I instructed, when I instructed.” I didn’t want to make matters worse so, I fest up. Next thing I knew I was grinding out too many pushup to count while the rest of the company stenciled away. Never do anything unless told. Got it.

Back to PS Form 1260, we move down to the next line, enter date and ring type OL and a time of 1200. OL stands for Out to Lunch. Next line, date and ring type IL (In from Lunch). Next line, date and ring type of ET (End Tour), 1530. You’ll get paid for seven and a half hours. You won’t get paid for lunch. I haven’t punched a clock in over thirty years and it was a bit humiliating to be honest. Having been a salaried employee for so long, the mature thought is that, just get your work done and frankly, if you need to do something during the day, go ahead. If you take an hour and a half for lunch, fine but, just get your work done. That don't fly with the Postal Service.

Having disbursed with the time card, it was time for the oath. Alan had us stand and raise our right hand and read from what was on the screen of the Power Point presentation.

"I, (state your name), do solemnly swear (or affirm) that I will support and defend the Constitution of the United States against all enemies, foreign and domestic; that I will bear true faith and allegiance to the same; that I take this obligation freely, without any mental reservation or purpose of evasion; and that I will well and faithfully discharge the duties of the office on which I am about to enter."

"Welcome to the United States Postal Service" Alan said.

I had said these words prior in my life at the Newark, New Jersey military processing center when entering the Unites States Navy at the age of eighteen. And, I did then, as I had just done, held one hand high in allegiance while the other hand was behind my back with fingers crossed. My little way of saying, "Well, yea, I'll defend the constitution but, …well, …there might be a time where I don't completely agree with a given situation and might just have an issue with carrying out a given task. We'll take it issue by issue and see."

If issued a "Code Red", do you carry out the order to the letter or, as a thinking human being, do you question the action?

"What did we do wrong?! We did nothing wrong!"

"Yea we did. We were supposed to fight for people who couldn't fight for themselves."[1]

Again, we'll take it case by case.

Alan began to make a big deal about the next ninety days. Your first ninety days is a probation. You sneeze wrong and you're out! Attendance and safety is of paramount importance. This is what is looked at for advancement. Where you went to school and the grades you received is nice but, if your attendance and safety record is blemished, you're done! Do NOT take any time off during your first ninety days! Period! Take care of your feet. If you have a foot problem, you don't have a job!

Is that it? Don't take off during the first ninety days, be safe and be on time and don't have a foot problem. I think I can handle it.

Alan continued with covering the most asked question at orientation; "Do we get free stamps?". Answer: "This is the Federal Government, nothing is for free!". He explained the virtues of "Informed Delivery". This is a relatively new process and service that the Postal Service has where, if you sign up for it, they scan each piece of your mail and send you an email with a picture of the scanned piece of mail, notifying you that you should be expecting this mail soon. I had just cancelled this service of my own mail a few months earlier as it proved to be a major pain in the ass. I have to get an email telling me that I'm receiving paper mail in the box

---

[1] *A Few Good Men*, 1992, Castle Rock Entertainment, Columbia Pictures

soon? Seems redundant. It's like calling someone and asking them if they've received your email.

Perhaps reading people's minds, Alan said, "There are NO firearms allowed on postal property, EVER! It's a federal crime!" I thought, the irony of that. The 2nd Amendment of the United States Constitution (ya know, the one I just once again swore to uphold) provides for the right of the people to keep and bear arms. How can one create a well-regulated militia to secure a free state (against a tyrannical government I presume), if you can't go on the property? The tyrannical president isn't going to just let you in when you ring the doorbell to the Whitehouse! Some rules are going to have to be bent I can see. I guess that's where the crossed fingers comes in.

We quickly went over the health benefits where the USPS participates in the Federal Health Benefits (FEHB) program where it covers general health, dental, vision, flex spending, and long-term disability. But again, not eligible to participate in such a program until one makes career. Until then, the USPS will contribute $125 toward a plan, later found out to be cost prohibitive, even with the $125 contribution. I found it very odd that there is any question in providing health care for a job such as this. Driving government vehicles, walking on private and public property, etc. The potential for major health and financial issues, was alarming, it seemed to me.

As a conclusion to Alans initial preamble, we were instructed to go around the room and introduce ourselves. Tell your name, location, position and a fun fact about yourself. I always hated doing this type of thing. Does anybody really care? It took a seemingly long time to get around the room. Some had language barriers and seemed perplexed at what was being asked of them. And then, once they understood, stumbled their responses that dragged out the already painful exercise. In response to what their position was, I kept hearing a lot of CCA or RCA, and I got little nervous in that, I wasn't really sure what my actual position title was. To me, I was to be a mailman. Was there an acronym for mailman? If so, wouldn't it be MLMN? I was not sure what a CCA or RCA was. I know what an RCA plug is. Anyway… As I sit there waiting for my turn, I rifle through my paperwork and emails, searching for an official title for my position. As it turns out, CCA stands for City Carrier Assistant and RCA stands for Rural Carrier Assistant. Thinking of Deerfield Beach, I'm not really sure if its considered City or Rural. I finally found where it stated that I was to be a City Carrier Assistant in Deerfield Beach. But, my mind keyed on the differences between City and Rural, not so much the Assistant part. The assistant part to me was what was initially described in the job posting as a part-time carrier. That made sense to me in that I'd be assisting the career carrier and not really doing the full blown job. So, I dismissed that part of the title. The rural part of the job title, I came to learn, was for non-incorporated areas of a town. Not necessarily rural, meaning, out in the sticks, as one might think. Just, non-incorporated. Apparently RCA's go by a completely different set of rules from the CCAs. RCAs basically are on a salary. They deliver the mail and if they get done with their route, they're done. Same pay each week. And, if inundated with mail and it takes ten hours a day to delivery, there's no extra pay. CCA's get paid on an hourly basis and are eligible for overtime pay. In my mind, however, call it what you want, I was to be a mailman.

One guy, after stating his information said that a fun fact about him was that, "He loved God!". Oh boy. This guy sounds like a lot of fun at parties. A woman with purple hair, Pam, skirted the whole fun fact part and posed a question to Alan. Referring to the USPS logo, she asked, "What's that logo supposed to be, some sort of bird?!" Taken aback slightly, Alan deadpanned his response, "It's an Eagle. You know, the United States of America. Eagle." Purple hair, "Ohhhhh". I could barely contain my laughter. I looked at Tim across the room and with mouth agape, he looked dumbfounded. We shared a WTF? glance with a disbelief head shake. We're going to be running this place in two weeks if this is our competition. We painfully finished our personal introductions and took a break.

Looking for coffee in this place proved to be futile. How is that possible? I went to the break room, nothing. I asked about it and was told no, there's no coffee. Unacceptable. How can there be no coffee. And, this is our first day of orientation, where's the breakfast spread? No bagels? No donuts? And, the final insult, no coffee! Nothing. There's a hundred year old water fountain in the hall. Knock yourself out.

This is going to be a long day.

Back from break, we settled in. Alan started having the obligatory computer problems that temporarily halted his presentation. No matter to me, gives me a minute to check on what people are complaining about on Facebook. After much trial and error, the presentation was back online after an extremely long Windows reboot. Alan jumps with a USPS history lesson

As with the beginnings of most poorly executed good ideas, the Postal Service had its inception in a bar. In 1639, the

Massachusetts court chose a tavern in Boston as its official place of business to handle correspondents delivered from and to England. Perhaps downing a few pints while sorting mail helped in the endeavor. I would later realize this to would be very true. Local Post routes were created and radiated out of from Boston, first reaching New York where the route became known Old Boston Post Road. The road ran through the Bronx in New York, not far from my birthplace, and is currently referred to as Boston Post Road or US Route 1.

Growing up and living in the area, this moniker was lost on me. However, origins of names must come from somewhere, I suppose, and that Boston Post Rd was actually used to carry Post mail between Boston and New York, may only have been known by local resident of nearby Coop City, and fellow mail carrier himself, David Berkowitz, aka, Son of Sam.

As is typical of me in a classroom setting, this last thought triggered a walk down memory lane. Having been in high school during the years that Berkowitz terrorized New York City and the surrounding area, I was fascinated by the story of the "Son of Sam". I remember that my sister, having long brunette hair (a seemingly main target of "Sam") considered cutting and bleaching her own hair to be less of a target. Years later, after having read the enthralling book, The Ultimate Evil, by Maury Terry, the hook was deeply set in me. The book described how investigators traced one of the threatening letters that Berkowitz had written to then reporter for the New York Daily News, Jimmy Breslin, to a mail box in Englewood, NJ, perhaps a mere two miles from where I had been living at the time. The story of Son of Sam is rife with conspiracy theories of satanic cult membership that spread throughout the area with far reaching connections to Minot, North Dakota, of all places. A sample of the Breslin letter read:

"Hello from the gutters of N.Y.C., which are filled with dog manure, vomit, stale wine, urine, and blood.

Hello from the sewers of N.Y.C. which swallow up these delicacies when they are washed away by the sweeper trucks.

Hello from the cracks in the sidewalks of N.Y.C. and from the ants that dwell in these cracks and feed on the dried blood of the dead that has seeped into these cracks.

Mr. Breslin, sir, don't think that because you haven't heard from me for a while that I went to sleep. No, rather, I am still here. Like a spirit roaming the night. Thirsty, hungry, seldom stopping to rest; anxious to please Sam. I love my work. Now, the void has been filled."

On the back of the envelope, in place of a return address it read:

Blood and Family

Darkness and Death

Absolute Depravity

.44

The book reported the general location of the mailbox from which the letter was mailed. Inquisitive in my own right, I conducted my own investigation. I did what any normal person would do to try and dispel the conspiracy theories, I went to find the mailbox.

I was disappointed to find nothing there. I walked the entire area and found no mailbox in existence. The conspiracy theories mounted. It had been about thirteen years since that summer of 1977 that I was seeking this information but, I pursued and went to area Post Offices asking if they knew if there ever was a mailbox on the corner of Myrtle Street and Lorraine Court, or anywhere in the area in the past and, if so, why would it be removed? The clerk at the Post Office gave me the familiar to most, vacant stare. One did acquiesce and retreat to the back to ask the Postmaster. The final answer was that no one there was ever aware of any mailbox in that area.

Hmmm, are they covering up? Are THEY part of the satanic cult with standing orders to throw this reporter off his track? Why would Terry report on this if it wasn't to be true? Why would the Postal Service remove a mailbox? Do they monitor the mail accepted at each mailbox and if, after a period, the amount of mail received within the box declines or disappears altogether, is it then decided to remove the box for lack of business?

I snapped out of my ADD moment and my hand was up before I could stop it.

"Yes?"

"Sorry to interrupt but, do you know if the Postal Service removes mailboxes from given locations after a period of time, for whatever reason?"

Pause…… "Sure, it happens all the time".

Alan returned to his history lesson but, not before I detected a slight eye-roll.

He continued sharing with us that these Post routes spread out from New York and further away from the Atlantic shoreline as the need for a communication network was realized.

However, my eyes were starting to glaze over. Not that I don't find history interesting, I do. It's that monotone "lecture voice" pulsing at me from a 7:30 am start and the lack of coffee smell in the air that triggers the eye lids to droop. I tried to fight it.

During my classroom history lesson haze, I was able to retain some nuggets of information on the history of the USPS:

In 1692, the Central Postal Organization was created to satisfy the need for a communications network within the colonies.

In 1737, Benjamin Franklin would be named as the Postmaster General of Philadelphia and later, Postmaster General of all the colonies in 1753.

In another example of "You're doing the job SO well, we're going to have to let you go", England fired Franklin and dismissed him of his duties in 1774. They claim that he became too sympathetic to the cause of the colonies and so, they handed him his walking papers.

On July 26, 1775 the Continental Congress agreed that a new postal system should be created and that the position of Postmaster General should be bestowed upon Franklin (because he was so sympathetic to the cause, and all.)

Benjamin Franklin held the position of Postmaster General until November 7, 1776. He was in office when the Declaration of Independence created the United States of America in July 1776, which made Franklin the first Postmaster General of the United States. The present Postal Service of the United States of America is a result of the system Franklin placed in operation.

After a certain point, Alan decided that the glaze over the faces of the "students" was enough for him to announce that we break for lunch. Certainly, I thought, they would provide a nice spread for the prospective mail carriers of the United States Postal Service. I wondered what it could be; assorted mini sandwiches? Dare I dream that they might have some chafing dishes set up for a hot lunch? Certainly, as a last resort without much thought, a few assorted pizza's would be presented. And, there HAS to be an urn of coffee so as to get through the rest of this history lesson after lunch. I waited for direction as to where to go. I figured that, even if they weren't going to provide a lunch, I'd just go to the cafeteria and be on my own.

Alan dictated that "It's 12:15pm, be back at 1:00pm and we'll try to get the rest of the history done today". And with that, he started his departure. Someone asked about the availability of food. He hitched up in his step and, almost as an afterthought said, "Oh, right; well, if you go out those doors, there's a 7/11 across the street and, a little further down the road there's a Burger King." And out the door he went.

7/11 and Burger King were my only choices. No cafeteria? Wonderful! I hadn't had it "my way" in a while and so, Burger King it was. As I sat there with my Whopper, I wondered if this was the first salvo in a future battle of poor gastrointestinal choices being on the run for this job. Again, I would learn that "poor" eating habits would not be the issue, rather, being able to eat at all, was.

Sitting back in the classroom, I knew that the Burger King was not going to sit well in a classroom setting. Hard plastic chairs don't lend themselves well to learning in comfort on a post Burger

King visit. But what choice did I have? Was I supposed to get one of those spinning, hot lamp, hot dogs from 7/11 that's probably been there since 9/11? I don't think so.

Alan bounds into the room and announces that we have a lot to cover and to hold questions until he can get through it or else we'll have to pick up the history part of the presentation the next morning. Silently, we all telepathically agreed to pipe down as we wanted this over with as soon as possible.

He went on to describe how the growth of the country placed higher demands on the Post Office Department, causing it to create even more routes and perform faster delivery and the trials and tribulations that the service face to present day. A few bullet points stood out:

1847 the 1st Postage stamp was used.

1863 the 1st usage of a ZIP code.

1970 the US Post Office became the United States Postal Service

However, the biggest take-away to all of this was that Alan told us that the United States Postal Service gets no financing from the United States Government. The USPS is its own entity where it satisfies payroll and other operating expenses from the Postage it charges for delivery.

Mail volume dropped between 2001 through 2003 causing massive debt. This was the first time since the Great Depression that mail volume fell during consecutive years. The cause of this shift was due to the proliferation of electronic media and the means by which communication may be accomplished. Between 2000 and 2010, overall mail volume dropped by 18% and First-Class

Mail (the service's most profitable) dropped nearly 25%. However, the Postal Services operating cost continued to increase.

The events of September 11, 2001 changed life as the nation knew it. It was no different for the Postal Service. Soon after the attacks in New York City and Washington, D.C, anthrax spores were detected in mail processed for delivery at various locations throughout the country.

By the end of the anthrax scare, there were five deaths and seventeen cases of anthrax poisoning. Among others, Senators Tom Daschle, Patrick Leahy and news anchor Tom Brokaw were targets for anthrax exposure. While the message within the letters mailed contained handwritten rantings of:

"09-11-01

THIS IS NEXT

TAKE PENACILIN [sic] NOW

DEATH TO AMERICA

DEATH TO ISRAEL

ALLAH IS GREAT"

The motive behind them remains a mystery. The FBI concluded, upon their investigation, that the letters were mailed from Princeton, New Jersey. Although, return addresses on the mail containing anthrax read:

4th Grade

Greendale School

Franklin Park, NJ 08852

Franklin Park, NJ does, in fact exist, however, ZIP code 08852 is the code for Monmouth Junction, NJ and there is no Greendale School in Franklin Park OR Monmouth Junction. There is a Greenbrook Elementary School in adjacent South Brunswick Township, NJ, however.

Investigators found anthrax spores in a city street mailbox located at 10 Nassau Street near the Princeton University campus. Over 600 mailboxes were tested for anthrax which could have been used to mail the letters, however, the Nassau St box was the only one to test positive.

After clearing initial subjects of interest, the FBI's main focus fell to Bruce Edwards Ivins, a scientist at the government's biodefense labs at Fort Detrick in Frederick, Maryland. Ivins was put under surveillance and at 1:00am on the morning of November 8, 2001 the FBI observed Ivins throwing away a book entitled *"Gödel, Escher, Bach: An eternal Golden Braid"* published in 1979 and a 1992 issue of *American Scientist Journal* which contained an article entitled "The Linguistics of DNA", and discussed hidden messages.

It was believed that the letters sent to the New York Post and Tom Brokaw contained a hidden message as the characters "A" and "T" were sometimes bolded or highlighted by tracing over the letters.

"09-11-01

THIS IS NEX**T**

TAKE PEN**A**CILIN [sic] NOW

DE**A**TH **T**O AMERICA

DEATH **T**O ISRAEL

ALLAH IS GREA**T**"

The book *Gödel, Escher, Bach* contains a lengthy description of the encoding/decoding procedures including an illustration of hiding a message within a message by bolding certain characters.

When the investigators extracted the highlighted letters from the message, they got TTT AAT TAT. The 3-letter groups are codons, meaning that each sequence of three nucleic acids will code for a specific amino acid.

TTT = **P**henylalinine (single-letter designator **F**)

AAT = **A**sparagine (single-letter designator **N**)

TAT = **T**yrosine (single-letter designator **Y**)

The FBI derived two possible meanings from the hidden message.

"FNY" – Fuck New York.

"PAT" – A nickname of Ivins's former colleague.

Ivins was known to hate New York City and four of the media letters had been sent there. No connection to Ivins former colleague (PAT) was ever made. The FBI's report claimed that it was impossible to determine with certainty that these translations were correct, however, the important part of the investigative analysis was that there was a hidden message and not so much of what the message was.

The FBI finally concluded that there was one "lone Individual" responsible for all of the anthrax attacks and they pursued further investigation of Ivins. Due to the grand jury finding the evidence as "largely circumstantial", Ivins was never indicted. On July 29, 2008, Bruce Edwards Ivins died by suicide with an overdose of acetaminophen.

One of the anthrax letters reached Robert Stevens, a photo journalist at the now defunct STAR magazine published by American Media, Inc. in Boca Raton, Fl, causing his death. The reason he was chosen as a target remains unknown. During this time, and seemingly unconnected to the anthrax attacks, America

Media also received a large envelope and was addressed, "Please forward to Jennifer Lopez c/o The Sun".

The envelope contained a metal cigar tube with a cheap cigar inside, and empty can of chewing tobacco, a small detergent carton, pink powder, a Star of David pendant, and a hand written letter to Jennifer Lopez. The writer of the letter spouted his love for Jennifer, asking her to marry him.

After the anthrax scare the Postal Service formed a mail security task force. Directives were given to authorize all employees to wear protective gear while the task force looked for ways to sanitize the mail, including irradiating it with electron beams. In November of 2001, the Postal Service began irradiating mail addressed to Congress, the White House, and federal agencies in Washington, D.C. They ended the irradiation at the end of 2019. In 2004, biohazard detection systems were installed at mail processing facilities nationwide. The equipment regularly collects and tests air samples near mail processing equipment to help protect postal employees and customers and remains in place to this day.

In 2009, the USPS faced harsh financial challenges mainly due to an increase in online shopping, where package delivery revenue made up for the lack of first class mail delivery. Later that same year, the Postal Service began Sunday package delivery service for the ever growing, monolithic, Amazon Corporation, affectionately referred to as, "Amazon Sundays".

In 2016, Postmaster General, Megan Brennan (the first woman to be Postmaster General in the 240-year history of the organization) testified before the House Oversight and Government Reform Committee and claimed that the Postal

Service's financial dilemma was "serious but solvable". In 2017, she spoke again to the Committee and said:

"The Postal Service is a self-funding entity. We pay for our operations entirely through the sale of postal products and services and do not receive tax revenue to support our business. ...

During the last decade, we have responded aggressively to the challenges that confronted us. ... These efforts have resulted in cost savings of approximately $14 billion annually. ...

Despite these achievements, our efforts have not been enough — and cannot be enough — to restore the Postal Service to financial health, absent legislative and regulatory reform. ... "

Some of our most significant costs are fixed by law and are outside management's control. Further, our ability to earn revenue to pay for those costs is constrained by law. This fundamental imbalance is the root of our financial instability."

In 2018, postal reform bills were introduced in the House and Senate, but stalled. Meanwhile, then President Donald Trump created a Task Force to study the Postal Service's operations and finances to help chart a course to financial stability for the service.

The Presidential Task Force ultimately concluded that comprehensive postal reforms were urgently needed. Brennen pledged to work with key stakeholders to find the best way forward.

On July 26, 1775, the Continental Congress agrees that, as the first American communications network, our postal system not only promoted commerce and strengthened the bonds of family and friendship - it united a nation. The Founding Fathers believed that to succeed, a democratic form of government depended upon the free exchange of news, ideas, and opinions. In 1804, Thomas Jefferson wrote:

"No experiment can be more interesting than that we are now trying...that man may be governed by reason and truth.

Our first object should therefore be, to leave open to him all the avenues to truth.

The most effectual hitherto found, is the freedom of the press."

And with that, the history lesson was over. And, of course I am paraphrasing here as, a full history of the Postal Service is beyond the scope of this journal.

Alan shut everything down and told everyone to be back the next day at 7:20am. I packed up and left the facility. As I walk to my car, I reflected on the history of the Postal Service. Alan really seemed to try to drive home the fact that the Postal Service was its own entity and took zero tax dollars in its operation.

Once in the parking lot, I see Purple hair (Pam) seemingly lost. She had that confused look about her. She mumbled something about not remembering where she parked her car. In her defense, it HAD been a long day but, I wondered if SHE'D be responsible for delivering someone's needed medication soon. I supposed she'll be alright, I thought.

Days 2 - 4.

I prepared a little better for days 2 and 3. I brought a traveler cup of coffee in the car with me in anticipation of going without for the rest of the day. At least that'll keep me going for the first hour or so. I was glad that we were done with the Postal Service's history. I mean, I suppose it's important to know the history of something in which you are about to undertake. As in, "He who ignores history is doomed to repeat it". And, I certainly don't mind getting paid while just sitting there being lectured on how some old white guys in white wigs decided on the future skeletal structure of a nation. Still, one wonders about the financial efficacy of the exercise.

Alan handed everyone a new time card (PS Form 1260) and we began our sign in. Clock in at 7:50. Yes, that's 7:30am. He began to lecture on a variety of subjects; shoes (no mesh tops) needs to be something substantial like, leather or leather-like. We were advised to not purchase anything too expensive as, they will wear out very quickly and you'll just have to buy again. There is the potential to go through four pairs of shoes per year. Alan pointed to the fact that, there will be a uniform allowance allotted after three months but, he advised not to buy the shoes that the Postal Service has available on its uniform site as they are very expensive. They were made in the U.S.A, as was all authorized Postal uniforms.

The subject of dogs is a sensitive one. Dogs can make you have a very bad day. If attacked, we are to use the issued satchel as a first defense. We are to "feed it" to the dog. The idea is so that it latches onto the bag instead of bone! And, as the dog chomps on the bag, you reach for your pepper spray if needed. Do not run from a dog; stand your ground. After giving the dog the satchel, back away slowly. If in a dire situation, our health takes priority and one must do what one must do to protect oneself. The USPS will back the carrier legally and financially for impending legal issues should they occur after a dog attack. The carrier must fill out the proper forms if it is found that there is an aggressive canine on any given property. This triggers the proper notification and alerts other mail carriers, through their GPS enabled scanner, that there is a dangerous dog in their area. And when the carrier approaches an address where the aggression has been noted, it gives a warning to the carrier to be vigilante in their approach. Should the mail delivery at a given address be impeded because of an aggressive canine, notification is given to the resident that mail will be withheld from delivery until the carrier is comfortable that the dog is restrained enough for a safe mail delivery. Should the resident refuse to take action on restraining the dog, neighboring addresses will have mail delivery suspended due to the volatility of an unmanaged aggressive dog in the area. This will initiate peer pressure from neighbors and the issue is usually resolved. If not, the residents are advised to visit the local Post Office to retrieve their mail, as no mail carrier will continue to attempt to deliver at that address.

Postal vehicles – don't back up, EVER! Even with all the mirrors, you can't really see what's directly behind you. If you miss a stop and need to go back, either continue forward and circle around or, stop the vehicle, turn it off, exit and walk back to where a delivery was missed.

Purple hair piped up; "Who pays for gas?"

I honestly didn't hear Alans response to this, as I couldn't hear over the groans of pain I was letting out at such a bizarre question.

I shouldn't be too hard on Pam as, I came to learn that Rural Carrier Assistants may end up using their own personal vehicles to deliver the mail. Perhaps Pam is an RCA. In that case, I suppose the question is certainly valid. But I thought, "using your own vehicle to deliver the mail?", there's no way in hell!

Safety is one thing concerning Postal vehicles, security is another. No one will ever really question a Postal vehicle. If entering a gated community, the guard will usually just open the gate as the Postal vehicle approaches. Other secure areas are just as easily breached by the mere presents of a Postal vehicle with a uniformed Postal employee driving it.

This appears to me to be of great concern should anyone with devious intentions wish to pursue. It's not such a stretch to obtain a Postal looking vehicle as well as reasonable facsimile of a Postal uniform and have almost unfettered access to secure locations in order to do the unimaginable.

Alan then introduced to us a website that we can go to for a variety of employee related issues; Liteblue.usps.gov. This is the site to go to for payroll inquiries, downloadable forms, find discount deals only available to postal employees, and a host of other areas of interest for the employee. Our attention was brought to the Employee Assistance Program (EAP) by visiting EAP_4-YOU.com. Should anyone have personal problems dealing with job or home related issues, this is the place to start seeking emotional assistance. "Things can get pretty stressful and it's best to seek assistance before they get out of hand.", said Alan. He enforced, "Going Postal – is a term that we don't ever use!" And he left it at that. I thought it odd that he didn't even mention the occasions where postal employees have...well...lost it. Since 1983, 35 people have been killed in 11 Postal offices. In 1993, the St. Petersburg Times newspaper in Florida first coined the phrase reporting that, "The USPS does not approve of the term and has made attempts to stop people from using it." However, many within the postal community feel that it has a rightful place in the vernacular. Since then, the term has been generally adopted as a descriptive for one who has become uncontrollably angry, often to the point of violence, and usually in a workplace environment, not necessarily within the Postal Service. But, as I sit here, even I can assert that the Postal Service doesn't cause it's employees to be overly stressed any more than any other employer to the point of public demonstrations of frustration. At least, I'll give it the benefit of the doubt at this point.

The LiteBlue website was also the place to visit should one want to view open job positions within the Postal Service. These positions are only available and viewable from within the Postal Service. They are not viewable or available to the general public, yet. Once job fulfillment is pursued within the Postal Service, it will exhaust all internal candidates first before making the position available to the general public. Hiring from within, probably a good thing, I thought.

Alan said that we were coming in at a good time as it appears that there are many people retiring at the moment. The United States Postal Service is the nation's second largest employer at over 600,000 employees. Second only to the massive Walmart at 1.5 million as of this writing.

The Equal Employment Opportunity (EEO) with the Postal Service seems to be standard stuff. No need to dissect what appears to be common sense to what most people who've gone through any sort of employee onboarding have experienced. Don't be abrasive, rude or discriminating in any way, and you're good. I would imagine that, in a place as diverse as the Postal Service, this would be especially true. Say something just a little colorful and someone, somewhere will be offended. It's just a matter of time. What you have left after all that filtering are bland interactions with blander existences. But, as long as no one feels uncomfortable…

At this point we had a special visitor in the classroom. We were visited by the instructor who would be giving classroom driving instructions the next, and final day of orientation. She came in and gave a quick introduction about what we'd be covering and told us that, instead of reporting at 7:30am, to meet at the turnstiles at 8:00am and she'll meet us there and we'll enter the building together and get situated in the classroom and start the day. There was an Asian lady in the class who wasn't able to grasp this instruction so easily. She kept asking about what she should do the next day.

"Meet at the turnstiles at 8am", said the instructor.

"Where, in the back?", asked the student in very broken English.

"At the turnstiles! Where you've been coming through for the past three days!"

"By the gate?!"

At this, Purple Hair piped up; "HOW ARE YOU GOING TO DO THIS JOB!? IS THERE A PROBLEM WITH ENGLISH!?"

So much for not being abrasive or insensitive in the workplace. Purple Hair comes at you straight between the eyes!

The fourth and final day (half day really, as we were supposed to only go to noon) came and I was looking forward to the driving instruction and ending this classroom instruction part of orientation. The instructor came in and got started right away with setting up the presentation. The Driver's Safety presentation consisted mainly of videos of potentially dangerous driving situations.

Chapter 3

One can appreciate the over emphasis on safety when it comes to driving a postal vehicle. They're basically handing the keys to a clunky vehicle to people who hail from a vast variety of walks of life. As with any job where there are mass hiring's, the law of averages says that there are going to be some people who are reasonable and considerate in their driving etiquette and there are others where it will be clear that they should never be allowed to operate a vehicle such as these, or any other for that matter.

The video's showed many examples of safety concerns including showing why it is imperative that you engage your hand break every time you leave the vehicle. When you need to dismount, you place the truck in Park, engage the hand break, curb the wheels (this is so that should the truck roll, it will roll toward the curb and not back into the street), turn the truck off, dismount, lock the truck. When ready to remount the truck, you are to first walk around the entire truck before entering to be sure no little children have decided to hide and play around a mail vehicle, which is common.

The presentation showed a few examples of this process when not completed property. One LLV (Long Life Vehicle) was left running without it's hand break engaged. The vehicle slipped back into gear (reverse in this instance) and began slowly moving backward. The wheels were turned toward the street and as the vehicle gained speed, kept circling round and round with no operator in it. Thankfully, it actually never hit anything until it circled around and hit a tree before the operator could reach the controls and shut it down.

Another incident depicted a true story of a mail truck backing up and striking and killing a small child that wanted to play "mail man". The videos showed the potential problems with texting while driving, using earbuds or some sort of headphone or other similar distractions. Over and Over again, the videos drilled in safety.

Common causes of Postal collisions are:

- Misjudging clearances and hitting stationary objects such as parked cars, low-hanging branches/limbs, or mailboxes.
- Failure to yield right-of-way to vehicles and pedestrians.
- Backing the vehicle.
- Inattention. Never finger the mail while driving. (Fingering the mail is when a carrier "fingers through" the mail to find the appropriate mail for the next address on the route. This should never been done. The carrier is to get to the next address first, park properly and then finger the mail.)

We were then told to take a short break before returning and we'll finish up. Upon returning from break, we couldn't quite get started again because not everyone was back yet. Pam was missing. We waited. The instructor began to get a little heated. We waited some more. Finally Pam strolls in as if nothing was wrong and is questioned as to her whereabouts. Pam dismisses the inquisition and expresses exasperation at having to endure more vehicle safety.

We push on. For the remainder of the presentation, we are instructed on how to proceed in the event we have an accident with a Postal vehicle. It's pretty much the same procedure as with any vehicle except with the additional responsibility of safeguarding the mail until it can be redirected with a replacement vehicle.

Alan takes back the reigns of orientation and once again added that, not only is it not a good idea to get into an accident while in a postal vehicle, should you have an accident during your probationary period (90 working days) it is cause for immediate separation, regardless of fault. That's comforting, I thought.

We were then instructed that we would hear from our offices as to when to report for a shadow day and when to report for on-road drivers training. We were dismissed. I bid good luck to Tim and left.

On the way home I received an email telling me to report to the Deerfield Beach Annex the next day at 8am for a Shadow day.

Chapter 4 – Shadow Day

I'd been looking forward to shadow day. I like to observe before actually doing anything. I get a better understanding of what needs to be done if I'm not doing any "heavy lifting". Also, I can assess, as I always seem to do, what needs to be done, how it's being done, try to determine a better way of doing it and, finally, how I'M going to do it. There may be the official way, there may be the right way, but it may not necessarily be MY way!

I was to report to Nick Compello at 8am for further instruction. I show up at the loading dock area at 7:50am and ring the bell. Someone opened the door and asked, "You the new guy?" "Yes", I replied. "I'm looking for Nick Compello". I was directed to a gentleman sitting at a desk that looked like it had been salvaged from an 1944 bombed-out, East Berlin building, in the middle of a large mail sorting room.

I approached the desk and waited for an opening in conversation as he looked extremely frazzled by a variety of people asking about this or that. I introduced myself and he quickly dealt me off to the mail carrier that I was supposed to shadow for the day. "You're with Jeremy Simpson today! He's over there by the time clock! HEY SIMPSON, HERE'S YOUR SHADOW!"

I looked over at Jeremy and saw an athletically built man holding his head with two hands while leaning his elbows on the time clock as if the weight of the head was just a little too much for his neck to carry at that moment. I'm familiar with this feeling. He managed a strained, uninterested glance in my direction. I walked over and introduced myself with a pre-COVID-19 handshake. He said to just hang back for a few minutes until we can get started. A few minutes later I was standing a few feet behind Jeremy while he got situated at his sorting station. He casually explained where to get your "Flats" and to then bring them to the sorting station and sort them first. He began his sort and was almost placing these "Flats" consisting of magazines, advertisements and other periodicals into the appropriate address slot without looking. While his arms were busily reaching to and froe, I stole the opportunity to look around the room. I was surprised to see a whirl of activity. I had done my homework and, Deerfield Beach was a smaller town than its neighboring towns. I figured that it would be a good place to experience this endeavor while avoiding the crush of larger neighboring towns such as Boca Raton and Pompano Beach. "How much mail can there be?", I reasoned with myself. And given that, how many possible mail carriers would be needed to accomplish this distribution? The amount of people buzzing around in this mail annex seemed to this uninformed mail carrier to be an over-exaggeration. And yet, there they were, crisscrossing the floor, giving missorted things to other mail routes. There was a lot of, "This isn't mine, this is 52!" and, "This goes to Bruna, why am I getting this!?"

I kept taking a step back, and then forward, and then back again, to avoid being run over by heavy bins loaded with parcels. While continuing to observe Jeremy sort his Flats, I see the Manager of the annex come to the mail sorting station next to Jeremy and approach the mail carrier there. Their voices slowly start to rise in that all-to-familiar parent/child inquisition fashion.

Apparently, there was a complaint from a customer that their mail is being delivered late and the manager was questioning the carrier about it. Late?, I thought. Like a NYC subway, is there an actual schedule? It's either delivered, or it isn't, I reasoned with myself.

Jeremy interjected without even lifting his head, "Someone has to be last Bill!".

Quite right. Mail routes are carefully and methodically planned out for the most efficient use of time and effort. The route begins at one point and continues on a specific course until the very end of that route. A typical mail carrier will be done with their sorting and loading of their vehicle and out for delivery by about 10am, 11am at the latest. Their first stop on their routes are usually businesses as, well, let's face it, we have to keep commerce moving. If businesses are waiting for incoming checks in order to process their wears, better to receive them as early in the day as possible. If received later in the day, commerce is halted until the following day. It's not so important that a private resident receives their political flyer at 11am vs 5pm.

Customers will further complain and request that they be realigned within the route to receive mail at an earlier time of day but, this will almost always be rejected as, it just doesn't make sense for a carrier to start a route in one geographical location, cross town to deliver to another location to appease specially requested time deliveries and then, backtrack to the point at which the carrier left off. It's just not efficient. And time is money. If the customer persists, the recommendation is to have the mail held and the customer can pick it up at the post office at their leisure. This is usually met with a huff and a hang-up.

I didn't quite understand the complaint, really. If a piece of mail is put into a mailbox at 5pm on a Monday, and a customer checks their mail at 7am on a Tuesday, well, then, weren't they the first to receive mail on a Tuesday? And if they had checked their mail at 5:30pm on that Monday, they would have been the last to receive their mail! I guess it's how you look at it.

At 8:30am there was an announcement over the loudspeaker simply stating that it was "Break-time!". I questioned Jeremy, "Break-time? Didn't we just start?". He smirked and said, that I was free to take a break but, he usually doesn't take one because, he just wanted to "get outta here!" I noticed that most of the workers stopped what they were doing and sort of disappeared. I'm really not sure where everyone went.

Ten minutes later I hear another announcement that "Break time is over! Get back to work and get outta my office. 4 o'clock comes fast!". I wasn't really sure what all that meant at the time but, I was intrigued that an organized break would occur a mere thirty minutes after the work day actually began. Everyone picked up where they left off and continued with their assignments.

During this din of activity in the annex you'd hear verbal bursts like, "Two years, 11 months!" Then, silence. More shuffling of cages and bins and redistributions of paper products and then again, "Two years and 11 months!!!" Apparently, a woman standing at her sorting station felt the need to share her countdown to retirement between "business" conversation. Ahh, a short-timer, I thought. Two years and 11 months. That's 1,060 days. A "Four Digit Midget" as we used to say in the military. She's got a ways to go! She's got to make it another two months before she can be a "Three Digit Midget" to even remotely be considered a short-timer for real. And, even THAT'S a stretch. While in the Navy, I started my "short-timer" calendar at 1,335 days! Now THAT'S a long time to be checking days off a calendar!

And then I see Greg. A crotchety curmudgeon, street worn veteran, who is also about to retire at some point in the near future and, very much looks like it. It's clear that he's done. His facial expression and skeletal positioning in which he carries, all reveal the result of someone who's been doing the same thing the same way for thirty-five years.

A voice from somewhere close shouts, "Greg! I thought you were dead! Hey Greg, when you gonna die so someone can take your route!?" From another area of the annex a woman shouts, "Bill, can you come here, I need to show you something!" Greg jumps in with, "Yea? C'mere, I need to show YOU something!"

Ahh, now they're talking MY language. My kind of people!

Jeremy shows me how he loads his vehicle, a "ProMaster" (a van type of vehicle), so that the delivery of route can go smoothly. Trays of mail were lined up neatly on shelves in the van. The trays themselves contain a combination of the Flats that he sorted inside and the DPS mail. DPS mail, (Delivery Point Sequence) is mail which is automatically sorted by sorting machines prior to its arriving at the local post office. DPS is sorted to the delivery point so that the carrier should just be able to pick up the trays of DPS and take to the vehicle without further sorting. However, in reality, there's always the need for further sorting. Jeremy told me that he always incorporates the DPS in with the Flats while inside because he felt that it's just more efficient to grab a pile of mail for an address from one source instead of two. And, he does this inside, before loading the truck because, in case I hadn't noticed, "It's hot as fuck outside!"

Made sense to me. Why would you do it any other way? Sort everything so each address has all of its mail in one bundle and then delivery it! Why take from multiple sources?

Also in the van, he showed me how to do the "Load Truck" feature on the scanner so that each parcel is property "loaded" into the system. This operation tags the parcel as "Out for delivery" and, should a parcel go missing, at the very least, it is identified that it had been loaded into a vehicle at a specific time on a specific date. The parcels are then arranged in the van in an order that mimics the flow of the route, somewhat. Due to the variety of sizes and weights and customized delivery instruction, sometimes parcels are just put out of the way and it's up to the carrier to be aware of where and when it should be delivered.

We "mount up" (get in the vehicle) and I get situated in my little jump seat that folds down on the passenger side of the van and I buckle up. Jeremy states, "I know they told you that you should never back up a Postal Vehicle but, "How the hell are we gonna get out of this parking spot if we don't!?" True enough. You either have to back out OR, to prevent from backing out when you go out for the day, you must back IN at the end of the day. Another Catch-22!

And we're off. We don't go very far. The first stop is literally across the street and in a small corporate park. At the entrance of the corporate park is what's called a "Cluster Box". The word "Cluster" is probably going to be used, a lot, during the rest of this book. So, stand by.

Jeremy tells me that it's frowned upon to "dismount" from the driver's door OR the passenger side door. We're to worm our way to the cargo area of the van and exit and enter through the sliding side door. Seems a waste of energy to me but, back we go. I crank my head on the metal threshold that separates the front cab from the cargo area and I see stars. "Watch your head", says Jeremy with a snicker.

He slides the heavy door open and I'm on the street. Like a butcher slicing out fillets, he swings his "arrow" key from his belt and inserts and twists and unlatches and opens all four cluster boxes in the blink of an eye. He removes any outgoing mail from the slots designating as "Outgoing Mail" and skillfully flips them into the designated "outgoing mail" bin he had set up in the van specifically for the situation. He then knowingly grabbed all the presorted mail from the trays he has customized to his liking and steps back down onto the pavement and starts doing a similar action to that which I just witnessed back at the annex. Back at the annex, the mail is thrown into slots which are organized specifically as the route is set up to be most efficient. The slots within the cluster box are set-up as the offices within the corporate park are laid out. I noticed a problem already.

Some of the slots were not labelled. I asked Jeremy how he knows what mail to put in what slot if it isn't labelled. He said that, there ARE labels on them, but sometimes you just have to look around. They're not in the same place all the time. At closer glance, I DID notice that what WAS labelled was done so in a meticulous way. Nice red Sharpied block writing that was easily readable. I asked, "Who does this?" motioning to the labels, thinking that it was a specific job within the Postal Service that maintains this type of thing. "I do", he replied. "Sometimes I take care of things like this on my own time because, there just isn't time to do it during a normal day's route. But, I feel that it's worth it because, the CCA's who fills in for me on my days off would have a hard time if it wasn't there." And then he added, "As for the occasional box that isn't labelled, …you do it every day, you tend to just know!"

Jeremy closes and secures the cluster boxes with the same skill in which he opened them. We climb back into the van and we're off to the next stop. We drive in a seemingly indiscriminate pattern known only to the driver, which is dizzying to me. The constant speed pumps in our path is causing the jumper seat to drive my spine up, and through, the base of my skull. We stop, grab the next batch of mail and walk the loop which had been carefully setup by…someone. In this corporate park, you check the doors, if it's unlocked, you go in, deliver the mail, take their outgoing and move to the next office. If the door is locked, you put the mail through the slot. Sounds easy enough. I look forward to creating relationships on a route of people that you see every day. Nice to have concentrated conversations with those taking the mail from you. "Nasty weather! You stay dry now!" "Would you like a cold bottle of water?" "How's that bathroom renovation coming?" "Thank you, have a nice day, see you tomorrow". Ya know, pleasantries without really "getting into it".

We pull down a section of corporate offices and Jeremy hands me a 3"x5" card of heavy paper and says, "Want to make it official? Take this and go put it into the slot over there". I take it and dismount the van. Of course I eye-ball the card and it's an advertisement of no real significance and I walk (probably too slowly) up to the office door in question and push the slot open and slip the card in. I release the metal slot and it snaps home with a clank. There, I'm officially a mail carrier. Piece O' cake. The sun is warm, the palm trees are swaying, I'm not in a cubicle....this could be good!

I return to the ProMaster and Jeremy congratulates me and we're off to continue the route. He explained that, this being Saturday, most businesses were closed. If this were a weekday, there'd be more effort to walk into the business to hand deliver the mail and to take their outgoing from them, which could be significant based on the type of business. Jeremy stated that, "Some days, I come back with more mail than I went out with!". This was yet another slap of reality for me in that, my blind bias of being a mailman was to "delivery" the mail, not to "accept" the mail. But, I guess this is part of the job as well.

We finish the corporate area and Jeremy states that he likes to take lunch at around 11am. Ok by me. I didn't know how things worked so, I didn't bring anything with me and we find ourselves pulling into a Wendy's. Wendy's....ooph! But, when there's nothing else... I solicit fast food joints about twice, maybe three times a year and now, this will be my second trip in a couple of days. This can't be good. I'm sure it's a fluke. I ordered my food and while waiting, I noticed that a Wendy's employee comes to the counter with a bag and hands it to Jeremy. I questioned it and he admitted that, "I come here every day at the same time and get the same thing so, they have it ready for me!" Hmm...

We choke down the food and remount the ProMaster. Jeremy informs me that we have thirty minutes for lunch. No more. The scanner that each mail carriers has is GPS enabled and each carrier is tracked at every moment of the day. They know where you are and how long you've been there. If the scanner hasn't moved for longer than thirty three minutes, they know it and an investigation will be pursued.

We drive to a rather run-down apartment complex and I'm witness to a whole new process. In this complex there are imbedded mail cluster boxes within a common exterior wall. Once it is unlocked, the whole box, consisting of about ten individual mail boxes opens up. Jeremy not only brought the corresponding mail to this apartment unit but, some pieces of those plastic mail trays that hold the mail. He said that he had to do some maintenance.

He began cutting and shaping the tray pieces to be inserts into the bottoms of the boxes. He said that, these boxes, over time, collect all sort of nasty things and, when you jam you hand in there, day after day, you're bound to catch on something. So, these "inserts" prop the mail up so that both the carrier and the recipient don't have to dig way down into the depths of the box. Jeremy said that at times, the carrier needs to remove mail from boxes as well and this helps facilitate that.

We move from complex building to complex building and I felt that I got the gist of how things need to go and my mind shifted gears from, "Let me see what needs to be done." to "Let me get inside the head of a mail carrier a little bit". And so, I struck up mild social conversation just to get a feel for what it's like being a mail carrier. Jeremy had been on the job for fifteen years. He claimed he loved it. He didn't understand why so many back at the annex complained about everything so much. He said that those people who started the job in their early 20's or even late teens and going on 20, 25, 30 years of service, are jaded. "It's easy for them to complain because, this is all they know. They don't know what it's like to have shit jobs. They don't know what it's like to work your ass off for shit pay and not be appreciated for anything! They just complain because a car is parked in front of a cluster box and will bitch all day about it. I'm not on the overtime list so, I do my 8 hours and I go home. That's it."

I can appreciate what he's talking about. No matter what the occupation, you do it long enough and you lose sight of relativity. Or, in the case of many within the Postal Service, you do it long enough and, there aren't many options to the individual that garnish the same benefits. You stay in the Postal Service long enough and become a square peg in a world of round holes. But, that doesn't stop the square pegs from complaining about being a square peg.

Jeremy tells me that his mother is a retired postmaster so, at least he's keeping it in the family. His son had just started working for UPS. Jeremy claims that he was unable to get his son into the Postal Service. I didn't bite on that but I did find it odd. His mother is a retired Postmaster, he's on the job for fifteen years and, he was "unable" to get a 23 year old young man on the job? I thought of how relatively easy it was for this "old man" to get to this point of the process. Perhaps the son just didn't want the job. Not sure, and I didn't press it.

Jeremy admits that he had gone out the night before to celebrate something, I failed to catch the reason, and his brother-in-law kept him out later than he wanted and drank more than he should and was feeling it today. That would explain the head-in-hand-resting-on-the-time-clock I had witnessed at the beginning of the day. He tells me that he also had a young daughter of four or five at home. I exalted him for having a 23 year old and a 5 year old at the same time and, once again, I see how it's necessary for the individual to find a balance between what we choose as our daily grind and our overall life's pleasures. I believe he mentioned that his wife was a nurse and so, I drew the conclusion that, the wife works odd shifts and, he needs to be available for his young daughter. Life choice. It works for him. Show up on time, get yourself organized, do your job, go home. It's really just that simple.

We continue to different parts of town and deliver to different types of residences. Different residences require different procedures and approaches. The assisted living homes need extra care required. Depending on the residence, you go in and take a hand truck they have and come back out to the van and load it up and then haul the whole thing back in where you drop parcels at the front desk, where they are then either delivered by the residence support staff or are retrieved by the residence themselves, and then you haul the First Class mail and Flats to a large bank of mail boxes within the depts of the residence. I observe Jeremy at these large banks and, while he cordoned off the area with those retractable ribbon separators you see at movie theatres, an elderly gentleman needed to get in to do "his thing". I listened to their conversation and, apparently the man was a 35 year retired mail carrier and, the resistant mail representative. He distributed flyers and announcements to the residents in a common mail area next to the locked U.S. Postal area. It really is nice hearing stories from older people. It's a history lesson and, if you can drop your ego long enough, you just might be fulfilled by the wisdom of someone who's "been there and done that".

Jeremy finished up and we're back in the van and he states, "That's it! We're done". It was about 4pm and we start heading back to the annex. Once back at the annex (I did notice that he pulled straight into his parking spot. I guess he'll be backing up tomorrow again!) he meticulously organized the outgoing mail, any mail being returned for whatever reason, empty bins and his personal items into a hamper and we retreat back from whence we came hours earlier.

Other carriers were already back from their route and saw me and I heard variations of, "You made it!" and "Are you coming back tomorrow?". Jeremy told me that, they used to have the shadow day after training but, they soon learned that, better to expose the person to how the job really is BEFORE spending the money on training as, many people get out on the street and decide that it just isn't for them. This way, exposing the person to shadowing a mail carrier gives them an idea of what it's like and they can bail out now and save the Post Service a lot of money by discontinuing the onboarding process.

I thanked Jeremy for allowing me to observe and ask questions. Nice guy. I could tell that he genuinely cares about doing his job well. He was very pleasant to customers on the newly added addition to his route, introducing himself to anyone on the route that he sees. Perhaps a little overly sweat at times but, I suppose it's never too soon to start laying the foundation for a nice holiday tip. Jeremy's most vehement piece of advice that I made a point to remember was, "Always deliver to the address, not to the person." I guess that would help explain why I'm living in my home for close to three years and I'm still receiving mail from the previous owner. The address is correct, therefore, it goes in the box. The name is insignificant.

Before leaving the annex, I make a pit-stop in the men's room and I find myself standing next to Greg at our respective urinals. Greg murmurs, "New guy, how's it goin'?... Hey, how old are you?" "Fifty eight", I reply. "Ooph!!", says Greg. "It's a young man's game. They're going to kill you!"

Hmm, maybe Greg isn't completely washed up after all!

Chapter 5 – Driver's Ed

After completing my shadow day, I received an email indicating that I should report to the Fort Lauderdale annex three days later at 6:30am for driver certification. I'm a morning person but, I thought that taking a driving test at 6:30am in the morning might be a little early.

I arrive at the address given to me on January 28th at 6:14am. Even in the sunshine state, it's dark as night at that time on that date. I didn't see any activity as I tried to determine exactly where to report. I saw that the only area with lights glowing was about a quarter mile away on the other side of the complex. So, I go there, park and start to look for some human activity. I find someone and explain what I'm doing there and the man told me that we were standing in the maintenance garage where auto maintenance occurs for the local Postal vehicles. He pointed and told me that I probably have to go to the other side of the complex (where I had come from) for drivers instruction. I walk back to the car and drive to the other side, and again, saw no one. I got out and checked all the doors of the loading dock and all were locked. I don't even know who to call to try to reach out to someone. And even if I did, it's 6:30am! By process of elimination, I drive to an area where I hadn't yet been and I see one person walking from a parking area to dimly lit turnstiles. I drive to that location and I now see another person standing outside the turnstiles. I gather my belongings, lock up and walk toward the entrance but, as I now see that it is 6:32am, I put a "gittyup" in my step and I greet an older, black lady.

"You Stallone!?"

"Spallone, with a "P", yes."

"YOU'RE LATE!"

Oh boy…

I apologized and stated that I had been there for almost twenty minutes looking for exactly where to go but, she didn't seem impressed by my excuse. She escorted me into the building as I didn't have clearance to enter on my own. We entered a cavernous mail processing plant. It was enormous. Rows and rows of electronic sorting machines, empty bins, full bins, signs indicating the specific area that an operation is performed and…no people. I followed closely behind the instructor who introduced herself to me while we walked as Maggie. We get to an office and I'm told to sit and fill out some paperwork that she will give me. While I'm filling out all of the paperwork, I perk my ears to the conversation going on between a gentleman and Maggie on the other side of the office.

Apparently, the man was upset that a request he had made for a case of water was denied. "So and so can order a $300 chair, that I had to put together by the way, but I can't get a case of water for driver's instructors to take out on the road!?" Maggie received the complaints with nods of understand.

Having completed the paperwork, Maggie takes me outside to where the vehicles are parked. They're parked right next to the garage where I had the quick conversation with the mechanic twenty minutes earlier. Going around in circles would be a theme to be repeated in the coming months. Maggie first takes me to a

Postal vehicle called an LLV, (Long Life Vehicle) manufactured by the Grumman company. A typical looking "modern" mail truck that most people are familiar with. I later found out that these vehicles are prone to spontaneous combustion. The Postal Service hired an engineering firm in 2014 to investigate the cause of the fires. When no single reason was discovered, the agency increased efforts to stick to mandated maintenance schedules and fine-tune repair and maintenance procedures.

The instruction started just like a car rental; "Here's the key, here's how you turn the lights on, etc." and we went over all of the necessary safety concerns. "Always wear your seat belt, be mindful of the various mirrors. There is no rear view mirror so, be mindful of that. And, above all, never EVER back up". Then she showed me with the wave of her hand the obstacle course for which I was to "mount up" and listen to and adhere to her instruction".

I mount. I bring the truck to the starting point of a Stop sign. Maggie then instructs, "Ok, listen carefully; make a left, then come back to the next stop sign. Make a right, then come back to the stop sign. Go straight, come around to the curbside mail boxes and reach out and touch the mail boxes remembering to put your flashers on. Pull up to the other mail box, touch it. Pull up to the mail box with the garbage can in front of it and stop just before the garbage can. Put the vehicle in park, set the parking break, roll the window up (manual window, of course), take the mail destined for that address, lock the vehicle. Walk to the mail box and deliver the mail. We don't have any mail today so, just go ahead and open the box and close it to pretend. Come back to the vehicle and do a walk around to be sure that no children are playing near or under the vehicle. Mount up, put your seat belt on, start the vehicle, disengage the parking break, put your signal on and pull up to the area where you will demonstrate how to parallel park and curb your wheels. You get two chances. Then pull out (remembering to put your signal on) and pull up to the stop sign and then back-in between those two orange cones over there by the loading dock. Ok, whenever you're ready, go ahead!"

How the hell was I supposed to remember all of that!? Frankly, I kind of lost her after "Listen carefully…". I was further distracted by the whole "back up/don't back up" contradiction as well. But, off I went. I did the best I could to duplicate her instructions and, it wasn't as bad as I thought it was going to be because she shouted out the next steps to take at each increment. I took each step methodically choosing to show care instead of speed as I thought a show of concern for safety would go a long way toward my evaluation. I get to the parallel parking bit and pull it off perfectly in the first shot. Feeling good that it was almost over, I throw it in reverse and carefully back in to the designated spot at the loading dock between the two orange cones. I shut down properly, dismount, and lock up and confidently dangle the key before Maggie's eyes in a "how's that?" gesture. "Very good", she said. "You just forgot to blow your horn before backing up!" "Ok, pull up to the Stop sign and do it again!".

Blow the horn?….before backing up?…when did anyone say anything about that? Again, distracted by this latest addition to what I WASN'T supposed to do, I circumnavigate the obstacle course with just a little more speed, pull off yet another perfect parallel parking job and complete the course with the added horn "toot-toot" before backing into the designated space. I refrain from the key dangle this time however.

"Again!", Maggie shouts. Off I go for a third time. Having memorized all the moves that are required to make at this point, I blow through the whole thing with no hesitation. But, before coming to the "backing up" part, Maggie approaches the vehicle, tells me to put it in park and she gets in and buckles up in a temporary jumper seat that I just now had noticed was slightly behind me for the first time since entering the vehicle. "Ok, you seem pretty confident. Let's go out on the road!".

The safety within the confines of an obstacle course was one thing, out on the road was quite another. Especially, "out there!". One of the reasons I relocated to Florida was that I couldn't deal with the congestion of the tri-state area of New York/New Jersey/Connecticut any longer. No matter where you went, you were choked. To my surprise, I hadn't realized that southern Florida was FAR worse! And, what added to the frustration was the quality of drivers. For lack of a more gracious description, they're all insane! I feel much more comfortable driving through mid-town Manhattan than simply driving around the block in southern Florida. I really don't know what it is. Perhaps the concentration of part-time residences from all over the country congregated in a very small area and the idiosyncrasies of their regional driving "habits" are more pronounced? I really don't know. All I know is, it's guaranteed that you'll witness some sort of bone-head driving move within minutes of driving the area, that's for sure. And then there's the red signal lights…..

Having been a troubled sleeper since my early teens, I remember pursuing a sleep study later in life and one of the questions on the questionnaire to determine ones level of sleep dilemma was, "Are you able to fall asleep while in a car and stopped at red signals light?" Of course, was the answer! And that's a New York red light. In southern Florida, the red lights are so long, I can take a nice refreshing nap that gets me through the rest of the day! I'm enthralled, and annoyed, when the changing signal lights go in such an odd pattern that at one point, all traffic in all four directions are completely stopped. No one is moving. How can NO traffic be moving? It doesn't make any sense! I realize that sitting at a red light for five minutes is probably coming off as complaining by a semi-privileged white guy is a society where there are far more life threatening and serious problems in the world but, fuuuuuuuuuuuck meeeeeeee…every quarter mile and it repeats! How does anyone get anywhere around here?

So, I was a little apprehensive with the thought of taking this bucket of bolts with a steering wheel and all the other automotive controls on the right side, with someone watching me over my shoulder, "out there!".

But, I think I put Maggie at ease with my awesome display of driving prowess on the obstacle course and can tell that she had a confidence in me about her with an air of taking the LLV out into the jungle of real southern Florida driving as, just a formality.

I followed her directions and, after a while, fell into a blasé' execution of movements. We navigate through the streets of Fort Lauderdale, far from any resemblance of any sea or sand, and finally end up, where we started. I was directed to back the vehicle into its final resting spot and lock up. Maggie then suggested that we take a break and then we'll move onto the ProMaster.

After a quick fifteen minute break we were back on the obstacle course, only this time, I was to be certified on the Postal vehicle called a ProMaster. This is the same type of vehicle that I had been in for my shadow day with Jeremy the other day. Now, this was no problem as, at least all the controls were on the right (correct) side of the vehicle, meaning the left side. Anyone who's ever rented a moving van, knows how to drive one of these babies. It drives like a car. But, again, I find myself executing the demands of the obstacle course. Again, nailing the parallel parking like a boss and completing the course confidently and efficiently. Maggie stated, "Damn, YOU can teach ME how to parallel park!". It's a New York thing Maggie!

We broke for lunch and I found myself sitting in the dingy break/lunch room with a multitude of vending machines hawking anything and everything from chips to soda to ice cream. There were ratty looking toasters and microwave ovens for use but, I chose to sit and enjoy my cold spaghetti that I brought with me. One or two other people were scattered around lunch tables and we all stared at the little tv suspended into the air at one end of the room.

I try to always be conscious of the moment and appreciate the humor in things. At this moment, I was shoveling cold spaghetti into my mouth in a dingy Postal Service break room in Fort Lauderdale, Fl, getting certified at driving, 42 years after receiving my driver's license, while watching Donald Trump be impeached on this tiny tv hanging from the ceiling. What the hell am I doing here? I'm in a circus, watching a circus, that took a break from its normal circus activity. Three rings!

After lunch, we take the ProMaster out on the street and perform the same lefts and rights that we had done with the LLV. The ProMaster, needing less "care" than the LLV, allowed us to slip into the obligatory and slightly personal social discussions. We discussed our children, and the driver's education we both administered to them and the ever-present fear that a parent has, even when they grow into "responsible adults" when operating a vehicle. "It's not YOU that I'm worried about, it's OTHER people!" That sort of thing. Maggie commented that I had been pulling just a little too close to the car in front of us when stopped at an intersection. "You know that you're a safe distance behind a stopped car if you can see their rear wheels touching the ground. You need to able to get around that car and keeping that distance allows you to do that! If you can't see their tires touching the ground, you're too close!" Fair enough Maggie. I find myself remembering this trick to this day.

The driving certification, done at this time in my onboarding, was approached in the same way that the shadow day was. No need to further train an individual if they simply cannot show capability with driving various Postal vehicles. I thought of Purple hair with not the best of outcomes after having completed what I had just done. We settle up back at the office with signed paperwork and such, and Maggie asked if I was supposed to do the 2-ton today. I had no idea of what she was referring to and she stated that I did so well and we went through it so quickly that we had time to get certified on the 2-ton truck, the next vehicle up in size in the Postal Fleet. We agreed that, since we didn't actually have anything in writing stating that I should be trained on the 2-ton, to wait until I'm on the job and have my office indicate if that's something they want me to do in the future.

I bid her thanks and farewell. On my way out to my car, I looked back at the Postal vehicles that I had just been certified on and parked in their positions waiting for the next student. I see that the LLV had a crushed orange cone under its left rear wheel! Had I done that? Maggie would have said something, I think. Nahh, probably someone had taken it out after me.

I'll always remember what Maggie had said in parting and I realized that it very well described the way I've always driven; "Remember", she said, "Slow is smooth, smooth is fast!".

Chapter 6 – Carrier Academy

The next day, I received an email to report to the Western Delray Beach Post Office a week from then for Carrier Academy. Another week of marking time. It's been two full months since I followed the link to apply for this position. Oddly, when meeting Bill during our "interview" and I asked about starting time frame, he mentioned that I was being fast tracked but, still, when the ball is passed from entity to entity for processing, things tend to get bogged down. Carrier Academy is the Postal Services training effort. It's supposed to last four full days and I look forward to rolling my sleeves up and getting down to the nuts and bolts of being a mail carrier.

I showed up at the address given to me extra early (6:45am) so as not to be met with further attitude about being late and found the area to be baron. It didn't look right. But, there was another person there who looked like they were looking for the same thing I was. The door to the inside of the Post Office, where the private Post Office boxes were located, was unlocked and we entered. Still, no one around. We found a door that looked like it might have led way to the interior of the building and I knocked. A woman answered and I explained that we were there to attend the Carrier Academy. The woman replied very curtly, "You didn't follow directions, did you?"

Here we go…

Chapter 6

The woman couldn't be bothered and proceeded to over-explain directions, as if we were idiots, to; "...leave the parking lot, make a right, then make another right at the light where the WaWa is and stay to your right. Make another right and go all the way to the back and park there and someone will be there to meet you."

We did this and saw a few people waiting outside of the back of the building and we were greeted by yet another attitude. No, "Good morning", no "Welcome to Carrier Academy training" just, "Follow me. Anyone who shows up now is late!"

We entered the rear of the building and I immediately see the woman who greeted us in the front of the building. I realized that, where we stood was just on the other side of the door that I had knocked on! She couldn't just let us in THAT door?

We were ushered into this tiny room with no windows containing a long table with chairs on either side. I thought, all day in here is going to be a challenge, especially if the attitude keeps up.

I take a seat and try to get situation but, the area is so cramped that I find it hard to lay out what I feel is necessary to take notes. There are files of paper and plastic baskets filled with this and that and paper-clipped smaller pieces of colored paper and various pens and such. But, no real room to spread out.

All of us got situated in their seats and no one was saying a thing. There's an uncomfortable air in the room of not being really sure how to behave. There's no chit-chat, there are no greetings, just grown people sitting quietly in hard plastic chairs with two feet on the ground and two hands on a table waiting for the next step.

The "instructor" then introduces herself as Sharma Williams, a Technical Instructor. I found out later that Technical Instructors are mail carriers that act as regular mail carriers and fill-in for regular carriers on their regular routes when those carriers are on "off" days. Again, I wonder where that leaves the CCA? I thought that that's what THEY did? A TI also acts as a trainer in situations where needed. Some are in-classroom (like Sharma), others are the designated on-the-job trainer at a given Postal Office and others act as driving instructors. I wondered if a TI's salary is adjusted to include the additional responsibilities.

I immediately get the impression of Sharma as a no-nonsense type of instructor. No-nonsense, on the surface, is certainly the way to try to command respect and therefore, expect results. However, this approach doesn't bode well for me in a training situation. I've always believed that you get more flies with honey than you do with vinegar and I seem to approach my efforts in communication in that manner with good success. Well, Sharma didn't aligne herself with that sort of thinking, it would appear. Her approach was very stern, militaristic, rude…really, and I feel that it is not only unnecessary but, ineffective.

I've been in the military. I've been barked at, seemingly for no reason, by the best of them. This Postal employee seems to be coopting a strong arm approach to training in a classroom environment and, it just doesn't work! And frankly, it's unbecoming. It has the opposite effect on me. You throw papers at a person with zero facial expression and zero communication using actual words and expect a positive outcome, you've got no business training people. I ignored the antics for the most part but I could see that her methods were causing more confusion in the class then were necessary. We're here to learn how to properly put paper products into metal boxes, not storm the beaches of France!

Sharma mechanically read from previously prepared scripts on what the expectations and responsibilities of the carrier were. What is obvious is that the primary responsibility of a mail carrier, who is the most visible of Postal employee to the public, is to provide reliable and efficient service, which encompasses obeying instructions of the local postal manager, reporting to work on time, completing time records accurately, displaying a willing attitude and put forth a conscientious effort in developing and refining skills necessary to perform duties assigned, be prompt, courteous and obliging in the performance of duties.

That last one got me. Sharma might want to review the courteous and obliging part of her duties.

The mail carrier is charged with preserving and protecting the security of all mail from unauthorized opening, inspection, destruction, tampering, delay, reading of the contents, or other unauthorized acts. The employee is not to place mail in their pockets or clothing, lockers or desks, or in parcels, handgrips, personal vehicle, lunch containers, other luggage, or dispose of or otherwise discard the mail. They are to protect all mail, money, and equipment entrusted to their care and return all mail, money, and equipment to the post office at the end of the workday.

With very few exceptions, no one, except those employed by the Postal Service for that purpose, may break or permit the breaking of the seals of any class mail matter without a federal search warrant, even though it may contain criminal or otherwise nonmailable matter, or would furnish evidence of the commission of the crime.

Infringement of these statutes do not afford Postal Employee immunity from arrest for violations of law. Any postal employee committing or allowing any unauthorized acts is subject to administrative discipline and/or criminal prosecution leading to fine, imprisonment, or both. Title 18, United States Code, Section 1709, Theft of Mail Matter by Officer or Employee states:

"Whoever, being a Postal Service officer or employee, embezzles any letter, postal card, package, bag, or mail, or any article or thing contained therein entrusted to him or which comes into his possession intended to be conveyed by mail, or carried or delivered by any carrier, messenger, agent, or other person employed in any department of the Postal Service, or forwarded through or delivered from any post office or station thereof established by authority of the Postmaster General or of the Postal Service; or steals, abstracts, or removes from any such letter, package, bag, or mail, any article or thing contained therein, shall be fined not more than $2,000 or imprisoned not more than five years, or both."

Two grand and not more than five years in prison? Seems kind of light to me. Further, the mail carrier is to practice to reduce financial losses. All postal employees are responsible for safeguarding the Postal Service from loss of revenue. As carriers, we are to serve as ambassadors of the organization and have unique opportunities to promote benefits of using postal products and services. Our diligence to revenue protection practices and identifying revenue generation opportunities are vital to the success of the Postal Service.

This translates to me not so much as "selling the Post Office" to customers but, offering improved methods to the organization.

Isn't it your responsibility as an employee at any position to offer improved methods of functionality? I already see that this onboarding process, as drawn out as it is, is a terrific time bog. I certainly understand that there needs to be a proper vetting out of individuals who are entrusted with the responsibility of delivering some very private and well needed information and medications but, it's my personal belief that this process, so far, can be improved upon to be more efficient. I'm just not sure who it is I can convey this observation to at this point. Sharma would probably not be kindly receptive.

The carrier is to maintain a neat, clean and generally creditable appearance. The carrier is the most visible postal employee and their appearance should reflect pride in work and duties. We are required to wear an approved Postal uniform which includes correct footwear. This helps promote the corporate image and professionalism.

Sharma quickly went over the various types of postal positions available within the organization:

City Carriers: Case, delivers and collects mail on foot or by vehicle under varying road and weather conditions in a prescribed area and maintain professional and effective public relations with customers and other.

Rural Carriers: Case, delivers and collects mail along a prescribed rural route using a vehicle and provide customers on the route with a variety of services.

Carrier Technicians: Serve a designated group of routes on the regularly assigned carrier's non-schedule workdays and may provide job instruction to newly assigned carriers.

Mail Handlers: Load, unload, and move mail. They also perform other duties incidental to the movement and processing of mail.

Clerks: May perform a variety of sales and customer support services for products or may separates mail in accordance with established schemes, including incoming and outgoing mail.

Custodians: Perform duties in connection with custody of an office or building.

Customer Service Supervisor: Overseas a group of employees in the delivery collection, and distribution of mail, and in window service activities within a post office, station or branch, or detached unit.

Postmaster: Manage the operation of post offices.

Manager, Customer Service: Directs, with the assistance of supervisors in activities of a carrier station or branch providing delivery and collection services, through a large number of routes; window and box services; mail distribution and dispatch; and the processing or sale of non-postal products.

Manager, Post Office Operations: Oversees all operations of a designated group of post offices within the jurisdiction of a customer service district, monitoring performance and ensuring compliance with national, area and district objectives for service, budget, and productivity.

This is just a small list of positions within the United States Postal Service. The diversity of occupations within the service is as vast as the people who work there. Auto mechanics, Human Resources professionals, Postal Investigators, as well as many other occupations, add to the support of the Postal Service's infrastructure.

Chapter 6

Sharma discards her notes and brings up the importance of accurate timekeeping when it pertains to reporting to work and for the various moves within the work day. At this point, she decided to berate the class as to why no one had asked for a 1260.

“It’s YOUR responsibility to keep your time card complete and accurate. If you don’t, there will be disciplinary action taken. Didn’t they tell you about filling out a 1260 in orientation? I know they did.”

A young man, who I later found out left a sweet job at Kentucky Fried Chicken for this, piped up, “Oh, right, yes, they did go over that.”

“Then why didn’t you say something about it when you came in this morning?”

“I don’t know…I….”

“Never mind, I’ll hand out one to each. Be sure that you Begin Tour at 7am and to be sure to put your employee ID number where indicated. If you don’t want to get paid, that’s your business!”

“…courteous and obliging in the performance of duties.” Ok…

And, of course, someone has to fill out the form incorrectly and was forced to ask for another one. All with heavy sighs and eye rolls, the torturous job of somehow having to prove that we were actually there and needed to get paid for it, got completed.

We quickly went over personal safety; if something is heavy, lift with your legs. If something is too heavy, ask for help. I found out later that, if something is heavy OR too heavy, it’ll be brushed off onto someone else to carry!

The Workplace Violence Prevention Program provides employees with resources and awareness of prevention and response measures. Workplace violence is a problem worldwide and the third leading cause of death in the workplace.

Zero tolerance means that every act or threat of violence, regardless of the initiator, elicits an immediate and firm response. The response could result in corrective action, up to, and including removal of the offender from employment with the Postal Service.

The concept of zero tolerance is based on the belief that no employee should have to work in an atmosphere of fear and intimidation. Every threat and every act of inappropriate behavior must be addressed.

The zero tolerance policy provides the foundation for prevention, but that is only part of the preventative efforts and strategies.

The Joint Statement on Violence and Behavior affirms the intentions to make the workroom floor a safer, more harmonious, as well as a more productive workplace. The following statement is posted on bulletin boards in all postal installations:

"The United States Postal Service as an institution and all of us who serve that institution must firmly and unequivocally commit to do everything within our power to prevent further incidents of work-related violence.

This is a time for candid appraisal of our flaws and not a time for scapegoating, finger pointing, or procrastination. It is a time for reaffirming the basic right of all employees to a safe and humane working environment. It is also the time to take action to show that we mean what we say.

We openly acknowledge that in some places or units there is an unacceptable level of stress in the workplace; that there is no excuse for and will be no tolerance of violence or any threats of violence by anyone at any level of the Postal Service; and that there is no excuse for and will be no tolerance of harassment, intimidation, threats, or bullying by anyone.

We also affirm that every employee at every level of the Postal Service should be treated at all times with dignity, respect and fairness. The need for the USPS to serve the public efficiently and productively, and the need for all employees to be committed to giving a fair day's work for a fair day's pay, does not justify actions that are abusive or intolerant. "Making the numbers" is not an excuse for the abuse of anyone. Those who do not treat others with dignity and respect will not be rewarded or promoted. Those whose unacceptable behavior continues will be removed from their positions.

We obviously cannot ensure that however seriously intentioned our words may be, they will not be treated with winks and nods, or skepticism, by some of our 700,000 employees. But let there be no mistake that we mean what we say and we will enforce our commitment to a workplace where dignity, respect, and fairness are basic human rights, and where those who do not respect those rights are not tolerated.

Our intention is to make the workroom floor a safe, more harmonious, as well as a more productive workplace. We pledge our efforts to these objectives."

(Signed by the D.C. Nurses Association, Federation of Postal Police Officers, National Association of Letter Carriers, National Postal Mail Handlers Union, United States Postal Service, National Association of Postal Supervisors, National Association of Postmasters of the United States, National League of

Postmasters of the United States, National Rural Letter Carriers' Association)

Dated: February 14, 1992

Source: Postal Bulletin, 21811, 3-19-92, page 3

So, it would appear that the Postal Service is serious about keeping the Postal employee in a safe operating environment. Still, that they don't provide health care initially to the employee stands in contradiction to their ethos.

At this point, Sharma decides that it would be a good time for all of us to go around the table and introduce ourselves and offer why we are interested in working for the United States Postal Service and what career we are leaving in order to pursue one with the USPS.

The group is diverse, as one could imagine. The gentleman who isn't quite ready for retirement and could barely speak understandable English having emigrated from Italy years earlier, the gum-snapper who didn't seem interested in sharing her name or what she's done in the past and a pleasant young black man of thirty who felt that a career at Kentucky Fried Chicken simply wasn't going to work out to provide for his family in the future. As for me, I made something up, as per my usual Motus operandi. We dispensed with the always pleasant introductions and took a break after having being barked at about taking a ten minute break and not be late upon returning.

Thankfully no one was delayed in returning back to the classroom as, that would just add to the tension already felt by those present.

The Mobile Delivery Device (MDD) is a device used by the Postal Service to which provides real-time scan data, GPS data transfer, two-way test messaging with supervisor, and signature on glass. It's claimed that the best way to generate revenue is to keep improving the customer experience. The MDD serves in this respect as the customer will be able to receive text or email messages if a parcel is delivered, out for delivery and proof of both and provide delivery information in real-time. The device uses cellular and GPS technology that uploads data every 10 seconds. The device also provides a means by which the location of the mail carrier may be tracked.

Sharma handed out a device to each of us and walked us through on how to log into the system. Once in, we stepped through each of the most often used functions of the device. We practiced scanning different pieces of mail and processing them as required within the system. Anyone who's been witness to a group of people stepping through the operation of a technical device on mass knows that it's just a matter of time before someone has a problem. Either the individual has moved beyond the current step that the instructor is on and has entered an area of confusion or, they are trailing behind for some reason or, technical difficulty. We had all three. Next to me was a young lady who didn't seem interested in much other than snapping her gum every three seconds and viewing her phone. She just plowed ahead on the MDD and was lost in an area within the scanner and didn't know how to back out of it. My MDD just locked-up completely. As I handed the scanner to Sharma to take a look at, she asked, "What did you do?". I refrained from making some sort of snide remark and handed it over quietly. She was unable to get it unlocked and had to replace the unit. Not a good sign, I thought. I received a new one and, logged in and caught up to the class quickly. Pierre', the KFC guy, seemed to have the most problems. It became clear that, as young as he was, he was having difficulty actually seeing the text on the smaller glass screen of the scanner. When meaning to select one option, he chose another, which brought him to a completely different screen. He would bring his misdirection to Sharma's attention and then, three or four steps later, be faced with the same misdirection due to his poor eyesight. I almost laughed out loud when Sharma almost word-for-word channeled Purple-haired Pam weeks earlier in orientation when she shouted, "How you gonna deliver mail to the proper address if you can't even see the scanner?!".

Pierre', clearly hurt, claimed that he's waiting for his first USPS paycheck so that he can get new glasses. Another reminder to myself that people around us may be dealing with a great deal of problems on a daily basis that a lot of people can't appreciate or sympathize with.

Having all gotten on the same page, we reached the point on the scanner training where it was instructed that, at certain times, delivery of an item needs to be signed for. We stepped through the screens on how to scan the bar code on the deliverable item, acknowledge that it is being delivered and where it is being delivered (Mail box?, Front door?, Parcel locker?, Front desk?, Neighbor? Etc.) and if a signature is necessary to receive the item. If yes, the carrier is to approach the residence and knock or ring bell. Usually anyone within the domicile is considered an approved signatory and you are to hand the scanner to that person with the attached screen pen and have them sign where appropriate. If no one answers the door, this is to be captured on the menu's provided on the scanner as well as having to fill out PS-Form 3849.

PS-Form 3849 is a pink/mauve colored rectangle piece of paper with a Post-it like sticky area at one edge so that it can be filled out with the appropriate information with name of person the item is addressed to, where the item is coming from, where the item can be picked up from, what date the item will be available to be picked up from that given location and if there is any postage due or if a signature is required and, placed on the front door of the residence giving notice that a parcel was attempted to be delivered to the residence and what action the deliveree needs to take.

Giving a cursory look through the menus, (while Sharma worked with Pierre' yet again) I could see that the scanner had a great many functions outside of what we were being exposed to. I assumed that they all would come to light when normal functions on the job became a practice.

We then discussed the importance of proper vehicle inspection. Before a Postal vehicle is driven, it must be inspected to ensure that it is in proper operating order and no damage or defect exists. All inspections of these vehicles are done on-the-clock and are done every day before heading out on a route.

Notice 76, *Expanded Vehicle Safety Check*, is used in the process of a vehicle inspection. Label 70, *Safety Check and Vehicle Dimensions*, is found on the dash of all postal owned vehicles and is another reminder that all safety checks should be performed daily before operating the vehicle. Notice 76, *Expanded Vehicle Safety Check* is designed to take the driver in a logical sequence around the vehicle during its inspection. The following are the steps to be followed:

- Inspect under vehicle for fluid leaks.
- Inspect front tires for uneven wear and under-inflation.
- Check that the hood can be latched securely.
- Check front for body damage.
- Check left door lock (check for complete accident report kit if stowed on inside left of vehicle.
- Check for rear end leaks.
- Inspect rear tires for uneven wear and under-inflation.
- Check rear for body damage.
- Check right door lock(s).
- Open door and move into driving position.
- Check for complete accident report kit.
- Start engine.
- With assistance, adjust pot-lid mirrors and rear-view mirrors.
- With assistance, check headlights, tail lights, brake lights, flashers, and directional signals (front and rear).
- Check operation of windshield wipers and washer.
- Check operation of horn.
- Check gauges for proper operation.
- Check foot brake.
- Check emergency brake.
- Check seat belt and fasten.

Is that it? I wondered. No checking the oil dipstick? No making sure that the tire pressure is balls-on accurate? I kid. I do agree that at the very least, these vehicles, which are being rolled-out on public streets should be at the top of their game. There should be no chance of any mechanical malfunctions causing harm to anyone or anything and I can appreciate the extra care taken by the USPS mechanics as well, as the steps taken in preventative maintenance by each carrier, each day before heading out on the road.

Should deficiencies be found such as body damage or inoperable items during the vehicle inspection, a report needs to be submitted to the supervisor using PS Form 4565, *Vehicle Repair Tag* so that the conditions can be corrected or another vehicle provided.

The next day of training keyed on the importance of handling the mail correctly. And in order to do so, one must have general knowledge of the classes of mail. My naiveté was in evidence here in that, I wasn't to be working at a Postal Office customer service desk where it might be needed to know the various options that a person could send something, and so, probably not that important for the mail carrier to know. However, this couldn't be further from the truth. All classes of mail are important, but delivery standards vary according to the class of mail. The class of mail also determines how the mail piece is handled when it is not deliverable as addressed. Another point of naivete' on my part as I had never even considered that something might not be delivered. As far as I was concerned, this is a one-way effort. Mail class is determined by mail piece characteristics and postage paid by the mailer.

As it turns out, there are six actions in which a carrier may take with a mail piece:

- Deliver
- Forward
- Hold
- Place in Throwback Case
- Return to Sender with a reason for non-delivery (when properly endorsed)
- Place in tub marked UBBM (Undeliverable Bulk Business Mail). Authorized personnel will verify and discard as appropriate.

The class of mail can be identified by markings in the postage area of the mail piece (Except for Periodicals that are not enclosed in an envelope or wrapper) and specialized packaging or labeling.

Starting with the Postal Services top level premium service is Priority Mail Express. Priority Mail Express is the fastest (as most expensive) way to send a piece of mail (up to 70 pounds) to its destination. This service guarantees delivery by the next or second day and delivery may occur 7 days a week, 365 days a year to most destinations and specific delivery times of 10:30am, 12:00pm or 3:00pm may be chosen depending on the service commitment and local instructions. Delivery is guaranteed by the time and day indicated or else a full refund of postage is given to the mailer. Priority Mail Express requires scanning and a customer signature on glass or PS FORM 3849, *Delivery Notice/Reminder/Receipt*, if the mailer indicates a signature is required on the Priority Mail Express label. The mailer may choose to require a signature and if so, it will be noted on the Priority Mail Express label. If a signature is not required, the carrier scans the mail piece as delivered and selects the appropriate response on the scanner when prompted and places it in the customer's mailbox or front door. There is an international version of Priority Mail Express called Global Express Guaranteed (GXG) and Priority Mail Express International (EMI). GXG offers expedited delivery service provided with an alliance with FedEx Express. EMI offers fast reliable service with date-certain service only to select worldwide destinations.

With the exception of restricted material, any mailable item, including postcards, letters, Flats, and small packages, may be mailed as First-Class Mail (FCM). Items containing handwriting or typewriting, personal information, bills, and statements of account must be sent as First-Class Mail. FCM is protected against postal inspection. Postage for a single piece of First-Class Mail (FCM) is determined by weight (in ounces). First-Class Mail weighing over 13 ounces will need to be sent as Priority Mail. At this writing, postage for a single piece of First-Class Mail weighing under 13 ounces is fifty five cents. FCM is to be delivered on the same day that it arrives at the delivery office. Undeliverable FCM must be forwarded if a forwarding address is provided or endorsed with a reason for the non-delivery before returning the mail piece to the sender.

Priority Mail is mail weighing over 13 ounces. Although not guaranteed, Priority Mail offers 1, 2, or 3 day-specific service. Priority Mail is a sub-class of First-Class Mail and does not require a signature on delivery unless additional postage for Extra Services is applied. Like FCM, undeliverable Priority Mail must be forwarded if a forwarding address is provided or endorsed with the reason for non-delivery before returning the mail piece to the sender. Priority Mail cannot be discarded. Priority Mail

International provides service for international shipments of document and merchandise.

The Periodical class of mail consists primarily of magazines, newsletters, and newspapers. Postage payment is indicated within the publication in an identification statement. Periodicals must be delivered on the same day as received in the Postal Office. Undeliverable pieces are forwarded for 60 days if a forwarding address in on file. Undeliverable as addressed pieces with no forwarded address on file, are endorsed with a reason for non-delivery and returned to the publisher. Periodicals may not be discarded.

Standard Mail, and frankly, what makes up the majority of product which is placed inside a residences mail receptacle generally consists of advertising such as, circulars or flyers and cannot contain personal information. There are two types of Standard Mail, Regular and Nonprofit. All Standard Mail is presorted and must be marked as such.

The low cost is the primary reason why Standard Mail is so attractive to customers. It provides economical prices for mailings of 200 or more pieces or 50 or more pounds of mail. The delivery of Standard Mail may be curtailed at management's discretion using PS Form 1571, *Undelivered Mail Report.* Standard Mail must weigh less than 16 ounces and may include saturation mailings utilizing simplified address. These are the mailings you receive which may be addressed to "Postal Customer" or "Resident". Standard Mail is not forwarded unless it is endorsed with one of the following Ancillary Service Endorsements (ASEs):

- Change Service Requested
- Return Service Requested
- Address Service Requested
- Forwarding Service Requested
- Temp-Return Service Requested
- Electronic Service Requested

And even with that, the ASEs must be placed in one of four specific positions or the mail should be considered fraudulent. Those positions are:

- Directly below the return address
- Directly above the delivery address are (which includes the delivery address block and any related nonaddress elements such as a barcode, keyline, or optional endorsement line)
- Directly to the left of the postage area and below or to the left of any price marking
- Directly below the postage area and below any price marking

If a forwarding address is on file, the carrier will send properly endorsed Standard Mail (and all other classes of mail that can be forwarded) to Computerized Forwarding System (CFS) or Postal Automated Redirection System (PARS)

If no forwarding address is on file, endorse the mail piece with the reason it is undeliverable and check local procedures for handling this mail. Undeliverable, unendorsed Standard Mail is placed in a container identified as UBBM (Unendorsed Bulk Business Mail). Authorized personnel will verify the contents of this container and will process for further handling.

I listened to Sharma spout these specifics but, I was starting to glaze-over. I had a flash-back to the interview where (Mike) made the statement, "There's more to this job than just shoving envelopes into boxes!" I supposed so but, I couldn't really believe at this point that mail carriers were on the street dissecting the various mail categories and markings of such and stopping to determine the proper action for each piece if undeliverable. It seems daunting and I haven't even been exposed to the daily grind yet. I sure hoped that there wasn't going to be some sort of test on all of this. I think that at that point I had already decided that, it either gets delivered or it gets thrown out! I'm posturing of course. I would never do that.

Standard Post is a competitive retail product whose parcels generally contain merchandise and matter that is not required to be mailed as First-Class or Periodicals. Pieces may not exceed 70 pounds. Standard Post prices are based on the weight (in pounds) and the zone to which the item is addressed. Delivery is not guaranteed within a specified time; however, these parcels are normally delivered the day they are received in the office. Pieces must be marked "Standard Post" or "SP" in the postage area.

Package Services may consist of items such as; merchandise, printed matter, CDs, and DVDs. Prices are based on the weight of the piece (in pounds). Delivery is not guaranteed within a specified time. Parcels are normally delivered the same day they are received in the office. Items may not weight over 70 pounds. Package Services pieces are subject to inspections to verify eligibility for postage rates. There are three subclasses of Package Services:

- Library Mail – Consists of items sent to, from or between a school, college, university, public library, museum, herbarium, or authorized nonprofit organization.

- Media Mail – May consist of books, films, sound recordings, computer readable media, manuscripts, educational reference charts, etc.
- Bound Printed Matter (BPM) – May weigh no more than 15 pounds and be permanently bound, forwarded if endorsed with an Ancillary Service Endorsement, Unendorsed BPM is discarded in the UBBM container.

All undeliverable Library Mail and Media Mail with Address Change Service (ACS) are endorsed and handled according to local procedures. Pieces, for which there is a change of address order on file, should be forwarded by appropriate personnel.

Undeliverable parcels should be returned to the sender with the reason for non-delivery. Package Service Mail should not be discarded as UBBM unless it is an undeliverable, unendorsed Bound Printed Matter Mail piece.

My head was spinning. Was all this really necessary? At this point I was already starting to cultivate my end-around approach to convoluted things such as this. There'll be someone there who can deal with all the minutia, I supposed.

Sharma doled out packages of a variety of mail to the six trainees at the table and, as an exercise, instructed us to separate the mail into two piles, First Class and Standard mail. Even though the many categories and sub categories of mail didn't seem to compartmentalize too well in my head, I figured that this couldn't be too difficult. We all sat in relative silence, flipping through our piles and organizing them as such. And when done, we were to bring each pile to her and she would check if we were correct.

I was the first one done and stood to bring my piles for review. The room, being so small and cramped, I had to weasel my way through the others. The gum snapper couldn't really comprehend that she needed to "suck it in" so I could get by and the result was a half-assed reaching over movement to hand the piles to Sharma.

In my mind, I was expecting to hear, "Good job" and then I could go to lunch. Instead, I heard, "Try again!" as she handed back my now comingled pile to me. I sat back down slightly disappointed but, undaunted. I'm sure I missed one. Probably a tricky one. I was rifling through my pile again when another person finished and submitted their piles for review. "Try again!". Then another person's attempt was met with, "Try again".

I finished my second sort with confidence and did the whole contorted moves again to get to where Sharma was and was met again with, "Try again!". Hmm, what's this now? I sat back down and went through it more slowly and carefully than I had previously done. While doing so, every couple of minutes I'd hear, "Try again!". Pierre' was even further admonished when he frustratingly just switched his piles in an opposite way and handed them back to Sharma. "You just switched piles!", she yelled!

"Well, if the one way was wrong, if I switch them, then the other way must be right!"

"Try again!"

I came up with six different configurations of how to sort these pieces of mail into two piles and all were wrong! For a solid hour, six adults sat at a table and shuffled pieces of mail into two piles over and over again. The result, after Sharma felt that we had put enough time into the exercise, was that one out of six got the sort correct. I was part of the five out of six on the wrong side.

It was an exercise in futility. We sat there exhausting all possibilities of logic. If we were still getting it wrong, we were just spitting into the wind and hoping for the best. A complete waste of time. It does no good to tell someone that they are wrong when the correct way is not offered. It would appear to me that the best way to teach is to lecture, give the student the opportunity to review, test, and then….and here's the most important part, go over what the student got wrong. If you just leave it at that, the student will never know the correct way to do the things they got wrong. To this day, I don't know WHY the mail pieces that I chose for each pile were incorrect. And so, I have no idea how to identify these mail categories. There's an hour of my life that I'll never get back!

We left for the day and felt my frustration growing.

Back the next day, the students gathered in our spots at the table, a little bleary-eyed. 7am IS a bit early to be reporting for a day of training. But, everyone is there with best intentions.

Sharma comes in and barks, "Ok, get up and let's go!". I stand but see that no one else is reacting. A beat more and Sharma repeats, louder this time, "GET UP and LET'S GO!". Now movement. Sharma is already flushed at the lack of enthusiasm in the group. I guess this group aren't morning people. "Get up and let's go" at 7am, just doesn't wash for most people I suppose. Me, any excuse to get out of this chair, and I jump at it.

We're taken out onto the floor of the West Delray Beach post office. We're given a tour of how a typical working floor of a post office is set up. Signs hang from the ceiling over the area for which a typical procedure takes place, including that of the supervisor,

Flats, hot case, etc. Sharma passes off to a few postal employees on the floor already seeking explanation of the various requirements for a given procedure. This is my first of many experiences within the Postal Service that I realized that there may be a serious communication problem. There seems to be many Haitian and Jamaican transplants present and, I was having a hard time filtering through the heavy accents. Another example of Charlie Brown's teacher "wah-wahing" about something or other and my eye and mind began to wander. "I'll figure it out", I figured. Let's face it, the best way to learn to do a job is to just go out there and do it. Sure, that might not be the best practice in performing brain surgery but, every job has a learning curve. Even a brain surgeon has to cut into their very first brain. They figured it out somehow.

We were all then brought to the casing area where there were six casing stations. We were to learn how to properly case mail. Now we're getting somewhere. Finally, something to do.

Accurate sorting of the mail saves times and helps preserve and maintain the Postal Service's standards of proficient, timely and accurate mail delivery. The carrier case is the primary tool that the carrier uses to organize residual mail in delivery order sequence. This process is referred to as casing. Residual mail is mail that has not been automated into delivery sequence.

The layout of the case follows the line of travel that the carrier will use in delivering the mail for that particular route. The line of travel is determined by management with input from the carrier most familiar with the route.

The carrier case is set up to follow the line of travel with the first delivery starting at the bottom left section, continuing left to right, and ending with the last delivery in the upper right section of the case.

We were each assigned our own casing station and instructed to take a cursory look around. The casing station consisted of three sections of shelving units with each section at 90 degrees to its adjoining section. Each section contained four rows of slotted shelving which started at about waist height and reached to about six to seven feet in height. Each slotted area within each section contained some sort of identifier.

A route book and the Edit Book (Carrier Route Listing Report) are required to be located at the carrier case.

We were given a tub of Flats and told to begin the sort. As we all dug into our tubs, Sharma instructed that we should grab about a two inch bundle of Flats and position them in the crook of the left arm and to first acknowledge the street name. Find the street name in the case and then find the specific address with that street and then case. Sounded simple enough. We all started our journey into casing mail in silence. There were a couple of occasions where Sharma would correct the way a person was placing the mail into a slot (so that the label could be read quicker once the mail is pulled down and loaded into trays and then gathered back into the arm for delivery) and some further investigation as to why a particular address couldn't be located but, it went relatively smoothly for the most part. However, after a while, the eye-mind-hand connection began to slip and, while the eye saw one thing, the mind perceived it as something else and the hand stopped, waiting for further, more confident and accurate information. I had to reset all three and begin again in order to continue. The longer we cased, the harder it got. It sounds easy but, reading the address off of differently labelled Flats in different fonts, in different locations, orienting the piece of mail so that it can be read legibly, find that address on the case and placing it properly within the slot is easy, the first couple of times. At the three hundredth point, it made me wonder if I really did have ADD. It was difficult maintaining whatever level of concentration was needed in order to perform the task.

About an hour later, Sharma told us to stop and take a break. While on break I pass by Pierre' on the way to the rest room and I give him a confidence inspiring slap on the back. His glasses are in his left hand and he's rubbing his eyes with his right. A sharp pain in the back of my own eyes began to grow. Upon returning from break, we each see a pile of mail on the ledge where we were casing. We were told that all that mail on the ledge was cased incorrectly and to do it again.

Well, I figured as much. We get back at it. 23388 SW 3rd Way turned into 28833 NW 3rd Place, 913 NE 8th St became 618 NE 3th Ave, etc. It was dizzying. Within the next hour, different levels of frustration presented itself to different people at different times. Having placed a few pieces of mail on the desk that I just couldn't find a slot for, Sharma came over and asked what was wrong with them? I said, "They're undeliverable. No address in the case." She took the bundle in her hand and methodically flipped each piece into its corresponding mail slot in the case and then, walked away. It's true, I'm an idiot! But, in my defense, you just stop seeing. It's as simple as that. Anyone who's done a marathon read knows the feeling of, "I can't see the words anymore" and you slap the book closed. That's how it feels when you reach that point with casing. And it makes it all the more tiring when your eyes are darting left, then right, up, then down (the floaters in my eyes having a field day with me in their snow globe way) and your head and eyes scan up, left, then down, right then up, right then down, left..... It's maddening.

But, I did realize even then that, what's making this exercise extra difficult is the fact that, we are all unfamiliar with this route. Give me a day and I'll have the whole thing memorized and at the very least, I'll know that 8th Street is somewhere up and to my right and that 3rd Ave is somewhere to my left and down, and then the search can be further refined from there. So, I was comforted with the fact that, once out in the field, I'll become more comfortable with the routes and this will be much easier. Sharma was nice enough to announce that, what had taken us 2.5 hours to case should have been completed in 20 minutes.

We spent the rest of the morning going over the Carrier Route Book. The Carrier Route Book provides relevant information about the route, such as delivery method, type of route and line of travel. This is normally located in a slot under the center of each case ledge.

The Carrier Route Book consists of:

- Item 391-M, Binder
- PS Form 1564-A, *Delivery Instructions*
- PS Form 1564-B, *Special Orders*
- Handbook M-41, *City Delivery Carriers Duties and Responsibilities*

The Carrier Route Book may also contain PS Form 1621, *Delivery Management Report* or the Edit Book.

PS Form 1564-A, Delivery Instructions (found in the Carrier Route Book) information includes:

- Method of delivery – annotated on PS Form 1564-A, *Delivery Instructions.*
- Collection Points – Locations of street letter boxes and mail chutes are listed in the order the carrier collects them on the route.
- Relay Boxes and Location of Park and Loop Stops – The relay boxes are listed in the order they appear on the carrier case labels. Park and Loop Stops are also entered here.
- Possible deliveries are listed for each relay, loop, wing, etc.
- Route Schedule – This scheduled reporting, leaving, returning, and ending time on the route is listed here.
- Line of Travel – This shows line of travel to and from the route.
- Transportation – The time the public transportation leaves and returns and the locations where boarded is listed for each trip.
- Lunch Information – This shows time of authorized lunch, location of authorized lunch stop(s), and location where carrier is authorized to leave route for lunch.
- Break Information – This shows approximate location of authorized break stops(s)

PS Form 1564-B, Special Orders (also found within the Carrier Route Book) information includes:

- Information on hold mail.
- Days Businesses on the route are closed.
- Dog Warming Information.

- Additional delivery instructions.

Mailing address errors cost the U.S. Postal Service millions of dollars annually. Correct addressing is critical to reducing the costs associated with handling returned mail for the Postal Service and its customers.

Normally, the full time carrier on a route is responsible for maintaining the information about the route in the edit book. In some instances, other assigned carriers may be responsible for this task. Accuracy of this information is critical. This benefits both the mailers and the Postal Service. Mailers are able to properly address their mail piece and the Postal Service's automated sorting equipment can rely on an accurate database. This translates to speedy and efficient processing of mail.

The Carrier Edit Book includes:

- Deliveries added or deleted from the route.
- The line of travel.

I familiarized myself with the Carrier Route Book for the route for which I was casing but, it felt detached in that, I was casing for a route in a fictional Wisconsin neighborhood, while I stood in Southern Florida and somehow the connection was lost. We broke for lunch and the headache grew.

We spent the rest of the day mostly recasing what had already been done and correcting the mistakes we each had made. For the last half hour of the day we found ourselves back in the now comfort of the cramped room where Sharma, almost as a relief from the day's grind, discussed real life working schedules. Starting salary for a City Carrier Assistant is $17.29 per hour. If a person makes it passed their 90 day probation period, they're bumped up by $.50 to $17.79 per hour. Having recently relocated from New York to Florida, I was still taken aback at the salary differentials. A quick search revealed that this federal government salary was geographically universal. You get $17.29 in South Florida, $17.29 in New York City and $17.29 in San Francisco! Being a person who prides themselves on having a good work ethic regardless of the quality of the financial contract entered into a given employment situation, I still couldn't help but wonder how they expected people to survive on a salary such as this. And, I wondered how the relative low wage affected a person's performance over time. Having done some research on the subject, I was surprised to hear a smattering of people describe working for the Postal Service as, "At least the pay was decent!", and it further confused me. Certainly, for someone like Pierre', this is probably a boon coming from the employment of Kentucky Fried Chicken where I would imagine that the salary would be much less than the gold-strike of $17.29. However, there has been recent political discussion of raising the minimum state wage to $15.00 per hour and I then wondered how that might affect a shift up in salary at the USPS. Or, should it? I adjusted my thinking and thought that this must be the salary for the originally advertised part-time job , which sort of makes sense. But I couldn't believe that this was the base for a full-time 40 hour per week salary for the standard mail carrier.

Sharma went on to explain that time and a half for over-time would be paid for any hours worked over 8 hours per day and/or over 40 hours per week. There is also a contingency where the hourly rate doubles if the work day extends past 10 hours. After asking if there was a limit to the amount of hours a person may work during the week, I was told that 56 hours per week was the limit that a mail carrier could work in one week but that, we'd probably never see that. As a matter of fact, Sharma indicated that, based on the size of the office, some of us may only work 10 hours per week.

I thought that this latest news at least made a little more sense in the feel of a "part-time" gig at $17.29 and the "assistant" part of the job title fell more into place in that, I guess we would be scheduled based on need for the work. The Italian gentleman expressed much concern over this. "I didn't take this job to only work 10 hours a week? How can I survive on that?" Sharma just shrugged.

We ended the day on that note and the confusion of an existence as an employee the United States Postal grew more intense.

The third day of train had us outside. We had been warned to dress appropriately as we'd be outside all day. Although it was early February, in South Florida, sunscreen is a must. We were told to bring rain gear as, we won't stop for inclement weather.

We gathered back in the cramped room but were soon whisked out on the floor where a general request to have two heavy mail-filled orange bins rolled out of the office and down the ramp and into the parking lot where and obstacle course was set up, was met with one being pushed (by me) and the other one waiting for someone else to decide to volunteer to do the pushing. They were heavy, that's for sure. But once you got it rolling, it was manageable. Someone else finally relented and started pushing.

We pushed the bins, affectionately known in the business as "pumpkins" due to their orange hue, to a shoddily set up obstacle course where Sharma had pulled an LLV to the starting point. We were then instructed on what we were to do. "Take the properly sorted Flats, the DPS, the parcels and the advos and load the truck. Using all the proper techniques and safety advise instructed, drive the route and deliver each piece of mail and return to this spot. There will be problems as they have been built into the exercise. Oh, and by the way, if anyone hits a mailbox with the LLV, pack your shit! Who wants to go first?"

I ALWAYS try to go first in situations such as these. I really don't know why. I just want to get it over with I guess. It's just my thing. There's probably some deeply seeded martyrdom in me that says, "I went first and even if I don't do well, I showed YOU how NOT to do it and therefore, you will be able to perform better than you would have if I hadn't gone first. You're welcome!" Or, something like that.

With the group standing by, I went into action. I pulled the appropriate Flats, DPS, parcels and advos and put them into the truck. Advos (advertisements) are those newspaper-like flyers with 10% off discounts for mattresses and gutter cleaning, that no one likes and no one wants. Personally, the ones that I get don't even make it into the house. I take it out of the mailbox and throw it straight into the recycle bin, and never look at it.

I go through the proper vehicle start-up procedure that Maggie had so patiently instructed and I was on my way. While slowly pulling ahead, I hear Sharma warn the rest of the class to always be sure to check inside a mailbox before you put your hand in there because, kids like to play tricks, especially around Halloween, where they'd put rats and snakes inside the box!

I pulled up to the first mailbox and throw in the appropriate mail like it was nothing. I close the mailbox and was on my way to the next. Once again, stop, open the box, finger through what I had, throw it into the box, close the box, put the LLV in gear and on my way. I get to the next box and see a problem. There's no door to the mailbox. Hmm, what to do? If I put the mail in, this might be considered a security issue. Better to not deliver it, I thought, and put it aside. Onto the next stop where there was a cluster box. I park and take the appropriate mail to the box and insert the arrow key into the cluster box and open the two doors. I put the mail in the individual boxes within the cluster box until I realized that there were a problem. There were boxes within the cluster that weren't labelled. Again, should I assume what the box should be? I guessed that it would be safe to not put mail into a box that I was unsure of and brought the mail back with me to the vehicle.

I pull the vehicle to the next box, open it and see a hornets nest in there. I quickly throw the mail in and close the door. Onto the next box. When fingering the mail for the next box, I see a piece of mail that was meant for the previous box. The hornet's box! So, I try to remember the procedure; I shut the LLV off, engage the parking brake, roll up the windows, dismount, lock the LLV and walk back to the previous address and quickly open-throw-close the mail box door and walk back to the vehicle where I do the walk around to make sure that there are no children playing around the vehicle. I mount up, start-up, signal my intention to pull out away from the curb and continue with the route. I came to an address where a parcel was to be delivered. The parcel needed a signature. This was a test course and therefore, no one was available to sign so, I scanned it as undeliverable and brought it back to the vehicle. I pull the LLV around and back to the starting point like a champ. Locked up and handed the key to Sharma.

She then proceeded to tear me apart.

"You didn't deliver to that box over there. Why?"

"There was no door on the mailbox. I figure that it was a security issue."

"It don't matter. If there's a box, put it in!" "Why didn't you deliver this bunch of mail into the cluster box?"

"The boxes inside weren't labelled. I didn't want to assume."

"If the first box is labelled #1 and the fifth box is labeled #5, you can bet that boxes 2, 3 and 4 are addresses #2, #3 and #4".

"Ok".

"When you stopped the vehicle to backtrack to the missed mailbox you failed to put on your hazard flashers!"

Damn!

"Why did you return with this parcel?"

"It needed a signature. No one here to sign."

"You should have just signed for it yourself!". "WHO'S NEXT!?"

Ok, I shit the bed a little. But, I'm done. Nothing to do now but stand in the South Florida sun and watch the others do their thing. I'm especially looking forward to seeing how Pierre' will do.

One by one, each of them went through the course, each with their own dilemmas. Except for one girl. She did pretty well, I'll admit. But, it turns out that she had been through this before. It seems that she went through the entire hiring process, was on the job for a few weeks, quit and now, three months later, decided to return. However, in accordance with procedures, she had to go through all the training again.

This took all morning and we had to roll the large pumpkins back up the long ramp and into the building before lunch. I jumped on the bin that I had rolled out earlier that day and repaired back to my car for a little lunch.

After lunch, we had to roll the pumpkins back out to the obstacle course. The class consisted of three men and three woman. Not the oldest man in the group but still, an “old man”, I felt that I had done more than my part in rolling out one of the large and heavy pumpkins on my own. It was someone else’s turn. Again, there was hesitation. I heard the young, tall, black gum snapper mumble, “I ain’t movin’ that thing!”. Two of the other women got on one of the pumpkins and the older Italian man and the last non-participating black man moved the other one.

Out on the obstacle course, we were then instructed to basically do the route again only, this time, we’re walking. Should be much easier, I thought. Less moving parts.

I was quickly proven to be incorrect as Sharma showed us how to carry the mail satchel and how to load it up with the mail in the most advantageous way. The bag is to be hung on the right shoulder where Flats are to be loaded in from the back to front and the DPS loaded in in front of them back to front and parcels crammed in anywhere there was remaining room. And the advos? Well, they’re to be carried in the crook of the left arm leaving the right arm free to manipulate the arrow key and open doors and such.

Again, I went first. I found it VERY difficult to coordinate this activity. Yes, I loaded everything up properly and was walking from stop to stop, however, when it came time to actually dig out the correct mail and deliver to the correct address, it seemed VERY cumbersome. The sweat beaded up and my brow and dripped onto my glasses. I couldn't see the addresses on the Flats (contributing to the problem was that I had put some of the Flats into the bag backwards and upside down) or the DPS. I found myself pulling individual pieces of plastic encased magazines from AARP and turning them over in my hands until I could make out the address. Once confident it was correct, I shoved it into the box and moved onto the DPS. Then I got to the Advos. They are flimsy, and trying to the hold thirty of them in the crook of your left arm and trying to grab the top one with your right (you know, the right arm that has had a 30 lb bag hanging from it) and turning it over to see the address with the wind blowing it all over the place was frustrating to say the least. I very slowly moved through the course and got to the end and realized that I had forgotten all about the two small parcels in the bottom of the bag. I was too fixated on the other stuff. So, I had to back track back to the addresses on the parcels. Surely, this didn't bode well in my performance for Sharma but, my real concern was thinking about the ramifications of this on the street. This is just a parking lot obstacle course, I can just walk over to the other side of the parking lot and deliver what I missed. What if I've walked a mile and realized that I missed a package delivery? This could be problem.

Sharma could see the frustration on my face, mixed with the sweat dripping from the top of my head and took a little pity on me and didn't say anything. "Who's next?" was all she could muster.

The rest of the class went through the walking obstacle course with varying levels of success and this took the rest of the day. Thankful that this was done and looking forward to getting out of there, we move to bring in the pumpkins and secure for the day.

Gum snapper was still adamant on not wanting to do any "heavy lifting", I overheard Sharma whisper to her, "Get one of the guys to do it!".

Uh huh….

We settled-up for the day back in the classroom and was given a forecast on what to expect for the following half day. We were to be visited by the president of the local Union and given a lecture on the benefit of joining it.

I was wiped out. Doing the mock delivery on the obstacle course was stressful in that, I felt I had to juggle things. Somehow, the original thought of taking an envelope, opening a mail box or slot and gently slipping that envelope into said box or slot, got lost in the shuffle. Doing the mechanical motion of mail delivery was clearly the easy part, getting to that point was an entirely different aspect of the job. And, it was one that I could see being problematic in the future.

At home that night I expressed my frustration at what I perceived to be a problem with having to juggle varying sized pieces and varying textures of mail pieces and having to manipulate them into some sort of cohesive order and get them to their final destination. My wife listened as patiently as she could while pouring me a nice cold beer but, managed to minimize it all the same; "Don't you just have to put an envelope into a box?".

The next and final day of training found us waiting for the Union rep. Actually, he was the president of the South Florida Letter Carriers (SFLC) National Association of Letter Carriers (NALC) Branch 1071.

I listened to his pitch in a respectful way but, at that point in my life, I was on the fence as to the merits of a union; any union really. Certainly there was a place and time for them. But, haven't we reached a point of evolution where their existence is somewhat...antiquated? We have national labor laws in place (yes, thanks to unions) and there exists an HR department and so, what is the real need here?

The union president went on and on about how they purchased land in Sunrise, Fl and built a state of the art Union headquarters where they hold monthly meetings and we're all invited and encouraged to attend. They also have a huge yearly b-b-q there. I wondered how they could afford to purchase land and erect brand new buildings? There apparently is a union representative mail carrier on site at every Postal Office should the employee have any employment issues. I wondered at how many issues an employee can have if there needs to be a union representative on site at each and every office? Seems a bit overkill to me. As the union president completed his presentation and extolling the virtues of the union, I piped up and asked if joining the union was mandatory. This question seemed to smack him in the face as, it would appear odd to him that anyone would not want to be a member of the union. He claimed that it was not mandatory but that about 98% of all employees are members and to, trust him, "It would be beneficial to join". Again, having to play the heavy, I asked what the cost was as he conveniently left out that little nugget of information. The cost was about $27 per pay period per member at two pay periods per month. I thought this to be a little steep considering the benefits in conjunction with the base pay but, decided to go all in and sign up to have my wages garnished automatically each month. My mind went into math mode and I pulled out my iPhone and opened the calculator app and did a quick tally; 600,000 employees, $54 per month, at 98% brings in to the union about $381 million dollars a year!

Three Hundred Eighty One million per year! Ahh, THAT'S how they can afford to buy land and erect brand new buildings for meetings and b-b-q's.

I walked out of there with a Union labelled shopping bag that contained a United States Postal service hat and a stress squeeze ball!

Chapter 7 – On-The-Job-Training

I was to report to the Deerfield Beach Annex at 8am on that following Saturday for my first day of on-the-job training. The work day was supposed to extend from 8am to 4:30pm with a 30 minute lunch and two, ten minute breaks. I noticed this "ten minute" break notion mentioned during orientation as well as during classroom training and wondered about it. I was always under the impression that a fifteen minute break was mandatory after 2.5 hours of work, or something like that. It turns out that the Department of Labor states that there really is no law mandating that a break be given at all but that, breaks of 5 to 20 minutes in length, if allowed, be considered compensable work hours that would be included in the sum of hours worked during the work week.

Ok, I thought, two ten-minute breaks it is. Although, I was used to working environments where, if you needed a break, you take a break. If you don't need a break, you don't take a break.

I was ready. I dressed for a potentially hot existence in the Florida sun. I had enough water and food for the day. I had mapped out and timed out my route to the job location and figured it would take seven minutes from door to door. I arrived in the parking lot at 7:45am, secured my vehicle and entered the annex ready to go.

The looks and stares I received as I entered ranged from disinterest to feigned interest to "Let's see how we're going to fuck with THIS guy!"

I went over to Nick and he greeted me quickly and said, "You'll be with Tina today. She's the trainer. Just stand by until she gets ready."

I stood out of the way and observed until I was called into service. As I stood there I noticed that the mass of workers were just standing around near the time clock. Apparently, they were waiting for the clock to click over to EXACTLY 8:00am in order to swipe their electronic time cards. This was another oddity to me in that, I felt that, if you were there on site, go to work. Clock-in and simply, go to work. Why wait around? It didn't make sense that twenty people were just standing around waiting for a clock to strike 8:00am in order to begin the chores of the day. If it's a money issue, and the employee is to be paid per hour and they are limited to 8 hours per day, have them start whenever they get there and have them clock out or, "End Tour" eight hours from that point (minus the 30 minutes for lunch, of course). Certainly I could understand that if there is an insurance issue that states that no one should be on the premises before or after a certain time. You could also dictate that no one is allowed to clock in, or "Begin Tour" earlier than fifteen minutes before their scheduled start time but, to have people standing around for five or ten minutes before their start time seems extremely inefficient and wasteful of time.

At 8 o'clock exactly, there was a flurry of people sliding their credit card looking cards through one of the two time clocks mounted to a wall. I noticed some were poking at the keypad on the clock and then swiping, others just swiped. Tina approached me and said, "Paul, do you have a 1260?". Still not up to speed on immediate recognition of the meanings of abbreviations and numerical references, I shrugged in the familiar way of not knowing, and I said that my name was Tom and that I had a son named Paul. Hardly acknowledging the small glimpse into my personal life and identification clarification, and a bit exasperated, she brought me to the desk where Nick was sitting and said, “He needs a 1260. He doesn’t have a card yet.” Nick whipped out the PS Form 1260 (Nontransactor Card) which I was to use to document my time for the day. I was to receive my own credit card-like time card in the near future but, I’d have to fill one of these cards out every day until then. With the best penmanship I could muster (and even then, it’s not that great) I entered the required information; Last name, First name, EIN (Employee Identification Number), the date, the ring type (I knew this; BT, for Begin Tour), OPN-LU (No idea what that was), Route and Finance No.(was told to leave blank for now), Time (0800).

While I was doing this, I lost sight of Tina. She was already off doing…something. I went over to where she was and she started explaining the routine. Some of it rang familiar between what Jeremy had showed me during Shadow Day and what I had experience in training.

Tina explained her method of sorting her Flats for this particular route. We were to go into a placed called Century Village and, as with each route, there are better ways of sorting than others and, eventually, each carrier comes up with their own method that benefits them and the Postal Service. As with Jeremy, I stood behind Tina and observed. Again, a flurry of pieces of mail kept flying back and forth between carriers and their routes. It appeared to me that, whatever happens prior to the mail getting to that point was in need of improvement as, it seemed that there was a lot of wasted effort in getting the mail into the correct hands for sorting and then delivery.

Tina then decided to relinquish sorting duty to me and I stepped in. As with most things, the action needed looks to be a lot easier than reality. Once again, take this piece of paper, read the address on it and find where it should go amongst all these slots on these shelves and place it in the proper position so that when we "pull-down" the mail, it will be organized in such a fashion to be delivered to its final destination in the most efficient way possible. No problem, I figured, as, this was the real deal. It wasn't some fictitious town in Wisconsin that we trained on a few days earlier. Well, I should say, I'm sure that the town that we trained on in Wisconsin actually exists, but, fictional enough for training purposes. But, now I'll be sorting real mail for addresses within the town in which I work.

I step in and felt immediately disoriented. The concept is easy but, somehow, manipulating all the different sized pieces of Flats and reading the differently fonted addresses in different positions and orientations, sometimes under plastic sheathing and then, finding those addresses on the casing shelves proved to be initially confusing and frustrating. Frustrating like golf, in that, all you really have to do is hit that little white ball which is sitting on the ground motionless, over to that area over there! Easy enough. But, in practice.....not so much.

I stood with my head slumped and did my best as I always try to do. The process flowed like January molasses in Vermont. This route contained some businesses and, I could already see that businesses were mostly delivered first in the sequence of the route but, the addresses for the businesses first appeared to be even more confusing than the private residences. The businesses were sometimes within strip malls or suites within buildings and the casing shelf may not be labelled too specifically to transfer a potentially mislabeled address to these places accurately. An address to a particular lawyer within a building may have the lawyers name and street address on it but, it may not include a suite number or letter. So, it is cased within the general street address for the building and the regular carrier (familiar with the route) would know where the actual office for which that mail should go, is located. To the unfamiliar, they'd just have to figure it out. I clumsily found some of the business addresses and place the corresponding mail in their slots hoping for the best and moved on.

Century Village in Deerfield Beach, Fl, is an over-55 community of condominiums. It is set up as villages within the village. The villages within the village have names such as, Durham, Newport, Ventnor, and Westbury and the like. They are further broken down into buildings within the village with an identifier. Further, they are specified by the individual apartments by their number. So, an address to someone living is Century Village might be:

Jane Doe, Century Village, Ventnor M, Apt 1204, Deerfield Beach, Fl 33442

Or,

Jane Doe, Century Village, Ventnor N, Apt 1204, Deerfield Beach, Fl 33442

At first blush, these are two completely different addresses. One can easily mistake an N for an M and, if the address was given over a cell phone with their iffy audio quality, and since they rhyme, one can easily be mistaken and interchanged for the other.

But, as Jeremy exclaimed, especially for the CCA (City Carrier Assistant), don't be overly concerned with the name of the addressee, deliver to the address. The address gets the mail, not the individual.

So, one of these pieces of mail goes to a Jane Doe who lives in apt 1204 in building M of Ventnor community within Century Village and, another one goes to a Jane Doe who lives in apt 1204 in building N of Ventnor community within Century Village. No problem (although, in the back of my mind I knew something seemed wrong). I'm not to question it. Just put the pieces in the appropriate slot. I found the section of slots on the shelves labelled Ventnor M. Ventnor M was further broken down into apartment slots labelled 1100 – 1139, then 1200 – 1239, then 1300 – 1339 then 1400 – 1439. I put the piece of mail for Jane in the section labelled 1200 – 1239. Done.

I find the section of slots on the shelves labelled Ventnor N. I figured that, all I had to do was find the section of Ventnor N that went from 1200 – 1239 and throw it in there and I can move on. Only, there was no section 1200 – 1239. Upon investigation, Ventnor N was broken down into apartment slots labelled 1140 – 1179, then 1240 – 1279, then 1340 – 1379 then 1440 – 1479. Sooooooo…which one is wrong? If I'm to ignore the name, maybe the apartment number for building N is incorrect. Or, maybe the apartment number is correct but the building label is incorrect and it should read M.

While I mulled this over, Tina sidled up and snapped, "What's wrong?" I showed her my dilemma and she just grabbed the piece of mail meant for Jane that was to go apartment 1204 in building N and threw it in Ventnor M section 1200-1239 without even thinking about it and without further explanation. Apparently I had run my course on my initial exposure to casing and she then grabbed the bunch of mail which was in my hands and started throwing mail pieces into slots without hardly looking. I watched her work and accepted the fact that, if you did this for a day or two, you'd learn the ideocracies of that particular route quick enough and it wouldn't be so confusing. It's the unfamiliarity of routine that created the jerky way of my performance.

8:30am, announcement blasted that it was break time. I chuckled at this. Tina turned and told me to go on break. I asked her if it would be ok if I just stayed and studied the case a bit more to try to gain more familiarity. She shrugged and skirted off. I tried to scan left to right and work my way up the shelves in succession and tried to memorize the sequence. Tina had already stuffed the slots semi-full with a variety of mail. Some of it extended out beyond the shelf, obscuring the shelve labelling, which made it even more difficult to see where this stuff should go. Around the case areas were bins full of miscellaneously sized pieces of Flats, some heavy machinery catalogs and just a mishmash of stuff which, I assumed, would eventually be cased into the appropriate slots.

Tina called me over and pointed to the men's locker room and rest room and showed me where I can choose a locker to use to store my stuff. I asked if there were any specifications on the type of lock to use. She said, "You don't need a lock!". She said to just pick one and put my name on it. I wondered at what "stuff" I needed to store in a locker if it wasn't to be locked. We went back to the case where she resumed casing, further explaining the idiosyncrasies of each type of mail and what should be done with it. For the most part, there were lulls of audio activity around the annex while the carriers processed their daily routine. It made the occasional outburst from a carrier even more stabbing when it did occur. “These mother fuckers!!!”, came from the neighboring casing station. “I told them a million fucking times, if your box is blocked, you don’t get no mail! It’s as simple as that! I don’t play that shit. Fuck them!”.

From what I quickly gathered, the carrier’s route is mounted where, the vehicle goes from stop to stop and places mail into the mail box which is positioned on the curb in front of the residence. Should a car, or other obstruction, be parked in front of said box, the mail carrier is supposed to pull the vehicle to a safe spot, curb the tires, shut the vehicle down, exit the vehicle, and walk to the box (which is blocked) and deposit the mail into the box. Well, apparently, this carrier, Jarod, a twenty five year veteran, has taken it upon himself to, not do that. Jarod’s method is to acknowledge that the box is blocked and therefore, their mail is deemed “Undeliverable” and is brought back to the office. When enough complaints come in about not receiving mail, and those complaints are conveyed to the regular carrier, it’s the carrier’s responsibility to rectify the situation. Apparently Jarod has tried, by informing them that, “If their box is blocked, they don’t get no mail”.

While I have not yet been “on-the-street” and experienced the real-life situations that each mail carrier must endure, my common sense tells me that Jarod probably had a point. I certainly wasn’t aware of how much work is needed to be done and in what time frame it’s to be completed by but, I thought that if he had to perform that function with the vehicle every time that a box was blocked, not much would get done. However, in my present state of naivete', I figured that the "office" is sympathetic to this type of job performance obstacle and, should a mail carrier not be able to perform all of their duties during the day, it's taken into consideration with empathy and support given by management. Perhaps they reach out to the residence to more forcefully explain that their mailbox needs to be accessible by the mounted carrier in order for the day's deliveries to be made efficiently. Or, IF the carrier were constantly faced with these types of obstacles, and they go about the required delivery calisthenics under these circumstances, perhaps a little financial bonus is rewarded at the end of the month for going above and beyond.

Tina finished sorting the Flats and then, brought me to where the DPS was held. A wall of metal carts contained labelled plastic trays approximately 14 inches wide and 2.5 feet long, filled with "regular looking" mail. Meaning; bills, letters, cards and other pieces that are more familiar as "standard sized" mail. Tina locates the trays for the route that we were working and loads me up with three. She took the other three. We took the trays of DPS back to the case and stacked them appropriately in ascending order. DPS is labelled by the route number and by lettered trays. We had six trays, therefore the trays were labelled "A" through "F" with "F" being on the bottom and "A" on top.

This mound of mail seemed daunting to me as, the Flats which "we" had just cased seemed to take a long time to case and this additional amount of mail would extend the casing time by a lot. Tina explained the process in that, this mail, DPS mail has already been presorted in a mail processing facility in West Palm Beach. It's already in the order for which the route takes. But, it needs to be further divided into slots in the case. But, instead of grabbing a bunch of differently sized Flats and orienting them and picking each one up, one at a time and casing them into the proper slots, the DPS may be taken from the tray is groups of numbered addresses labelled on the case. Businesses first, where this whole group of mail may be taken from the DPS tray and put into the whole building address which is labelled on the case and so on. The mail will further be divided into specific addresses from there. For this route, once we got to Century Village, it went pretty fast where, the group of DPS for Ventnor A 1100 – 1139 goes into that slot and Ventnor A 1140 – 1179 goes into that slot and Ventnor A 1180 – 1199 goes into another. These groups may contain a good number of pieces of mail and the casing of such went pretty smoothly and swiftly.

Then, Tina goes over to another area of the annex where bins of small enveloped packages were being sorted. She takes the bin for our route and brings it over. For the first time, I had noticed that there were already two full bins of these small enveloped packages under the desk of the case. These then needed to be cased with the Flats and DPS. These small packages are considered by the Postal Service to be "SPRs", or "Small Parcel and Rolls". These "SPRs" should be able to fit in a standard sized mail box. Like the Flats, they are not presorted and each one needs to be handled separately and placed into its corresponding slot in the case. Tina systematically took a SPR one at a time and manipulated it just so, so that it can fit into the slot. Sometimes there are multiple SPRs which are to go into a slot and I couldn't see how everything could fit. When there was an overflow, the SPR is jammed, as best as it could be, on top of the slot dividers. She spared me this process and did the whole thing herself.

Once the official casing was complete, the case station looked like a bomb hit it. All kinds of mail spilling out from all areas. It was painstakingly sorted but, to the uneducated eye, looked to be one hot mess. And speaking of "hot", once I thought that we were done, we had to get whatever was in the "hot case". What's THIS now, I wondered. In another area of the annex was yet another cubbied shelving area containing a few pieces of mail for each route. Apparently, these pieces were mail that has come back from either not being delivered the previous day or for some other reason. I guess they considered it "Hot" because, the clock was ticking on those pieces of mail in their journey to be delivered. There was only a handful of mail from the "Hot Case" and so, it was sorted quickly.

Having completed the sorting, the time was now about 10:30am. Tina instructed me to retrieve a few tubs and a few more of the plastic trays, like the ones in which the DPS had come. I gather up a bunch of these items and bring them back to the case. It would later be apparent to me that, as importance of properly casing the mail is, the "pulling-down" of the mail may be equal to, if not more important. It's all about being organized, and "pulling-down" has a good impact on how the day is going to go.

Tina rolls over a pumpkin and takes one tray and places it on the desk. With a fury, she starts taking mail within slots from the left/bottom most section of the case. She takes from a mound of rubber bands and bounds that bundle together and places it at the front of the tray, facing forward. She continues to do that same process for each slot within the case including the SPRs. I didn't really think that the rubber band would hold these large clusters of mail but, for the most part, they did. When she filled a tray, she wrote the number "1" on the first piece of mail at the head of the tray and placed it on the bottom of the pumpkin. She then took another empty tray and placed it on the desk and repeated the process. Having completed a second tray, she then placed it on top of tray 1 in the pumpkin. She then treated the "high-rises" within Century Village differently; she buddle up each division of apartment numbers within a lettered building within the village. So, Ventnor A 1100-1139 would be one bundle, Ventnor A 1140-1179 would be another and Ventnor A 1180-1199 would be another, and she would place them into a plastic tub. These tubs were about 2 feet by 1 foot by 1 foot deep. This was done because the "high-rises" (and by high-rise in Florida, it means four stories), receive much more mail as a stop and therefore, a larger vessel is required to carry. And, it organizes the mail better when in the vehicle so the carrier can be more efficient.

She continued to do this until there was no mail left on any slot in the case. Due to the addition of the Flats and SPRs, we had 6 trays and 6 tubs of mail, stacked on top of each other in reverse chronological order in the pumpkin.

Tina then went to retrieve yet another pumpkin overflowing with parcels. She instructed me to push that pumpkin out to the vehicle we were to use. She pushed the pumpkin containing the trays of mail and I followed her outside. We reach the far side of the parking lot and unlock a ProMaster. She showed me how to load the truck in an organized manner so that the delivery would go smoothly. She removed the top trays (which would be the last tray for the addresses on the route) and placed it on the shelve toward the back of the vehicle. And, with each tray, she placed it closer and closer to the front of the vehicle. The tubs, labelled with the village name and letter were placed in route order on the deck of the vehicle. Entering the vehicle through the side sliding door you'd see on the shelf above the floor, trays lined up from right to left with the first on the right (closest to the bulkhead that divides the cargo area from the driver) moving to the left, toward the rear of the vehicle where the last stop on the route would be.

Tina then moves the tub of parcels closer to the vehicle and scans each parcel as being loaded into the truck. This is called the "Load Truck" feature on the scanner. It appears to me that she's simply scanning each parcel and throwing it into the vehicle indiscriminately, however, there was definitely a method to her madness. When each parcel was scanned, the scanner would emit an electronic voice stating the section that the parcel is in. Beep "Section 2", Beep, "Section 6", Beep "Section 3, etc. I noticed that inside the vehicle were stenciled numbers on the walls as Section 1 through 6. I supposed that when the scanner tells you the section that the parcel was in, you'd place it on the top shelf within the vehicle so they would be easily identified. Tina organized the parcels within the vehicle to her satisfaction and we pushed the empty pumpkins back into the annex.

Back in the annex, Tina sought out the clerk who is charged, among other things, with issuing arrow keys. There is an arrow key for each route. An arrow key can not only unlock a cluster box or wall of locked mail receptacles, it can also gain entrance to gated communities. On most intercom boxes is a key receptacle with an envelope logo near it. This is what the carrier uses, with their arrow key, to gain entrance to the gated community or otherwise locked building. The arrow keys are kept in their own cubby hole within a locked cage for obvious reasons. The keys are issued to the carrier for the specific route on each day. The carrier signs for the key and is responsible for its return. Clearly, someone in possession of such a key with ill intentions could probably do a lot of harm. Frankly, I'm surprised that I have never heard of any situation where an arrow key was used to gain entry into an establishment for devious means. And I supposed the signing out of keys identifies the carrier of the daily ownership of that specific key and is opening themselves up for investigation should anything amiss occur while it is in their possession.

Tina asks the clerk for a spare key for the route that were we on and I took possession of the large key that dangled from a large brass chain and I signed for it. Tine showed me how to loop it through a loop on my pants for safe keeping and easy retrieval. She picked out a spare scanner from the banks of charging scanners and swiftly set it up for me so we didn't take any more time in the annex. She instructed me to get my personal stuff and bring to the vehicle.

Back again in the little jumper seat, we donned seat belts and made sure we were ready. I really didn't notice any sort of vehicle operational check going on but, perhaps she did it while I was futzing with something. And, with a "toot-toot" on the horn, Tina began to back up. Again, extolling the importance of being careful when backing up as there are many blind spots on this vehicle.

As Tina drove to our first stop, she explained that we didn't take the business section with us today because it was my first day of on-the-job training and, that would probably confuse me more than is necessary. I was happy for that. Apparently, a route can be further dissected into "pieces". The business section of a route can be a piece. Other sections of a route can be considered a "2-hour piece" or a "4-hour piece", however it may make sense to break it up from the overall route and divvy out to others as necessary. The business piece for our route was given to someone else to do. I supposed that I was making friends already.

While we travelled to our first stop we made chit-chat. Tina was a no-nonsense woman of Jamaican decent, approximately thirty years old with a new born baby at home. She was a graduate of the University of Florida and had been on the job about 5 years and loved it. Almost on que, she took a phone call from her husband and after a brief, seemingly one-sided instructional conversation, she exclaimed to her side-kick trainee, "That man…I've got to tell him how to do EVERYTHING!"

Perhaps my blind bias surfaced and I wondered why a young college graduate was fully ensconced in a job such as this. I gently prodded but the conversation was quickly ended with a, "It just works better for me." comment. My mind replayed a "Seinfeld" scene where Estelle Costanza questioned her under-achieving son, George;

Estelle: "Why don't you take the Civil Service test?"

George: "To do what? Work in the post office? Is that what you want me to do?"

Estelle: "I don't understand. You get job security. You get a paycheck every week!"

George: "I'm a college graduate! You want me to be a mailman?!"

We drove through the guarded and gated entrance to Century Village merely by slowing down as we approached. The gates parted in recognition as we crept closer. Apparently, what was said about a Postal vehicle never being questioned was true. On the other side of the gate was a sprawling complex of garden apartment type buildings mixed in with large, four story high-rises in the shape of a boomerang. We drove by the clubhouse that supposedly contained restaurants, gyms, administrative offices and other types of recreational jumping off points. In front of the club house was a large man-made lake with a spewing fountain in the middle. Tina navigated the ProMaster in and around little streets within the village until we arrived at our first stop. Tina explained where we were on the route and we went back to the cargo area of the van to retrieve what was to be delivered to this particular building. This first stop being a garden apartment consisting of perhaps 40 separate apartments, there wasn't much mail to take with us. She grabbed the rubber banded group from the front of the first tray and we existed out of the side door with a large step-down to the street. We wound our way up the sidewalk until we got to the central part of the building where an alcove containing the bank of mailboxes imbedded into the wall revealed itself. The alcove terminated with a door leading to the laundry room for that building.

Tina swung her arrow key from her hip and inserted into the key slot on the top level of the two levelled bank of boxes. The box, hinged on the bottom, swung out with a clank. She then opened the other bank of boxes next to that one. With a flash, she threw the individual pieces of mail into the separate mail boxes within the bank of boxes and reinserted the arrow into the locks and slammed the bank of boxes home and secured them with a twist of the wrist, swinging the arrow key back to home, in her pocket. She swung the key out again, forgetting to open the outgoing mail box. Opening the outgoing box revealed that it was empty.

That was pretty easy, I thought, as we walked back to the ProMaster. We open the side door and climb back in and I work my way to my little jumper seat and strap in. Thirty seconds later, we're at our next stop. We repeat the entire process, only this time, it was on me. This next building was in a slightly different design than the previous one. There were more apartments and therefore, more mail. I grabbed the rubber banded group and turned to slide open the side door and as I exited, I cracked the top of my head on the metal track where the sliding door slid on the van. As the needles in my eyes stabbed, I think I heard Tina say something like, "You have to be careful. You can get hurt real bad if you're not paying attention!". I thought, maybe if I didn't have to get in and out of this van through the side sliding door, this wouldn't happen, but I didn't say anything. Rubbing the already forming lump on my head I walked to the bank of mail boxes. I inserted the key, twisted and pulled and, … nothing. It was stuck. Standing behind me, Tina said, "Yea, these boxes are pretty old and sometimes you have to sort of jiggle it". With the bundle of mail in the crook of my arm, I used my left hand to try and pry the box open while I jiggled the key with my other hand. It finally gave way and opened with a bang. As it opened, I had to take a step back, and doing so caused the bundle of mail I was holding in my arm to fall to the ground, breaking the rubber band and splaying the mail all over the ground. "Gotta pick it up!", Tina quickly and unnecessarily informed. I bend down and gather the now unsorted mail from the ground and as I stood, I cracked my head again on the open bank of metal boxes. "Fuck me", I whispered. Tina, in a scolding way exclaimed with a chuckle, "Whatya doin'?"

Chapter 7

I wasn't bleeding. Bleeding might have somehow made the situation better in some weird way. As my head pounded, I tried to deliver the mixed bundle of mail into the boxes. But, because they were now unsorted, I had to stop, read each address, find the box, and deliver in a clumsy way. I found myself doing a sort of dance; three steps to the right and up, two steps to the left and down, one step to the right and down, then up, then down and left, then up and right. Made my already buzzing head buzz some more. Had I not dropped them and broken the sort, I could've taken the DPS and just followed the flow of the numbered boxes; two in here, one right next to that one, three right next to that one and bang-o, it's done.

I finally finished and locked the box back up and started walking away and Tina informed me that I was forgetting something. "Ah yes, the outgoing". I still found it somewhat odd that part of the job was taking mail back with you, for some reason. This time there were things in the box. There was one piece of stamped first-class mail and two pieces of standard mail. Tina grabs the standard mail out of my hand and with exasperation said, "These people…they have to go back." As explained, standard mail are basically advertisements; cell phone deals, an offer to lower your auto insurance rate, etc. We all get them. Most people throw them into the recycle bin if not interested, however, in this particular situation, a person may have had to walk from an end apartment to the mailboxes and, they'll be damned if they are going to bring this shit all the way back with them. So, they put it in the outgoing box to discard. This is technically illegal. The outgoing box is for properly paid for mail items. The standard mail has been paid for by the mailer and they have been delivered, satisfying the contract with the Postal Service. Taking that mail and putting it into the outgoing box is saying that that person wants it delivered elsewhere, without paying for postage. Sometimes, the addressee writes a note on the standard mail in the form of , "Person does not live here anymore" or, "Don't want".

It's up to the mail carrier on how to proceed at that point. The mail carrier understands that many people don't want this type of mail but, it's being paid for to be delivered and therefore, that's what needs to happen. If the recipients don't want it, they are perfectly free to discard. But, if asked to "UNdeliver" it, that's a no go. That's basically asking the carrier to do twice the work. It being standard mail, it cannot be forwarded or returned. Most carriers take this unwanted mail and return to the vehicle and deposit into a dedicated bin for UBBM, which will then be returned to the office where it will be gone through to verify if it is truly unwanted standard mail or wrongfully discarded mail by the carrier.

There are many more moving parts to this operation than I originally thought. Is this case, nothing was written on the mail and so, Tina felt that it needed to "go back". Back into the boxes, that is. So, another round of fighting with the key and opening the bank of boxes to REdeliver the standard mail advertisement that the addressee clearly doesn't want. Tina explained that, perhaps it was misdelivered to another box and that addressee put it into the outgoing so that we can deliver it to its proper address. They didn't write anything on it so, there's no way of knowing.

Still, I fell that the cycle of the seemingly easy process of delivering a piece of mail seemed to go in many directions and not as originally thought, from point A to point B.

We returned to the ProMaster, climbed back in and were on our way to the next stop. Tina maneuvered the vehicle to the mid-point of one of the 4 story high rises and backed-in. We went back to the cargo area and Tina told me to take the tub of mail destined for this building. The tub contained three large rubber banned groups of mail. While I fought with the side door again, I made sure there was no more chance for further brain damage, Tina stood in almost grocery store shopping mode, trying to ascertain which parcels on the top shelf should go to this particular building. The result of the shopping spree was an overflowing tub of parcels of various size. We walk to the bank of mail boxes, which were different in configuration from the garden apartments. In this case, the entire bank was separated into the three sections with the large door of each hinged on the right side. Next to this bank of mail boxes was the building's elevator. We placed the tubs on the ground and Tina went ahead and opened the first section of boxes. The mail bundle meant for that section was nicely wrapped in its rubber band and she quickly slipped the band from the bundle and onto her wrist and began inserting the pieces into the boxes. The DPS was in relative delivery order but the Flats were not and so, there was needed a similar side-step dance to the one I had just done previously in my dropped mail routine minutes earlier. Also bundled within the DPS and Flats were the SPRs. These were little paper and plastic enveloped packages which, I later realized, had be unspokenly sized up to fit within the mail box. If it was too big, it would've be included in the parcel pumpkin. Tina had me do the next section and I had a little trouble with the door. The key opened a little door the size of all of the other individual mail boxes and inside that, there was a sort of "squeeze and pull" type of mechanism that released the larger door, enabling access to the individual boxes. Tina showed me how to "squeeze and pull" and the door swung open. This deliver went more smoothly. Some of the individual SPRs needed to be scanned. Not being experienced with the scanner, this took a little time. You need to position the scanner's laser appropriately on the bar code or else it won't acknowledge it. Once it's scanned, you need to input into the scanner what you are doing. It being delivered was the first choice, where it is being delivery is the next choice. You have the choice of mailbox, or parcel locker, or front door or with recipient or with a neighbor or something "other". I find on the scanner menu where it states, "mailbox" and press the "Enter" button. A little "buffering" swirly thing appeared and after a few second beeped in its acceptance of the input. I pushed the package into the mailbox. I finished the section and closed and locked the large door with some more fumbling of the "squeeze and pull" mechanism to have to be seated just right so the key could turn in its tumbler and thereby, lock. I moved to the last section and the got the door open with more ease and processed the delivery of mail in that section only to be interrupted a couple of times by residences coming and going to get to the elevator, which the door of the mail box section was blocking. I had to close the door slightly, let them pass, open up and continue. I was almost finished with the section and only had one last SPR to process. I scanned it delivered to the box but, was unable to fit it into the box. I sought Tina for advice. She took the package from my hand, manipulated it within her hands and crammed it home into the box somehow. I closed the last section and locked it up feeling not all too disappointed in my performance this time.

Now it was time for the parcels. Tina said that she like to work from top to bottom. While she packed the parcels into the tub, she took mental note of where the parcels should be delivered. I picked up the tub while Tina called for the elevator. We exit on the fourth floor and walk to the end of the boomeranged section of the building. She digs out the parcel to be delivered to the address and I scan, mark as delivered to front door, place it on the ground next to the door and knock on the door as notification to the resident that a package has been delivered and should probably get it, lest it disappear. We move to the next delivery address, which is still on the fourth floor but, on the opposite side of the building. We walk past the elevator we had just exited from and continue to the end of the other side of the boomerang. I estimated the walk from the previous delivery to this one to be about a hundred yards. I repeat the delivery process and we're off to the next one. Tina explains that she like to take the elevator up but the stairs down. So, we take the stairs to down to the floor below and repeat the delivery process only, on the third floor, the distance between the deliveries wasn't a great as it had been on the fourth floor. The two deliveries on the third floor were only a couple of apartments apart. We walked the stairs down to the second floor as the tub of parcels which I had been carrying grew lighter and repeated the process. There weren't any parcels to be delivered on the first floor. We got back into the ProMaster, put the outgoing mail into the outgoing tub, organized the empty tubs and back in our seats, we moved on to the next building address.

We continued this way for the rest of the day. The process, while becoming more familiar, also seemed to drain this unaccustomed trainee. Little annoyances become big. My compromised ankles and knees (from way too many miles of jogging) started to scream every time I needed to step up or down from the ProMaster. While it was February in South Florida, the strained movements within the vehicle and carrying tubs of mail and parcels seemed to turn on sweat spickets that never seemed to stop. We stopped for lunch next to a pool area at one of the high-rises. Tina told me that there were rest rooms in the pool area and to go ahead and take a break.

I entered the rest room and washed up as best I could. I threw cold water on my face and head and headed went back out to the ProMaster where we both broke out our cold lunches. I believe she had some sort of rice and bean dish and me, with my cold spaghetti. As we ate, I asked if this exact stop was planned to be the lunch stop on this route. She said that it was and that, she knows where to go to use the restrooms in the area. Apparently this is important as, you never know where you're going to be on any given route and, rest room location knowledge is extremely important. Jeremy had told me that he keeps a piss-bottle handy and, if needed, he just goes in the back of the van and "fills-up". That's ok for us "boys" I thought but, what's to become of the "girls"? I guess proper rest room location knowledge IS important. And, this is taking into consideration Number 1, I don't even want to think about Number 2!

We finished delivering everything we had by about 4pm and returned to the annex. Tina then showed me how to end the day by emptying out the ProMaster and keeping it relatively clean. She then showed me where to put the returned UBBM mail, where the forwarded or unable to be delivered mail should go, where the empty trays and tubs should be stacked, where the vehicle keys should go, where the used rubber bands should be placed and, how to return the arrow key. She helped me fill out the 1260 and I handed it to the acting supervisor at the desk. I wondered where Nick was. I returned my scanner to its charging cradle and thanked Tina for her instruction. She showed me where the schedule was and pointed out that I wasn't due to come back until the following Tuesday. A couple days off, nice.

On my way out of the annex a woman who I hadn't been introduced to said, "You made it. You coming back?"

I responded that, "Yes, I supposed so."

I reported back to work on that following Tuesday to a similar din of activity from the first day of on-the-job training. I reported to the supervisor's desk and was told that I'd be with Arnel today. I sought him out and he instructed me to hang back until 8. He also asked if I had a 1260. I told him that I hadn't and in a déjà vu, went to Nick and informed him that I needed a 1260. Nick handed me one and I filled it out with moderate familiarly.

Arnel was a pleasant enough Haitian immigrant who had been working at a bank for years before taking the job as a mail carrier. He didn't like the stress of the bank and the Postal Service seemed to fit his personality better. He was a family man but, I couldn't get him to open up much more than that about his personal life.

He approached my training in similar fashion to the way Tina had where, I did some casing but, my slowness caused Arnel to step in and take over, lest we fall very far behind. While standing behind Arnel and observing not only him in how he approaches the job but, also the activity around me. The flurry of motion and audible bombardment was dizzying at times. Some of the conversations were important to the job (and something that I should probably pay attention to), while other banter was just bullshit that stepped all over some important information. I caught an auditory glimpse of a couple of people referring to me from a distance; "What's HIS deal?" "He looks like a banker!"

From somewhere in the annex, I heard Jarod's voice booming, "Fuckin' this,....Fuckin' that...!!!!" I couldn't really follow what the complaint du jour was. Tina catches me and tells me to listen to Arnel today and watch what he does but, remember all the things she told me the other day. Nick hears this and gives me what turns out to be wise instruction; "Tom, don't listen to ANYONE but me! Trust me!". I wasn't sure who to believe at this point.

Arnel and I pack up the necessary trays for that day's mail and load into the required pumpkins, same as Tina and I had done, with a twist. Today was Tuesday. Apparently, starting on Tuesdays of each week, the delivery of the newspaper-like advertisements, affectionately known as "ADVOs", commences. Due to the sheer volume of these things, depending on the volume of mail, the delivery of advos may be split between Tuesday and Wednesday. As I entered the office that morning, I did notice the mountains of these advos piled high in front of each casing station. They are bundled in groups of forty to sixty, dependent upon what information they contain for that week. I quickly flipped through a loose one that had fallen to the floor and it contained something from AARP, coupons for local markets, Burger King reporting that they offer delivery service for $1, Cricket wireless is offering 4 lines of unlimited data for $100 per month, BJ's wants your membership for $40, Aldi grocers are reporting that a 24-pack a PurAqua water can be gotten for $2.29 and bone-in frozen turkey breast may be obtained for $1.59 per pound, you can have an A/C tune-up special for $29 and the omnipresent mattress sale for up to 50% with fine print stipulations that make it all but impossible to get anywhere close to 50% off.

These bundles were bound by heavy plastic tie wraps and we loaded them into the pumpkins with the bundles labelled with the very first addresses on the route and buried them under those with addresses at the end of the route along with the trays of all the other mail. The parcels were again, in a separate pumpkin. We roll the pumpkin's out of the annex and are about to load the parcels into the truck physical, as well as do the "Load Truck" feature on the scanner, when Arnel realizes that there is no jump seat in the LLV for me. The LLV is MUCH smaller than a ProMaster and can become very cramped, even without a jump seat. Arnel rushes back into the annex and reports that there is no seat for me. Word gets passed around and the annex's maintenance personnel quickly installs a jump seat in the rear of the LLV. We load the truck but, this time, it appears to be a cluttered mess to me. There doesn't seem to be any order by which the mail should be delivered. It's just a mountain of trays of mail and parcels and bundles of advos. And now, I had to climb over everything to get into this jump seat.

Arnel scans one of the pillars on the way out and this was something that I had missed the other day with Tina. Apparently, the letter carrier must scan the vehicle out of the Postal office by scanning a barcode located somewhere around the exit of the office. Once it's scanned, the scanner asks what the outgoing mileage is on the vehicle. This must be entered accurately and, the reverse is done upon returning at the end of the day.

I squeeze my overweight body (doctors would describe it as obese) into the jump seat of the already cramped LLV. I'm sweating already. Arnel manipulates the set-up of the LLV like he likes it, with windows down, fan blowing and adjusts his seat. Again, the "59" point vehicle check went undone and with a toot of the horn, we were on our way. The shock absorption in a Postal vehicle such as an LLV was never meant for comfort. This was strictly a utility vehicle meant for hauling mail and parcels. The fact that a human must operate it seemed to be merely an afterthought. The jostling that occurred even when motoring down the most smooth of surfaces was bone rattling immediately and from behind, cramped in the back of the tin can and sitting on a temporary, hardly padded seat held in place with a single bolt, didn't help much either.

We were on a completely new route. Well, it was new to me in that I had only be exposed to two at this point; one with Jeremy on my shadow day and one with Tina three days prior. Arnel made our way to the start of the route, which, as I had mentioned, were businesses. We were in what looked like any standard strip mall that contained a grocery store, a dollar store, a nail salon and a Subway sandwich shop. Our first stop, apparently was, using the restroom in the grocery store. Sure, I thought, I can always go and, I never miss a chance to wash my hands. After that stop he showed me where the cluster box for these storefronts were located. He quickly opened the box and inserted the necessary mail but did not deliver the advos. He told me that they were only for residential addresses. We finish and I contorted my body back into the sardine can and we proceeded to begin delivery to residential addresses.

Arnel had a heavy foot. No easing into acceleration and stopping for him. It was a bone jarring hard start and hard stop each and every time we needed to move. We were on a curbside delivery route which meant that, the carrier stays mounted. You pull up to the curbside mailbox and insert the intended mail. Arnel did this and described his movements to me as he did it. He sat in his right side drivers chair, window to the sliding driver side door open. To his left was a metal tray platform containing a tray of Flats, a tray of DPS, a couple of bundles of advos and, parcels that Arnel had determined to be coming up for delivery at the point at which we were on the route.

Even at this new point in my little experience I took note that Flats were not comingled into the DPS and wondered why. It would appear that some carriers choose not to comingle the Flats with DPS based on a variety of circumstances. The amount of DPS, Flats and parcels is a main factor. It depends a lot on what else needs to be done for that particular day, as, not all days are equal in the mail delivery business. On this day, there were these advos to be delivered and so, the carrier determined, in conjunction with the amount of mail that needed to be delivered that it wasn't worth the time to comingle the Flats with DPS and, considering that this is curbside delivery where he'd be taking from trays and putting into mailboxes, it was easier just to take from the Flats tray already.

Still, it seemed to this novice that the mail carrier needed to draw mail from three sources in order to make the proper delivery. Four, if you include the parcels. This seemed confusing and rife with problems to me and, far from the original thought of taking whatever mail which was intended to be delivered, and just put it in the box. But, Arnel jerked to a stop, fingered the mail like a magician doing a card trick, reached through the window, flicked the mailbox open, jammed the mail with the advso into the box, flicked the mailbox close and jammed on the gas and we were off to the next box. He did this again and again without pause and occasionally grabbed a parcel and, if it was small enough, scanned it and placed into the mailbox. If it wasn't small enough, he'd have to shut down the vehicle, exit and walk to the front door of the residence and go through the steps for proper delivery to the front door. Get back in, start the vehicle and gun it to the next stop.

On a mounted route, you don't want packages that don't fit into a box. The time it takes to shut the vehicle down, get the parcel, walk it to the front door, scan for delivery, return to the vehicle and start up, times the amount of parcels for that route for that day, can cause serious delays in completing delivery on a given route for the day.

Arnel decides that it was time for lunch and we pulled to the side of a road under a large tree which provided some shade. Finding shade in South Florida is like winning a couple of bucks on a scratch-off; it's not going to change your life but, it sure does make you smile for second.

I grab my stuff and squeeze my way from the back of the LLV and out the driver side and sit down under the street and catch my breath for a minute before eating. The claustrophobic jostling that I had just endured had really taken the air out of me. The constant jerk stop and start and speed bumps and quick left turns and quick right turns, snapped my neck in a chiropractor's dream way! The coffin-like environment in which I was sitting in the back of the LLV provided no air and no room to have the ability to even shift in one's seat. The fan blowing hot air on Arnel never reached the rear of the LLV and it was never intended to. The sweat soaked through to the surface of my shirt.

Chapter 7

I dug out of my soft insulated lunch box my sandwich that I had prepped earlier that morning. Not a full-blown germaphobe yet, but I was in my Junior year and on my way to gradation, I was looking for a way to wash up before manhandling my sandwich. There'll be none of that, as we were too far away from any semblance of running water and soap. I made do with splashing some water from my jug onto my hands and wiped them on my shorts as, I didn't want to use the one and only napkin I had packed as I was intending on using it as a shield when I held the sandwich from the flesh-eating bacteria that I was sure I'd transfer from my hands to my sandwich to my mouth and into my run-down immune system.

I choked down my now soggy sandwich and watched Arnel as he sat in the driver's seat of the LLV, thumbing his phone. He seemed to take it all in stride and appeared to me to be a man driven to achieve a certain level for which certain things just needed to be endured in order to attain.

After lunch Arnel positioned the LLV at the head of a street and turned the keys over to me and said it was my turn. He propelled his slender frame into the jump seat in the rear of the LLV with a grace that made me feel a little silly, with my grunts and groans that emitted from me as I had done it. I pulled up to my first official mailbox and, I realized that I didn't know what street I was on. "You're on SW 3rd Way mon", said Arnel in his accent. Ok, got it. So, take the mail and put it in the box and move on. What mail? Well, let's see; I flip through the DPS and I don't see anything for this address, but, I see a couple of things in the Flats tray, I take those and position them in my hands. Then I look at the advos but, I can't really see the address without having to pull the whole, still bound bundle toward me. I see the upside down address and try to slip the individual advo out from it bundled home. They start to tear and Arnel jumps in to show me how he removed an advo from the bound bundle. I fold the Flats into the advo, reach and pull the mailbox door down. I neatly place the mail I had positioned in my hand into the box and closed the door. As I was about to pull away, the mailbox door opened. I reached out and shut it again. It opened again! I slammed it shut and it held but, it looked like it was going to pop open at any second again and so, I just moved on and hoped for the best.

I came to the next address but found that this time, this address had mail from DSP but nothing from the Flats. I removed the advo from the bunch without tearing any of it and delivered into the mailbox. I eased into acceleration and knowing how it felt being back there in the LLV, came to gentle stops in front of each subsequent mail box. I came to an address where I found that there was DPS and Flats mail but no address for an advo. Arnel said that some people opt out of getting the advos and so, not every address will get one. You have to read the address. I had come to the end of the street and read the next address on either the next DPS or the next Flat and apparently, it was on the other side of the street and then heading back in the direction I had come. In this particular situation, odd numbers ran one direction of the street and even numbers ran in the opposite direction. Becoming disoriented between matching the mail box numbers with the house numbers and aligning them with whatever comes next in the flow of DPS and/or Flats in conjunction with the advos became a problem for me. But, I was new and I was sure I would pick it up with more professionality in time. After the first few deliveries, Arnel left me to my own devices and resigned himself to thumbing his phone. I came to a point where he told me to stop and we traded places. I grunted my way back into the jump seat and right away Arnel said, “What’s THIS?!” I looked to where he was pointing and I saw a few small parcels on the tray. I was so focused on finding the right address and matching it with the correct DPS, Flats, advos, that I had completely forgotten all about the parcels. Sure enough, the address of the parcels were all the way back at the other end of the long street and we had to dead-head back to that spot and, not wanting to waste any more time, Arnel made the deliveries with perceived pep in his step that I absorbed shame in.

He jumps back into the LLV and guns it to the point where I had stopped and he picked up. He then explained to me that I shouldn’t take so much time fingering the mail and orienting and making it nice and gently placing it into the box. Time is a factor. Grab it, jam it and move on. I did notice him looking at the mail in the trays and he maneuvered the vehicle to the next stop in anticipation of what is to be delivered. Perhaps that saves time and something I didn’t do as I was concentration on driving this rickety metal box so that I don’t kill anyone or hit a mailbox.

He gave me another opportunity to delivery on the mounted route but, by that point later in the day, I had sweat through my shirt, my shorts, AND, my socks and the thought of twisting and bending this old(ish) body out of the jump seat and into the driver’s seat to once again try to make sense of the addresses and whichever pile the mail is derived from, was something that I wasn’t looking forward to. But, I grinded it out and did a few more streets with even more confusion as fatigue had set in.

Upon returning to the annex and doing the whole process of returning the vehicle with proper mileage scanned in, distributing undelivered mail, outgoing mail, outgoing parcels, returning empty trays and tubs and returning vehicle key and arrow keys and scanners, I was wiped out. And I suppose it was obvious, as people commented on my clearly drained and sweaty appearance; "Look at you!", "Did you go swimming?" "Tough day, heh-heh?". I mustered all the smile I could and 1260'd my ass outta there.

The next day my eyes opened from a restless sleep. I did the now familiar morning check; Am I breathing? Check. Do I know where I am? Check. Do body parts move? The knees sounded like popcorn popping but, ok, check! I shuffle to the kitchen to make coffee and prep food and water for the day. The body, especially the back is aching pretty good. Human beings weren't meant to squat on an uncushioned seat in the back of 30 year old rusting bucket of bolts with no suspension, no air conditioning, and no window, in 90 degree heat for 8 hours at a time. Even a submarine has A/C! I pack up and head back out for more punishment.

Back at the annex, the day begins in similar fashion to the previous one. I'm with Arnel again and this time, I'm left to do a bit more casing as, we had delivered all of the advos the day before. Had we split the advos into a two-day delivery, we'd be back out there delivering the 2nd half of them on this day, Wednesday. So, the day was looking less taxing without the dark cloud of advo delivery hanging over our heads. However, we still didn't comingle the Flats with the DPS as the route we were going on today (which was different than the previous day's) was a partial mounted and partial "park and loop". As I've said, it's up to the carrier to determine if time would allow the carrier to comingle the

Flats with the DPS and I supposed it was Arnel's call on this day based on volume and his trainee in tow.

We went through the whole casing, pull-down, loading-up, scanning out process again and we were on the road. Squeezing myself into the back of the LLV was even more difficult today as, soreness had set in and the body wasn't cooperating in a way that I would have liked. Arnel pulled into a strip mall, needing to do the business first and began to explain the idiosyncrasies of each business. Some weren't open yet and therefore, you'd have to go to the door and see if you could see any activity inside. If so, you try to flag them down so as to deliver what you had and take away anything they had to go out. In this specific case we were in front of a pizza restaurant, clearly not open as of yet and, we could see someone way in the back, prepping the kitchen for the day. We got his attention and he held a finger up in a "be there in a minute" gesture. We stood there waiting. There was no mail slot on the door and so, the only way to deliver mail to such places is to gain access and either hand deliver to an occupant or simply place somewhere within the establishment and make sure that someone is aware that you put mail there.

Being new to the whole process, even this smacked of a time drain. I'm not a businessman by any stretch of the imagination but, I was getting paid, Arnel was getting paid, and we were standing outside a pizza restaurant in a mini mall, waiting for someone to come and unlock the door so that we could hand them a small glossy cardboard advertisement from Midas for a muffler inspection. The thought that would enter my mind and appear on my lips for the next few months arrived in a blaze, "There's GOT to be a better way!".

Finally finishing with the pizza restaurant, we move onto the UPS store. "What the hell are we doing here?", I thought. Arnel had rifled through some parcels in the LLV and packed them into two tubs and we bring them into the UPS store. The store was open and active with customers sending and receiving various things and again, we had to wait to be "served". We finally get someone who worked there to receive the packages that we had for them and we scanned all of them as delivered. And I turned to leave, Arnel stopped and informed me that we had to take "these" with us. I look to where he pointed and I see a full U-boat of packages of various sizes. We roll the U-boat out of the UPS store and scan each package as Pre-Paid parcel and pack them into the already packed LLV. I return the U-boat to the UPS story trying to wrap my head around why we're even dealing with UPS. Apparently, UPS works with the USPS so as to provide pick-up, processing and interim transportation of mail, with final delivery being made by domestic and international Postal services.

Why not? I supposed. It's another revenue source and why not entertain it if it could be accommodated. But, once again, this deviated from my general idea of what a "mailman" was, or did. I thought I'd be whistling down a tree-lined street, happily delivering a birthday card with 20 bucks stuffed into it for little Johnny. Not, hauling packages out of a UPS store in a mini mall and scanning and cramming them into a decades old death trap to bring it BACK to the post office!

We completed the businesses and Arnel begin doing the curbside delivery. Again with the jerking… My back screamed in protest and the sweat marathon began. After a few streets he turned the reins over to me. I really wasn't interested at that point but, anything was better than being crammed back there in that jump seat with UPS packages falling all over me.

I managed to do a few streets of curbside delivery (parcels included this time) without too much problem or fanfare. But, of course, I was slow and Arnel felt that he had to take over lest we lose our “destination-at-a-given-time” momentum. If we’re five minutes late on this street, it’s makes us ten minutes late on the next street, then fifteen and, by the end of the day, you’ve got people calling asking why you are where you are and what you are doing that is causing such a delay?

We apparently completed the curbside delivery and moved into a townhome complex. I already hated being mounted and doing curbside delivery. Sitting in that vehicle and being thrown all about and trying not to hit anything in the obstacle course of a mail route while trying to coordinate the Flats, DPS, advos and parcels was circus-like. I envisioned the little clown car entering one of the three rings where clowns and things entered and exited, stopping and going and then, disappearing behind some curtain and forgotten until the next act appeared.

Within the Waterford Courtyards complex there numbered buildings containing four individually number homes within that. These were cluster box deliveries but what made it confusing was that the cluster box comprised mail receptacles of more than one cluster and hardly any of them were labelled. What also made it confusing was that the buildings had a mailing address of, say 29 and within 29, the home’s delivery address may have been, say, 2889, 2891, 2893, 2895 (Try making sense outta THAT!) and to then try to find apartment 2929 and finally finding it in building 25, was hard to figure on the fly when there are no building numbers on the delivery label. It made delivering to this complex painful. I'd been known to drive around in circles looking for an address. I'd even stopped people who lived in the complex and asked where a certain apartment might be and all I'd get is a shrug.

I picked-up on the fact that each cluster contained four residences and that their mailing addresses were labelled in multiples of two and some buildings contained odd numbers and other buildings contained even numbers but, I was unable to see the building number pattern. I tried to fix it in my mind with a "If I designed this…" and figured that if building 25 contained four individual homes, they should at least be labelled 2925, 2926, 2927 and 2928 and the next building number of 26 should contain apartment 2929, 2930, 2931, and 2932. Then, if I had a delivering that went to 2936, I could deduce that it must be within building 27! Something that made some sort of mathematical sense. Nope, not in this place. Well, I'm sure it does makes sense to someone but, it wasn't apparent to me at this point with my solid C/D grade High School algebraic mind!

The further problem with this was, the cluster boxes weren't labelled and you'd have no idea which cluster box went to each building AND, each cluster box covered multiple buildings and the individual boxes weren't labelled either so, delivering in this complex was maddening. I could take a guess at whatever cluster box might go to a specific group of buildings but, there's no time for guessing. Arnel tried to explain how it worked to me but, I got the sense that, if you do it long enough, it becomes apparent, like everything else. Fair enough, I supposed, that I shouldn't be expected to memorize how the number schemes worked for each individual complex within the city of Deerfield Beach, Fl worked in just a few days. But, it was disconcerting at the lack of common sense.

I tagged along as Arnel showed me how to open these types of cluster boxes (different from those I'd been exposed to thus far). Had to go around back and turn the key and lift and swing out one side of the box and with the other hand manipulate the other door. He did it swiftly with a familiarity that comes with time. These cluster boxes were positioned in the middle of a "U" shaped bank of bushes. Why it was decided that these bushes should be "sticker" bushes was beyond me. Just getting behind the box produces open scratches on legs and arms immediately. Arnel took out for me a bundle of Flats, DPS and parcels and handed to me and pointed over to a cluster of townhomes to deliver. I was thankful that he did that as, figuring out what mail goes to each building apparently is the key factor in efficiency here. You can't just bring ALL the mail with you and then try to figure out what goes where. You can only carry so much.

I get to the cluster box and pile the packages on top of it and as I work my way through the barbed wire I see a sign on the box warning residents to be aware that, rats had been seen in the area and to be reminded not to leave food out. Great, so, now I'm looking around waiting to be attacked by rats while being scratched to shit by these bushes. I struggled with opening the box but finally got it open and the mail delivered. Having that feeling of being pounced on at any second, I felt that any delay whatsoever makes me rat food. And, of course, I had trouble locking the cluster box back up. Even more sweat formed and dripped from the brow and I jiggled and twisted, looked down at my feet for rats, shook and rattled, looked down again, and finally landed the bolt home. I blew through the sticker bushes this time not really caring about the blood scratches. After walking what I thought was a safe distance away, I looked back figuring I'd see hundreds of rats scurrying in the spot where I had just been. But, no. No rats. Only, the packages I had left on top of the cluster box! Fuck me! I had to go back.

I approached the box gingerly and, when I felt the coast was clear, I swooped up the parcels and backed away. But, now I was spooked. If rats had been seen around the mail cluster box, what's to say they weren't…everywhere! I checked the addresses on each package and found their corresponding townhome and had to open an outer gate to get to the front door of the residences. Some people keep the homes nice, others, not so much. With rats on my mind, every nook and cranny triggered my mind with "I'll bet they're in there!". I was able to deliver the parcels without incident and returned to Arnel leaning up against the LLV thumbing his phone. Before looking up he asked absently, "How did it go?" and then sees me and said, "You bleeding mon!". The bushes had done a number on me but, no big deal, at least I don't have the bubonic plague!

We made it through the rest of the day in similar fashion and, upon returning to the annex, was given the green light to go out on my own the following day. Well, well, look at me, almost a full blown mailman. I was told to come in the following day at 10am. I could use the extra time in the morning to steel myself from what was to come. I was enthusiastic as, I work better alone anyway and perhaps all of the things that caused me confusion will have light shed on them when I don't have to deal with someone talking at me.

I thanked Arnel for his patience and guidance, and his parting words to me as an on-the-job trainer stuck with me during my time there, as hard as it was at times; "Go with the flow mon! Just go with the flow!"

Chapter 8 – Begin Tour

The day before, as I left, I checked the schedule and it had me down to come in at 10am. The schedule doesn't show an end time as in, 9a-5p or 8a-4:30p or 10am -4:30pm, just the number 10. In my mind I was still technically a part-time employee. That's what it said on the application anyway. And, with a starting time of 10am, the day's work for me was a customizable thing. Not like any full-time employee where their working hours are relatively fixed at say, 8am-4:30pm, based on workload. Of course, I'm referring to salaried employees but, I don't see how scheduling hourly employees should be any different.

A bit difficult to plan for but, I'm all in and, I'll assume that I'm there for the rest of the day. I report to the annex and go straight over to Nick to see what I need to do. He said, "You ready?" I told him that I thought I was and he explained to me that I was being put on a two-hour piece. Two hours? So much for the rest of the day and I thought of that guy in training who was concerned about not getting enough hours. Immediately my mind conjured up that I'd be home for a nice lunch and nap before I knew it. I thought further that, it made sense; why kill a person on their first day? They'll just get disillusioned and walk out if it's too much.

Nick brought me over to a bin that had contained mail which had already been cased and pulled down and nicely labelled as to where to start and what would be the next tray or bin to deal with once the first one was complete. I was sent over to the clerk's cage to obtain and sign for an arrow key. I was asked what route I was on and, having no idea, I went back to Nick and he yelled to the clerk to give me the spare key for 25. I signed for the key and threaded the chained key through my belt loop. I asked Nick what scanner I should take as the scanner for route 25 was already taken by the regular doing the majority (less 2 hours) of route 25. He gave me a spare scanner and I began to set it up by scanning the bar code on my ID badge and entering the necessary information. The scanner went blank. I tried reviving it but, it was a no go. I went to Nick with the problem and he opened the back section and took out the battery and reset it but, still dead. Another scanner was given to me and I was able to set it up with limited trouble. Nick handed me a key to a vehicle and told me not to forget to do the load truck feature.

I remembered to ask for a 1260 and wrote my start time as 10:00am and shoved it into my pocket. I wheeled the bin out to the parking lot where all the vehicles sat in readiness for the day. Some vehicles were already gone as, the out-of-office time for a carrier is dependent on the volume of mail and the carrier's enthusiasm in wanting to get going.

I matched the vehicle number with that which was labelled on the key and wheeled the bin to it. I started doing the vehicle check as I thought I should, being new. I went over it very thoroughly, as instructed. The tires looked a little low and I wondered if I should say anything. I continued. The rear bumper of the LLV had a nice dent in it and, I wondered how paranoid I should be. Should I treat this as a rental car and should I report every little scrape and ding, lest I be accountable for it. I wasn't sure.

I got into the vehicle and started it and it rattled to life. I noticed that the fan didn't work but everything else seemed to be operating. I forgot to check the blinkers and turned the right one on and got out to check the front (working) then the rear… "Whatya doing!?"

A weathered female carrier caught me. "I'm doing a vehicle check. Checking the blinkers." She said, "Never, EVER, get out of your vehicle while it's running! That's cause for IMMEDIATE dismissal! I didn't see anything." And she walked away.

Oops, strike one on the day. But, I figured that I was supposed to garnish assistance from another carrier in checking all that needed to be checked. How else does one check break lights? But, I looked around the parking lot and saw no one doing this and, since I was getting the feeling that I was taking too long in prepping for leaving the office, I just blew it off and called the vehicle check good.

I managed to do the "Load Truck" feature for the parcels but, I was unsure on how to process the information. With each scan, it spit out a section number to me and, I tried to put the parcels in relative section order in the vehicle but, this was an LLV I had, and not a ProMaster where there were nice shelves and stenciled delineations of sections on the wall of the van. The LLV had none of that. It was just a metal sweat box and you put things in there as you pleased and hoped for the best. Luckily there was only about ten parcels to deliver. I stacked the parcels in the LLV from largest on the bottom to smallest on the top just so they wouldn't shift around the vehicle so much.

I locked up the vehicle and rolled the empty bin back into the annex and retrieved my personal things from my locker, which now had my name on it. I went over to Nick and said that the vehicle seemed ok but the fan wasn't working. He said he'd take a note of it and asked if there was enough gas. I told him that there was three quarters of a tank and he said, "Might as well give you a gas card now anyway." We went back to the cage and he pulled out a binder containing individually enveloped gas cards, each assigned to a specific route. But before giving me the gas card for the route, he had to set me up with a special password to be used at the pump. He went on a computer and clickety clacked his way, processing me into the system and wrote down my password on a little torn piece of paper. He handed it to me and told me not to lose it. I shoved it into my wallet for safe keeping and he handed me the gas card for route 25. He said that I probably wouldn't need it but, just in case.

I was about to depart the annex to the vehicle and finally get going on my first solo outing as a mailman. I checked the clock and it read, 10:35am. I had my backpack and water jug and bid Nick a "See ya later!" With a smile Nick said, "Just stay calm. Don't get frustrated. I'll see ya around 12!"

Twelve? It's 10:35am. He just said he's giving me a two-hour piece. On the paper at the head of the first tray that describes what it is I'm supposed to be doing, it says, two hours. Apparently they determine how long a certain amount of mail should take to be delivered based on previous, experienced carrier times but, that time starts at the point of dropping the first piece of mail into a box, surely, and ends when the last piece is delivered. Am I wrong? Surely not from when I'm scheduled to start. I'm behind already? I haven't even begun! I've failed and I haven't even gotten out of the parking lot yet. Strike two on the day!

At least the two hour portion of the route I was doing was within Century Village and, at least at this point, was most familiar to me. I got myself as organized as I could and pulled away from the annex in the LLV. I've never driven in Europe and I don't know what it's like to drive on the "wrong" side of the road but, I must say that driving a vehicle on the "wrong" side of the vehicle itself wasn't as disorienting as I thought it might have been. As an occasional golfer, I can say that driving the vehicle had a very golf-cart-like feel to it. Nothing fancy, it just gets you to where you're going, barely. I tested the security waters as I approached the opposing guarded gates at Century Village, fully prepared to show my Postal ID but, the gates parted as I approached, nary a hesitation or glance. The power of the postal vehicle!

I knew the name of the village within the village but, wasn't quite sure how to get there. You'd think they'd provide some sort of map of the route? The speed limit within Century Village was 25 mph and I kept to it. Being on probation, I didn't want to test the water by speeding with a federal vehicle. At almost each speed limit sign there was one of those electronically displayed speed limit signs that tell you exactly how fast you're going and if you should "Slow Down". I kept it pinned at 25 mph, nothing more, nothing less. I pulled up into where I thought I should go but got turned around and finally found the very first building where my piece of the route was to begin.

The heat inside the LLV was already beginning to boil in the morning sun. I already wanted out of the vehicle, at least for a few minutes while I made the first deliveries. I gathered all the DPS and Flats (which were nicely comingled, thank you) and any parcels meant for that stop. The first stop was what they considered a “garden apartment” and there weren’t too many individual addresses for this particular building.

I rolled the windows up and locked up the vehicle and made my way to the alcove where the bank of mail boxes were. I inserted the arrow key and twisted and the bank of boxes swung out with a clank. I slowly and carefully went through the mail I was carrying in my left hand and placed everything in the appropriate receptacles. I closed the bank and locked it. I then opened the Outgoing mail box and retrieved a few pieces of mail and closed and locked it back up and headed toward the LLV feeling slightly proud of myself. First stop, done. No problems.

I unlock the LLV and climb in and realize that I had forgotten to take an empty tub with me from the annex and now I have nowhere to put the outgoing mail that I just retrieved. The first of many jury-rigged situations was evident. I put the outgoing mail into my backpack for safekeeping. I realized as I was doing it the potential problems which might occur having done that but, I didn’t want to put the outgoing mail anywhere where the wind (should there actually be any in South Florida) would blow it around or out of the LLV or, have it comingled with any of the other mail, especially the UBBM. It all looked the same to me at this point and didn’t want to risk it and so, I chose what might be the lesser of the evils and put the mail into my backpack.

I gingerly maneuvered the LLV around the maze-like Century Village and found the next building, which was a “high rise” and, throwing caution to the wind, backed the vehicle into the “no parking” zone as I had seen my trainers do. I loaded myself up with a tub and parcels to go to that building, rolled the window up, locked up the vehicle and made my way to the mail box area of the boomerang shaped building. I placed everything neatly on the floor and began to open each sections of the buildings boxes and delivered all of the mail with no issues. I had two parcels to deliver; one on the fourth floor and one on the second. I knuckled the call button to the elevator and waited. And waited. It finally came but, the thought that if I had to wait for the elevator like that much during the day, might cause some serious delays.

Up on the fourth floor I processed the delivery of a relatively heavy parcel. Scanned and delivered and gave a gentle three knocks on the door. I turned to leave and the floor few open as a gentleman came out professing his appreciation for my delivery of the parcel and handed out a five dollar bill and a diet coke to me. I held my hands up in protest that it wasn't necessary but he insisted AND persisted. "Please, you came all the way up here with that heavy package, I really appreciate it."

Is this a test? We're not supposed to accept gifts worth anything more than $20 and not to accept any cash whatsoever, no matter how small the denomination. Once again, going with what I thought was the lesser of the evils, I took the money and pocketed it rather than stand there wasting more time debating the merits of accepting a cash tip.

I took the stairs down to the second floor, following Tina's lead and delivered the smaller package there and went back to the LLV and unlocked and mounted up thinking, "Five bucks…and I've been out here less than an hour! This might be pretty lucrative if I play my cards right!".

I completed the rest of my two-hour piece and began the drive back to the annex. Upon parking and locking the vehicle up and checking the time, it read 2:00pm. Upon entering the annex, Nick said, “Four hours, that sounds about right!”. Well, I really didn’t start delivering until about 11am so, in MY mind, that was three hours. And, take off another ten minutes for the ride back to the annex. So, I’m thinking that, what is supposed to take the regular carrier 2 hours, took the new guy 2 hours and 50 minutes. That’s pretty good in my book. But, I don’t believe that it’s perceived that way by the Postal Service. How it’s perceived is that, it took me twice as long to deliver a piece of a route (Begin tour at 10am, back in the office at 2pm, four hours to do a two hour piece) and that is just not acceptable.

For my penance, I was sent back out to do another one hour piece. This took me two hours. By the time I had returned the scanner, the arrow key, the gas card and put UBBM in it necessary place and put outgoing mail (I remembered to take it out of my backpack before entering the annex) and returned the rubber bands to the route’s casing station, I exited the annex at 4:13pm.

Started the day at 10am and finished at 4:13pm. 6 hours and 13 minutes. But, would only get paid for 5 hours and 43 minutes due to the fact that, if any work-time is over 6 hours, 30 minutes is automatically removed for lunch. Kinda unfair, I thought. What lunch? I didn’t stop for a second. But, all in all, the day went off pretty well for my first time on my own and, a cool five bucks in my pocket. I decided to fess up and told Nick about the tip and he exclaimed, “I didn’t hear nothing”, and walked away.

As it would turn out, that first day, my first day on my own, would be the last day that I was offered any further financial gratitude in the future. And trust me, there were times where…a little somethin’ for the effort…would have been welcome.

I brought the diet coke home.

The next day, a Friday, considered to be one of the slowest of the week, I was scheduled to start again at 10am. I was given a four-hour piece of a route I had not been on or seen at all. The four hours consisted of two separate complexes a couple of miles apart from each other. Again, everything was cased for me and the parcels were even marked as to the order in which they would come up on the route. This was Enzo's route. Enzo Guaraldi was a super nice guy who, I'd come to learn, had many jobs before coming to the USPS. He was happy in his position as career city carrier and fill-in supervisor. I could read from his comments and just by his demeanor that he, "Goes with the flow". He is fully aware of the USPS's shortcomings but, like Jeremy, felt that he was better off now than where he had come from and tried hard to overlook the Postal Services idiosyncrasies and once he got home to his wife, all was good with the world. He'd been on the job for something like fifteen years and yet, managed to still be sympathetic to those starting out, remembering how hard it was when he started.

Enzo set me up for delivery very well so that I wouldn't have too many problems. However, it wasn't completely selfless as, if a CCA screws up a regular carriers route, guess who has to swoop in the next day and do damage control?

He described for me how I was to locate the first complex and again, I wondered why there were no maps for such things. This first complex was at the southern border of Deerfield Beach called "Discovery". I felt like I was driving a long time and, with the signal lights lasting an eternity, I really felt that, by the time I got to the complex, it felt like it took 20 minutes to get there. I turned left into the gated entrance and, I see the call box on the left side of the vehicle just where Enzo described it would be. I stopped the

LLV, turned the engine off, go around the vehicle and I locate the little envelope insignia etched into the call box where the arrow key should go to be able to gain access to the complex. I dig the arrow key from my pocket and insert and twist the key. The gates begin to open. I retreat the key and walk around the vehicle and dig the ignition key from pocket and start it up and put it in gear and begin to approach the gates. But, I guess I took too long as the gates began closing again.

I had to back up (uh oh) to the call box again and do it all over again. Faster this time. I checked behind me and of course, there was a car in front of the box. So, I pulled up and around the turn-around in front of the entrance and circled around behind the car. I thought of just following that car in as, I would image there might be enough time for me to fit through but, who wanted to chance it.

I pull up in front of the box, shut down the vehicle, walk around the other side to the box, insert the key and twist, ready to run, I withdraw the key, get around to the right side of the vehicle, quickly jam the key into the ignition, throw it into gear and punch it. Through the gates I went. I was told to go through the gates and go straight for a little bit and the cluster boxes will be on the right. I pulled up and saw a wall of cluster boxes stretching perhaps thirty feet from end to end. I found a spot with enough room on either side of the already parked cars to back into safely.

I was in a complex consisting of townhomes and these were their mailboxes. No mailboxes existed on the home itself or in front of the home on the curb. I guess residences arrived home, pulled into a parking spot, get out of their car to get their mail and pull out and continued to their specific residence. I think I would find that annoying but, that's just me.

I removed from the vehicle the first tray of mail as well as the first tub of SPRs and placed it on the ground at the head of the mass cluster box. I opened the first of many double doors that exposed the individual mail boxes within the larger box and began the job of putting paper products into metal boxes. Each individual double-doored box had its own outgoing slot and I retrieved whatever was in there and threw it into the empty tub that I had remembered to take this time. I went about the business of scanning and delivery each SPR into its appropriate slot and, when finished, locked up the first cabinet and moved to the next one in line. Along with the mail and the SPRs, were also parcels which needed to be delivered and some may be able to fit within two larger receptacles (parcel lockers) within each double-doored box. If they don't fit, they must be driven to the front door of the residence. But the same procedure applies, you scan it as delivered and where it was delivered, in the box or front door.

While delivering to this wall of cluster boxes, on many occasions people would simply approach me and give me mail to take away. I don't know why this bothered me as much as it did. Can't they put it into a slot? Can't they see I'm busy here? But, I take it with a smile and flip it into my outgoing tub and continue side-stepping to the next set of boxes. I glance up and to the right every now and then to see how much more I have to go and the distance needed to be covered didn't look promising. Every time I look down the line of cluster boxes to the end, my eyes did that thing that Hollywood does when the focal point begins to stretch out slowly and continually gets farther and farther away. After finishing with the cluster boxes I still had to drive around within the complex looking for the individual addresses for the parcels which couldn't fit in the parcel locker within the cluster boxes. I finally finish with the complex four hours after beginning!

I was thankful for the relatively short ride from Discovery to the next complex called, "The Lakes". The sun had been beaming and, although the cluster boxes at Discovery had an overhang to them, the heat and humidity works its way into a person. The little fan on the dashboard had two speeds, slow and a little faster. I cranked it as far as it would go and rolled the window down on the driver's side door and let the warm air wash over me. I guzzled the ice water from the insulated jug I had with me and tried to will myself to cool down.

I pull into The Lakes and was thankful that there was no gate controlled by the arrow key that I'd have to do a Chinese fire drill to gain access. I just drove in and found the first stand of three leveled apartments. I found a safe enough parking spot to back into, although, the parking area seemed tighter for some reason. I gathered all that I needed for this stop, shut down the vehicle, locked it up and went looking for the box. This particular apartment complex had the cluster box on the rear of the stairs leading up to the second floor. The Lakes seemed to be a bit tattered around the edges as an apartment complex. It was bordered on the east by railroad tracks and Rt 95 beyond that and to the north by SW 10th St which is a major east/west thoroughfare that, if taken further west turned into the Sawgrass Expressway that went through Parkland, Fl, (where a gunman had himself, "Gone Postal", at Marjory Stoneman Douglas High School and killed 17 and injured 17 more students a couple of years earlier) and, if continued to be followed, would lead to Alligator Alley, which crossed the state of Florida at the relative extreme bottom of the state. I supposed that, the closer you are to major roads and highways and railroad tracks etc., the less attention is paid to certain areas of residential design.

Standing behind the stairs within this complex didn't give me the most secure feeling and I could hardly see as there were no lights near the mail cluster box. You could transverse the building from the parking lot, through the ground level and to the back, which led to a pool and sand volleyball court in the center of the circular layout of the apartment complex. This caused a wind tunnel blowing in one direction or the other at times which was nice in a way as, it was dark and windy as opposed to being "out there" where it was bright as the sun itself and no sweat evaporated due to the stillness of the humidity.

I managed to open this type of cluster box, which was a different configuration from anything I'd been exposed to thus far and had to first unlock it with the arrow key and then pinch closed two opposing metal tabs to disengage the large metal door from its latch. The door swung to the right and almost fell off its hinges as the years of opening and closing seemed to have taken its toll. The outgoing box within this cluster was the very box where the key unlocked everything and it was very small along with the rest of the residences boxes.

The labeling of these boxes was a disaster. Some were labelled, others weren't. What made delivering to these boxes difficult was that they didn't seem to fall into the same pattern with their neighboring box. This cluster box was a rectangle shape with three boxes left to right, and seven boxes top to bottom. The code deciphering the apartment number in conjunction with the building number left me scratching my head and I had to stop and figure out where the sketchilly labelled mail in my arms might need to go within this cluster. I'm simplifying here but, if the lowest left box was labelled number 1 and the boxes ran bottom to top, any reasonable person needing to find the unlabeled apartment four, you'd just count from the bottom and work your way up to the fourth box in that row and, there you go.

If it were that easy, I may not have even decided to write this book! This building may start from the upper right as 1A, then the next box to its left is 2A, then 3A. Where should 4A go, directly down from 3A on the next row below or, all the way back to the right on the next row below 1A and continue in that pattern? It's a trick question, there is no 4A! The pattern in this building goes from 3A to 1B. But, again, the location of 1B might be directly below 3A or, it might be below 1A to the right, or, it may be somewhere else.

I mention this because, each of the building's pattern of boxes is different and, to try to get into a flow of delivery where you can give a shot at memorizing the pattern, makes it easier to finger through the mail held in your left arm and at least reach with your right arm in a general location of where the box should, logically be. Without that repetitive pattern, the newbie is spitting into the wind!

I moved from apartment building to apartment building very slowly, each with its own unique pattern of mail boxes within the cluster box. The boxes were all the same size, small, and I'd begun jamming and scraping fingers as I went through the delivery motion. I had originally dismissed Arnel's suggestion of wearing gloves as unnecessary but, I now believe it to be a good protective measure.

I reached the last apartment building within the complex when a golf cart came speeding up and the driver asked, "Habla Español?". I replied, "No, sorry." He then said, "Not even a little?"

I had to laugh at that one. No sir, my high school Spanish teacher will confirm, "Not even a little!". He was apparently the grounds keeper of the complex and needed to convey something to me. He decided it wasn't worth trying to communicate with me in his broken English or, in my even more broken Spanish, and drove off in the cart.

The last stop within this complex was the administrative office for the complex. As I walk into the office I was almost knocked over by the blast of cold air. They kept it, meat preserving cold in there. As I exchanged incoming with outgoing mail, I was asked, "Are you new?" A question which would be asked often in the coming months. I answered in the affirmative and was out the door into the thick air again and headed back to the annex, the day's delivery completed. The designated four hour piece took me seven hours from beginning to end. Paid for six and a half hours however, no break, no lunch.

Enzo was still there when I returned and asked how it had gone. I explained my frustration at not being able to see in The Lakes and the odd way that the mail boxes were set up. He said, "Yea, it's all fucked up. They recently redid the routes, and The Lakes was added to my route. I hate it. I haven't had the opportunity to label the boxes better. Do the best you can".

And with that, I left with a major stiff neck.

I was told to come in the next day, a Saturday, at 9:30am. Upon waking that morning, the stiff neck that I had gone home with the day before had now turned into a knot in the base of the neck with a pounding headache. I could barely straighten up.

The move here is, as you deliver to cluster boxes, you hold the mail in the crook of your left arm and you flip through it with your right hand and when you have a grouping of a certain address, you glance your eye up, with hardly moving your head, to find the intended box and you extend your right arm toward the box and make the delivery. The head is still in that down looking position and, after hours of this, the muscles knot up. This is something that minimizes with time as, once becoming more familiar with the idiosyncrasies of each route, there isn't the need for such head-hunch concentration, and the muscles are more relaxed.

But for today, the hunchback of Deerfield Beach pressed on. When I showed up, I was slightly relieved to hear that I'd be doing the same route as I had done the previous day, only, with the addition of a third complex in the middle of Discovery and The Lakes. I was happy that I'd finally have some redundancy so that I could start the process of doing things without so much concentration.

I got to Discovery and was ready for it this time. I turned the engine off but I left the ignition keys in the ignition this time to save time in trying to dig them out of my pocket. I twisted the arrow key, opening the gates and raced to the other side of the LLV and twisted the ignition keys. In I went like a champ. Of course, leaving the keys in the ignition is a major no-no but, one must figure out ways to make one's life a bit easier and weigh the consequences.

Discovery took "forever" again but then I was on my way to The Meadowridge apartments. This complex was split into two entrances and, of course, I went into the wrong one to start delivering there. I figured out my mistake and circled back to the other entrance to a whole other grouping of two leveled apartments. I found the first cluster box for the first building and began to deliver. I made the rounds without issue and soon found the need for a “biological break”. I saw that there was a pool/club house and headed there. It was locked with no one in sight. I looked around… lots of bushes and trees…but also lots of windows and decided against it. I pushed through.

I finished with the first grouping of apartments and moved to the next. As I delivered, an elderly couple asked if their million dollar check came in with their mail today. I said, “Well, if it did, don’t forget your friendly mailman.” They chuckled and we parted company.

I moved onto the The Lakes and performed the delivery without issue and without trying to “Habla” and I returned back to the annex eight hours and fifteen minutes later at 6:15pm. Not too bad, I thought. As it turns out, Saturday may be the easiest of the days of a mail delivery week and so, I probably shouldn’t get too cocky.

Once I got back to the annex, I washed up and stood at the urinal for a good ten minutes. I’d gone all day without, …”relief”. I’m a once-an-hour type of guy, this was a huge feat to be able to accomplish this. So, there were some high points to the day and I felt I was accomplishing something. However, before leaving for the day, I was told that two parcels which were my responsibility weren’t delivered. Huh? I said that I had delivered everything I had. Enzo pulled up on the computer screen a picture of two parcels. “Do these look familiar?”

I resisted the urge to say what was on my mind, “Are you fucking kidding me? They all look the same! It’s just one after the next!” But, I just said, “I dunno, I delivered everything I had and I didn’t come back in anything, so…”

He took my scanner and scanned the barcode of the package on the screen and marked it as delivered. Apparently, a picture is taken of every parcel that comes into the office and is also scanned and, the incoming scan needs to be answered with a “delivered” scan to complete the cycle. Why were parcels outstanding as not scanned delivered? I had no idea. I processed everything without apparent incident but, if left me with the feeling that, a carrier could be hung out to dry pretty well on this. What if I did just take the parcels for myself? What if I hid them in the bushes somewhere and then, on my way home, retrieved them for my own use? I just feigned ignorance by saying that I had delivered everything I had and, it was satisfied by scanning the parcels delivered at the end of the day. So, I could already see a minefield of potential problems occurring if one doesn’t cover their ass. But, I had no devious intentions. I really felt that I had delivered all parcels properly. Where was the missing link? Did the scan of those parcels not go through to the accepting server? If so, that can be a problem. I’ll have to monitor.

The following day, Sunday, I was to be trained for what is considered Amazon Sunday. The United States Postal Service is under contract with Amazon to deliver its overflow that they don’t have the manpower to handle. This mostly happens on Sunday although, there are plenty of Amazon parcels delivered by the USPS during the week.

I show up and am introduced to a very pleasant young gentleman (I say young but, he was probably at least thirty) of Haitian origin and he showed me the bin of fifty parcels that we needed to deliver. I basically sat shotgun in a ProMaster while he did the driving around and did most of the deliveries. Samuel was another Postal Employee I found to be very proud that he was part of the organization and felt a certain privilege in having the job as he proudly showed off his car to me and said, "If it wasn't for the Postal Service, I couldn't afford this car! It's nice, right?" It was very nice. Frankly, mine was the oldest car in the parking lot, clocking in at 19 years old and kicking. Once again, my blind bias arose when I spied a couple of late model Mercedes in the parking lot. "Hmph", I thought. "I guess not everyone is making $17.29 an hour!".

As Samuel and I enter Century Village, he said, in his very thick accent, "You see dis place? You see dis apartment complex? Only A-Rabs and Muslims live here. No normal people!"

I don't fault Samuel. The "A-Rabs and Muslims" to which he refers are, in fact, Orthodox Jews dressed in full regalia with white knee-high hosiery and furry Abraham Lincoln-like hats. Probably not a large population of Orthodox Jews in Port-au-Prince and so, I give him a pass at his unfamiliarity.

Throughout the morning he began to hand off to me various packages as he stayed in the car. The delivery of these parcels was no different than what is done with them during the week so, I was comfortable with that aspect of the day. What was the cause of confusion on this day was that, Amazon Sunday, as far as I could tell at that point, doesn't follow a set route. Those familiar with the town's subsections will be able to sort out the best approach to which carriers will take what parcels when leaving the annex. Not all Amazon parcels spew out a section number when doing a load truck feature when loading the truck and so, you basically just had to know where you were going to get to the delivery address. We went all over town. We were in sections that I didn't even think were still Deerfield Beach. We went to the dreaded "East Side" and delivered packages along the beach as well as in sketchy neighborhoods along the railroad tracks and I-95.

The "East Side" was "dreaded" but, at this point, I wasn't exactly sure why? I thought, the East Side was the beach side and so, how many people get to be a mailman delivering mail to luxury beachfront homes and condos. How bad could it be? All I know is that, while in the Annex, any time I heard the East Side referred to, people reacted as if the Devil himself just walked into the room. They quietly skulk back to wherever they came from so as not to draw attention to themselves from the evil which was present.

The following day was "Presidents Day", a holiday. No mail delivery to be done, only parcels. Working Saturdays, Sundays and Holidays, all for $17.29 a hour! Today was basically going to be the same as yesterday, an "Amazon Sunday" only, I'd be out on my own.

While getting organized for the day, Bill, the Postmaster, came up to me and asked how it went the day before, on my first Amazon Sunday. I said that it was no problem and he responded with a smirk, "Well, we're not doing brain surgery here!"

True enough. However, I'll bet brain surgery probably isn't performed on Saturdays, Sundays and Holidays.

Nick also stopped me and told me that I was doing a good job and asked, as if checking on my reasons for being there, if this was something that I'd want to do. I responded in the affirmative and he went on to tell me that it was a good job but, it was much better twenty years earlier. "Everything changed after 9/11!", he said. "I used to deliver mail in South Philly and people would greet me at the door is hazmat suits because they thought I was bringing them a terrorist package!"

Since he broke what I perceived to be a standard protocol of not really opening up to mail carriers (personal communication-wise), especially new ones, I took the opportunity and expressed that I was feeling more and more comfortable with delivering the mail and packages but that the miscellaneous procedures, such as processing returning mail for whatever reason, and actually finding addresses and the like, seemed overwhelming at times. He reassured me that it was because I was new and that after a while, it'll be nothing.

I was told to begin the day at 8:00am and I assumed it to be a normal eight hour day. However, I was initially sent out with twenty three packages within Century Villages. Even in my "newness" I was estimating that I deliver at a rate of about ten parcels per hour. This is shaping up to be an easy day.

After I had delivered about twelve parcels, I was called back to the office to pick up more packages for delivery. I drove back to the office and there was a bin with an additional forty-nine parcels to be delivered on top of the original twenty three. Why wasn't I given the whole seventy two when I went out initially, instead of killing the twenty minutes for returning to the office and then getting back to the point at which I suspended? I had no idea.

It ended up being a full eight hour day (7.5 if you remove the lunch, which I never had) and the delivery of 69 packages in total.

I had to bring back three parcels as, they had been comingled with the other packages and were to be delivered to certain businesses, which were closed due to the holiday.

Feeling good about my “performance” for the day, upon returning to the annex, Arnel was sitting at the supervisor’s desk. Apparently he was a supervisor-in-training, if there’s such a thing, and asked to see my scanner. I turned it over and he saw that I had delivered sixty nine parcels and I sort of waited to hear, “Great job, take tomorrow off!” Instead, he said, “Samuel did 125!”. There goes the day off.

The next day, Tuesday, I was told to come in at 8:00am. The parcels from the two previous days as well as the daily grind so far were already catching up to me. Everything hurts. It’s not so much that the parcels are heavy to carry, although some are very awkward to manipulate, it’s the constant motion of getting in and out of a vehicle and climbing stairs over and over again. Twenty five years of sitting behind a desk had taken its toll. I had looked forward to doing the job as mail carrier while researching for this book with the fantasy that, much like playing golf, you’re just taking a nice walk, while also doing some other activity. But, so far, the mail delivery game is much more than what the general public thinks it is. It’s a rough gig. I keep hearing people say, “It’s not for everyone!”. No, it certainly is not. I’m not sure at this point how it can be for anyone!” But, I’m sure that my frustration is due to the fact that I’m new to the game and there’s a learning curve which needs to be leveled out some.

And what would be my existence in the near future, when I show up for the day, I’m given the parcels for a route to deliver and then, by say, 10:00am, return to the office to get the mail which is being cased while I deliver the parcels. The weak link here is casing. To the unfamiliar, casing could take hours if you let it. And, there's no time for that. Better to have an experienced carrier who is familiar with the route, case it, case it properly, get it done and then, someone else can take it out for delivery.

Also looking for ways to improve a given situation, I was already wondering why they just don't have special casing positions within the Postal Service as a "part-time" gig. Come in at 8am, do the casing for the route and out by 10:00am or 10:30am. Could be a good job for retirees or other special situations. The combination of casing and delivering for an entire route can, in fact, be easy on some (rare) days but, normally, you're chasing yourself. And as a new person, I'd just assume have someone else do the casing, especially due to the fact that each day, you're on a different route and just can't absorb the differences in the layout of the casing station. If you can get one down, that's good but, you probably won't see it again for weeks, and then it becomes brand new all over again. So, every day there's that feeling that it's your first day. There's never a time where you can go home and know what you're doing the next day so that you can compartmentalize your actions beforehand which would make the day more efficient. You always have the feeling of being back on your heels and not on your toes.

What I didn't realize at the time was that, on this Tuesday, the day after a holiday, was similar to any given Monday. A fact lost on the general public is that, yes, first class mail is not delivered on Sundays, however, the mail IS delivered to the Postal Station in the town in which you live. It comes in, it just doesn't go out. So, on Monday's that means that twice the amount of mail needs to be delivered in the same amount of time. And so, on a day after a holiday, the same procedure applies and THREE times the amount of mail needs to be delivered, in the same amount of time.

There's no accommodation for it. Just, get it done. It's acknowledged that it will take a bit longer to delivery this amount of mail than on a normal day and so, there's usually overtime on Mondays and days after a holiday.

I went out with my thirty two parcels within Century Village and it was becoming more and more familiar. I had Googled Century Village and was able to find a map of the layout of the place and that helped find the villages within the village. Although, consulting the little map on my iPhone while driving was probably a sketchy move, stopping to find my bearings just took too much time.

I delivered nine of the thirty two and was called back to the office. I'd love to just finish something without being interrupted, I thought. The back and forth was tiring and inefficient in my mind. I stopped what I was doing and went back to the office to get the mail.

When I got back to the office, I saw what lay before me. The amount was massive! At least to me! However, as luck would have it, I was able to deliver all of the DPS and Flats and the rest of the parcels and get back to the office at 4:15pm. Perfect, I thought, settle-up and get outta there at 4:30pm. A normal 8a-4:30pm day. Still, no stopping for lunch. But, upon returning to the office, as a reward for my outstanding job of delivering triple the amount of mail and parcels for an entire route and for doing it without going into overtime, I was sent back out to help someone else out.

I went back out and located the carrier who needed help, took a piece of their route and delivered it, another hour. It all went smoothly considering what day it was and how new I was. The only outstanding issue was, during the day, I had two parcels which I just couldn't locate the address for. I was gunin' and runin' and I just couldn't find these addresses. I called the office for guidance and Tina answered and said that she'd look the addresses up in the database and get back to me. She called minutes later and said that the addresses were good and to try again. I went back to where the address should have been and, after taking a breath, saw them, clear as day, right where they should be. Why my mind and eyes just "dipsy-doodled" the whole thing is a testament to how tiredness and fatigue can alter one's perception.

Chapter 9 – Can't Pump Gas

The following day, Wednesday, I finally had a day off after going eight straight days. I did nothing but lick my wounds. I couldn't bring myself to do anything around the house. Just too tired; physically and mentally. I needed a Netflix day. Didn't really matter what was blasting from the tv. Just to have something yack at me and not have to respond to it and to be able to stare off in a daze, either at the tv itself or out the window and watch a bird bathe itself. It was strictly a battery trickle charge of a day.

The next day I showed up at the annex at 10am, as scheduled. While at the desk awaiting my assignment for the day, Bill said to me, "I had to answer for you!"

"About what?" I responded. "You worked eight straight days and I got a call!" Leaving me to deduce that working eight straight days is considered to be unacceptable. I mean, it's not like I WANTED to work eight straight days! They said to come in so, I came in! Perhaps a $50 bonus in the paycheck for that effort might be in the cards for me? Ya know, as a "Thank you for your dedication!" No, it wasn't to be. Just the feeling that I had done something wrong by adhering to a schedule that was out of my control.

I was on Enzo's route again and, again, he had it cased and set up nicely for me and ready to go. But today I was in a new vehicle. Not new in the sense that it was a new vehicle, just a vehicle that I hadn't driven before. This was basically a passenger minivan that had the seats removed and a cage separating the driver from the cargo area. At least it had air conditioning.

The vehicle needed gas and this would be the second time that I used a gas card with my password. I had previously used it successfully so, I knew that the password was valid. Putting gas in a Postal vehicle is just another time taker. The carriers always hope that someone else will do it. No one wants to have to stop and perform this necessary function. And, it takes a little longer than putting gas into your personal vehicle because, you must first answer screen prompts at the pump. It asks for the mileage of the vehicle and then asks to enter your password. Sounds easy enough but, what I had tended to do was pull up to the pump, turn off the ignition, get out and start the process. But, based on the vehicle that a carrier had on that particular day, to get the mileage, you needed to reinsert the ignition key and either turn the vehicle on completely or just engage the electronics system. This is yet another time taking obstacle. Surely, it can be overcome by simply remembering to acknowledge the mileage display before actually turning off the vehicle and exiting but, it's something that needed a habit to be cultivated.

I insert the gas card and it asks for the mileage and I enter it. It then asked for my password. I take the little bit of paper out of my wallet and enter it. Einstein said, "Why memorize anything if it can be easily looked up!?" But then the screen on the pump prompted that the transaction was cancelled. I didn't know why and I started all over. Same thing. I figured that there was something wrong with the pump and so I moved the vehicle to another pump. Tick-Tock, tick-tock….

After the third try and getting another "transaction cancelled" prompt, I called into the office. The impression that I got was that I was doing it wrong. Having grown up in New Jersey where pumping your own gas was something you just didn't do, I'm pretty sure that I was comfortable enough with the procedure and had many successful and uneventful fill-ups since first learning to drive over forty years earlier. But, apparently, so far today, I'd been "wrong" for working eight straight days and for not being able to pump gas successfully!

I was told to come back to the office. Tick-Tock….

Enzo got into the car with me and back we went to the gas station where he can witness my actions to see what it was that I was doing wrong. I went through the repeated action with the same result. He said that if you try to do it too many times, it locks up the card. He brought out another gas card and we tried it with the same result.

"Hmm, must be something wrong with your password!"

"Ya think?"

I had to mention that it worked the other day with no problem. Enzo entered his password and we were finally cooking with "gas". I drove him back to the office (Tick-Tock…) and went back out on the road. While having gone back to the office to pick up Enzo and try to figure out what the problem was, Nick (supervisor) said, "Eh, it happens..." "…but if it happens again, you'll be written-up!"

While I had limited exposure to Enzo's route in which I was on that day, it was quickly becoming more familiar to the point where I started getting into a groove. But, during the day I was thrown a little curveball when I had pulled from the Flats, a cover to a magazine to be delivered. It was just the cover, no actual magazine attached to it. Pretty useless I supposed but I tried to reason what my responsibility was here. There's something here with an address label on it. I'm supposed to deliver stuff that has an address label on it. So, I delivered it.

I thought that, perhaps the cover got torn off accidentally and the guts to the magazine had somehow found its way to the recipient and, by delivering the cover, make the delivery complete. About an hour later, I'm delivering to a cluster box across the street from where I had delivered the magazine cover and a guy comes out from his apartment with the magazine cover in his hand and walks across the street to me and said, "Hey buddy! What am I supposed to do with THIS!?", as he waves the magazine cover before my face. I explained my well thought-out reasoning but, he wanted no part of it and gave it back to me to take it away.

Back at the office, Nick said, "Yea, that's why its stamped with a "Damaged" stamp on it!. I'll handle it". And he took it from me. I'm not sure if the guts of the magazine was actually ever found!

Earlier, while setting up for the day where I'd been told I was working too much, I don't know how to pump gas and, what kind of idiot delivers just the cover to a magazine, I thought of Tim. Slightly trailing me on the road to mail delivery nirvana due to scheduling, today was to be his first day out on the road on his own. I sent him a quick text asking how things were going but, I didn't receive an immediate response.

On my way out for the day I ran across Tina who said that I was doing a good job considering that I "only" had three days of on-the-job training and shared with me the fact that there had been one women who she trained for seven days straight, only to quit after the seventh day. I'm sure that it's similar frustration felt by a teacher who has a student who isn't receptive. So much work, so little feedback.

While driving home that day I finally receive a text from Tim stating that, "I'm an idiot! I clearly can't do this job!". That made me laugh and somehow I felt at ease that the failed gas pumper was in similar company with feelings of inferiority.

The following day I was on the same route again. This is good due to need of redundancy. No one does anything perfectly the first time out! And even if you do, do it again! And again! This, like most things, is something that needs to be done over and over again on various days of the week on the same route to even begin to get into a flow where the precious minutes are accounted for.

The night before, I was able to log into the payroll system to see the breakdown of my latest paycheck. I noticed in the breakdown that it listed one minute of overtime. Just one! The paranoia over time keeping is off the charts within the Postal Service. To me, either round up or round down!

Today was a Friday and, keeping true to form so as far as I could tell, the mail and parcel volume was lite. I got to the office as usual at 10am to begin tour and everything was set up perfectly for me once again. Not needing gas (thankfully) I was out on the street with a good head of steam going. I completed the entire route by 3pm! I called back into the office and asked Enzo if there was anyone out there who needed assistance. But, apparently, it was a lite day overall, not just with that route and there wasn't anyone who needed help. Enzo considered the time frame and suggested that I hurry back to process the outgoing and undeliverable mail and clock out before 4pm so that I wouldn't be charged a half hour for lunch, which triggers at 6 hours of working time. More like, six hours and one minute.

It was 3pm and so, there shouldn't be a problem with that. Getting back to the office and bringing all of the outgoing mail, parcels and undeliverable back in, I was still confused on where all of this stuff goes. First, concerning the undeliverable, why were they undeliverable? Based on the answer, the action for it can be completely different. Outgoing First Class was the easiest; it just gets dumped into a large metal crate which gets rolled out onto a tractor trailer at 6pm every night, destined for all points beyond. The parcels were quite another story. Parcel Post, First Class, Media Mail, Priority, Priority Express…all get treated differently and all get collated into different bins or carts or trays based on the volume. The First Class parcel will get further differentiated based on whether its local or beyond. Local for us was anything between West Palm Beach and Key West. The problem I had was determining the location of the addresses printed on the parcels. Is Belle Glade north of West Palm Beach? Is Pahokee? I had no idea! This end-of-day distribution is supposed to go very quickly. Isn't there someone here that does this sort of thing? No time to consult Google Maps. Enzo tells me that the end-of-day procedure is supposed to take, technically, five minutes from when you burst through the doors until you punch out for the day. It took me five minutes to figure out where deceased mail went!

Finally having distributed all of the outgoing and returned mail and was pleased to see that I was going to make the 4pm, no charge for lunch, cut-off time, I went to clock out or, End Tour. I did so and made a bee-line for the door to the parking lot.

"Hold on!", shouts Enzo. "You didn't Move to office!"

"Huh?"

"When you return to the office at the end of the day, you're supposed to swipe at the clock that you are "Moving" from the street, to the office". I'll take care of it now on the computer but, in the future…"

Ok, so, even successful days must end on somewhat of a sour note, I supposed. Again, this time accountability seems extremely obsessive to me. I'm not only supposed to do the job correctly and quickly but, I'm also supposed to manipulate the time clock to the point that, when I return to the office, I'm supposed to tell the time clock that I'm no longer on the street and that I'm back in the office, only to tell the time clock that I left for the day five minutes later.

I wondered how much time could be saved by not having to play with the time clock!

A new day, Saturday, let's see if I can get through a day without messing anything up. I began noticing a weight loss. Oddly, the date was 2/22/2020 and when I weighed-in that morning, the scale read 222.2 lbs!

"You'll have to play that number!" My mother would have said. Big numbers game player, my mother. Not listening to my mother's prophecy, as I seldom try to do, I didn't have the guts to check if the lottery actually came out with a 2-2-2-2-2 hit! There's a good chance it didn't come out. Probably.

Again, did Enzo's route and lo and behold, did the entire route (without casing) in six and a half hours and, to my amazement, nothing went wrong! I even Began Tour, Moved to Street, Moved to Office and Ended Tour properly! I think I got this!

Chapter 9

The next day was my first Amazon Sunday all alone. But, as I've said, the only difference between Amazon Sunday and another day is that, you don't necessarily have a route to adhere to on Amazon Sunday when only delivering parcels. You can be all over the place.

Knowing that delivering within Century Village is probably the easiest to do while being a new carrier, I was given a bin full of parcels to be delivered there. But, not only was I supposed to deliver that bin, I was to split another bin Samuel.

I delivered the initial bin within Century Village and returned to the office where Arnel had put together an entirely new bin to be delivered to Century Village and then, took away half of the half of the bin I was to split with Samuel. Again, there didn't seem to be a cohesive method to determining who should be delivering which parcels. I went back to the Village.

Not wanting to wait for an elevator, I humped up a couple flights of concrete stairs with a package on my shoulder, a man chastised me by shouting, "You shouldn't be working on Sunday!". Add Saturday to that, and perhaps the occasional Friday and/or Monday and I couldn't agree more sir!

There is a large Canadian contingent within Century Village and a couple were beside themselves as they watched me manhandle a pile of parcels up the stairs for delivery; a women with husband in tow said, "We don't even have mail delivered on Saturdays in Canada!"

I said, "Maybe I should move there!?"

The woman replied, "You should! AND, you get Medicare!"

That stung a little as my knees and ankles were screaming at me as I climbed the stairs with thirty pounds of "stuff" in my arms while not having any health insurance through the Postal Service.

Later in the day, things calmed down a little and, as I played with the arrow key to massage yet another stuck cluster box open, a man came down the stairs from his second floor apartment looking very tired and haggard in his bathrobe. I read his body language and he appeared to be a man simply looking to get out of the house to talk with someone.

He said, "Oh my God, I got my sister-in-law staying with us! She came down from New York for a four day stay and it's now day TEN! I'm exhausted!"

I laughed and said, "Pfft, that's child's play sir! I got my step-daughter staying with us and it's been almost three months!" I got him to give me a sympathetic look while he put his arm around me and said, "My condolences young man! I'll bet if we lived in Canada we wouldn't have ANY visitors!"

Again with the Canada!

The following day, Monday, I was given parts of four completely separate routes that I had never been on before. I asked how I was to know where to go for these routes and it was suggested that I use Google Maps.

On MY phone? First of all, what makes them think that I actually have a phone AND, that I have it on me. And the gall to suggest that I use my data for such a thing. How about equip each vehicle with a GPS mapping system. The scanners have this ability but I was told that it's more trouble than it's worth to try to follow. I never did figure out how to use it. But, it certainly does seem to be a benefit to equip each vehicle with a mapping system. Of course, that's money.

I just found it odd that they would fully expect you to not only have a phone but, to have it on you all the time and, to use it for business purposes without question or reimbursement of any kind. How about issue phones to each carrier for this purpose, as well as for communication? Again, I found it odd that they expect to be able to call you on your personal cell phone while out on the job with further instruction like, "Come back to the office, we have more!" or "Go meet up with someone and take parcels from them". Didn't sit well with me. If I leave my phone home that day, what happens? I can't find addresses to deliver to and I can't be communicated with. The responsibility doesn't seem to fall to the carrier for this, in my mind.

I thought that I was going to get done for the day by 4pm but was delayed in trying to find some locations and didn't get back until 5:15pm. As of this point, I don't see how they can derive these "working times" that they come up with. If they say it's a one hour piece, it takes me two hours. If they say that it's a one and a half hour piece, it takes me two and a half! I'm going as fast as I can. My paranoia started to set in that they are coming up with these unattainable completion times simply to degrade the new carrier or, to provide a metric on a spreadsheet that says, "Look, the carriers are underperforming based on expectations and therefore, no salary increase!" Regardless, I wasn't getting the job done in the time that it was expected to be done on paper.

Chapter 10 – Bronchitis Pt 1

Over the next few weeks I was scheduled for a variety of times and a variety of pieces of routes to the point where I could no longer make cohesive determinations on how to approach a given day. I always felt disoriented. The disorientation extended into home life as well. My wife, while sympathetic, still felt that I was just complaining (as women feel men tend to do) and that, "Isn't it just walking and putting things into a box?" The resentment started building with the feeling of, "No one understands what this job is!" And again, it's not the actual job of delivering a piece of mail but, it's also the amount of hours worked, the time-frames, the not knowing from day to day what you should be doing, or when you should be doing it and not knowing when your next day off is and even, not knowing when you're working. The "schedule" isn't really a schedule at all. It's a moving target, always changing. Well, that's not a schedule by definition. It's hard to prep clothes washing cycles and food prep and, to simply get your head right, when you just don't know what you're doing from day to day or when you're doing it.

I finally got a real sense of the job when I reported for work on a Tuesday and found mounds of things in front of casing stations. It seemed like there was a massive amount of bundles of a variety of paper product to be sorted and made sense of. It was, after all, Tuesday, advo day. While I had been exposed to this phenomena, I hadn't really gotten the full brunt of their effect on a full day's deliveries. I was about to. Because, compounding the dilemma of juggling these unwanted, newspaper-like advertisements, there were also 5 by 8 inch glossy advertisement cards to be delivered. Doesn't sound like a big deal but, I'm here to tell you that, the originators of such cards have had their mother's referenced on more than one occasion.

Wearing gloves so as to protect your hands from scrapes and scratches and perhaps any biological contamination, made it almost impossible to finger, separate, grab and then deliver these slippery-as-a-fish like cards. Doing the juggle of holding ten pounds of advos in the crook of your arm, a banded bundle of regular mail, somehow dragging along SPRs and large parcels and THEN, having to manipulate these special advertisement cards, was taxing, to say the least.

The cards that we had to delivery on this day was from a local dentist with the picture of the dentist and his assistant with big, white smiles from ear to ear. They were hawking a $69 New Patient Special that included cleaning, exam & X-rays AND, $400 off each porcelain veneer (with a minimum purchase of 2!). All very important and all very noble of the dentist to offer such wonderful deals but, I wondered if people actually took these cards into a dentist's office, slap it on the counter and say, "I'm here for my $69 special!". The cards caused a MASSIVE waste of time and caused the entire day's "performance" to be called into question.

Also on this particular day, we were saddled with Valpak envelopes. These are envelopes chock full of coupons; car wash, air duct cleaning, eye exam, oil change, another dentist, plumbing, home security, best care for your pet, BJs, COSTCO, etc. All in addition to the advos which, basically advertise for the same things.

After a few hours on the street, one begins to really question what it is that we're doing here. A lot of money is being spent to deliver coupons to households where, I truly question whether or not they're used. I'm sure that the originators of the coupons deem it a success if just one coupon is used but, the army of mail carriers that are blanketing the country in this regard, doesn't seem to justify it. In this world of ever decreasing desire to use paper products, these advertisements and coupons are picking up the slack on a monumental level. As I've stated, speaking from experience, I get these things in the mail and I throw them right into the recycle bin! Never enters the home. I'm sure I'm not the only one. As a society, I'm sure that we could come up with something else that is better than this.

After hours and hours of performing the juggle of delivery with all these moving parts and feeling the frustration building, I receive a text message from Tim. It's a picture of the glossy 5" x 8" dentist advertisement that I actually had in my hand at that very moment, with the caption, "I'm gonna murder this mother fucker!"

I limped back to the office that day looking like a wet rag. The local Post Office union representative, Juno, called to me from across the room. She calls me "Bossman".

"Bossman, how you doin'?"

"I'm still standing!"

"That's good. Most people would have quit by now!"

I had, and needed the day off the following day and returned with a little breath in my lungs the day after that. I was on edge the whole day. Everything bothered me. The scanner crapped-out causing a massive delay, got called back to the office to pick up more parcels that caused me to not finish for the day until 6pm where I might have been done by 4pm. I started building a resentment toward customers as they made chit-chat. I simply don't have the time to get into little conversations with each and every person who is lonely and just wants to talk about anything that comes to mind. I begin to fend off their conversational advances in a pleasant enough way but, as time went by, a slight rudeness began to surface in my demeanor. This is foreign to me as I've always felt that I could muster at least a pleasant enough sidestep, no matter how I was feeling personally in most any situation. It's not their fault I'm feeling bitchy! I'm feeling very run down and on edge.

While readying to end tour for the day, Nick tells me (seeing the drawn look in my face and my slump) that, as of right now, he's going to schedule me for two days off in a row the following week! Wow, that's big! It never happens but, he did actually say the words, which is rare, from what I understand.

I was dragging so much, as the old joke goes, "As I walked, I felt something hitting my heels!. I looked down, and it was my ass!"

The next day I received a text from Tim telling me that this had been his hardest day to date. He was pushing all the way but then received a call from the office telling him that he's too slow and that he needed to pick up the pace. He said that he felt that he sucked at it and really didn't think he could do it anymore.

Tim is younger than I (even though he's no spring chicken) and is physically fit and intelligent but, this job tends to break down even the best of us. I don't know much about Tim's past but, my particular curriculum vitae can be perceived as having some pretty challenging and impressive aspects to it; surely, I can overcome any obstacles that the Postal Service throws at me. Granted, this job is NOT what I envisioned it to be OR, what it was advertised to be. It's understandable that in the courtship between employer and employee there isn't full disclosure of the minutia on either part, and, while not lying, it isn't telling the full truth either, but to advertise this job for what it is; no one in their right mind would apply.

I started not feeling well. Coughing, aching, etc. Can't call out sick. That's just not an option. So, I push on. At my age, it was a silly thing to do. At my age, every little thing has the potential to explode into something that it shouldn't have been. I cold medicined-up at night, and then coffeed-up in the morning, and I pushed on.

The next few days were a daze of notable interactions. A very pregnant black woman who came out of her apartment in a skin-tight leotard asked if she'd gotten anything after I had closed and locked the multi-box door. I asked her for identification (you're always supposed to obtain identification for anyone asking for their mail) and I opened her box to show that nothing was in there. Always the wit, I asked her if she was expecting something other than,…ya know.

She replied, "I'm just waitin' fo ma' tax refund!!!"

Dragging myself back to the office at the end of another day and looking angry and pissed off at the world, a regular carrier greeted me and said, "Don't let it get to you. You've only got twenty years to go!!"

I found myself delivering to a shooting range. A guy outside smoking a cigar said, "Gonna get your shooting in?" Not in the mood, I replied, "No, I'll just wait until I get back to the office and light the place up!"

Yet another Amazon Sunday arrived and I was happy to not have that many parcels to deliver. I could use an afternoon of couch nonactivity! I went out and finished by 12 noon. Perfect. Heading home? Nope! Was sent back out with just as much as I started the day with. There's no end to it. There's no sense of completion.

I wasn't getting any better and figured that I should see a doctor. Just by dumb luck I was off from work and I was able to get to a doctor at a moment's notice. After I did, the results were in, bronchitis. Got some cough medicine and pushed on. I hear from Tim that they gave him shit because he needed to take his daughter to an orthodontist appointment. Apparently there's just no wiggle room for this job.

While delivering on one particular route, an extremely beat-up and used-up individual came to chit-chat with me. He introduced himself as Justin Bieber "The Original". He was a 30 veteran of the Postal Service and, could barely walk. His name was, in fact, Justin Bieber, and was giddy at the connection to the pop star. Justin was telling me what a great job the Postal Service was for him. His pension gets a 3% raise each year and it afforded him the ability to buy three condos within the Village. He lives in one and rents the other two out.

As I am exposed to more and more of the villages within the Village, I realize that some of the multi-mail boxes within the alcove of the garden apartments have newer, larger boxes where some are very dated and small. The smaller ones are wreaking havoc with my hands and there is just no more room to cram anymore mail into those because the residences refuse to empty their boxes daily. The advos take up an enormous amount of room, causing all of the mail to have be folded and manipulated somewhat in order to get all of the mail into the box. And, the goal is, in fact, to get all the mail into the box. No one wants to come back with anything, especially when they know that, if they come back with a bunch of mail which can't be delivered because the box is full, they will eventually have to deliver all of that mail that was undelivered in the past, at some point in the future. And that's just too many trips and wasted movement. And so, the cramming into, continues! At times, you must remove all the mail from the box from previous days and nicely make smooth with the addition of today's mail and manipulate the whole bundle into the small box without causing bleeding to the hands.

On yet another Tuesday, advo day, I needed to get bailed out at the end of the day due to the fact that I had forgotten that advos could be divided into two days of delivery and I tried to do the whole thing in one day and was unable. You need to determine where the half-way point is on a route and then divide the advo bundles at that point and leave the rest for the following day. Surely, the person doing that route the following day is none too fond of that approach but, it allows for mail to be delivered on time if done properly. This is yet another incident where the CCA is lost as, they don't do the same route every day and would have a hard time determining where the halfway point is on any given route.

It was March 3rd and, during delivery, an elderly woman told me that she was a snowbird and was leaving for New York soon and that she had notified the Post Office to forward her mail. I acknowledged what she was saying and kidded, "You know, it's still cold up in New York!"

She said, "Eh, it gets boring around here after a while. I have a life in New York!".

Except for a short time during on-the-job training and some spotty times during slow days, I had been coming into the office and picking up mail which had been cased and sorted and nicely packaged in trays and placed in bins already. That, easy bit, had come to an end. Today, I was to case and deliver everything for a full route completely on my own. While casing, Bill sidled up and apologized that he hadn't been around much to talk but, said that I was doing well and that it should slow down in three or four weeks due to the departure of the snowbirds.

I appreciated the talk as, you tend to feel that you are simply thrown to the dogs without any support, even though people tell you to ask them questions and such. Actually, it got frustrating and they all know when there's blood in the water and, with good intentions (I assumed) offered advice. But, ten people were telling me what to do and ten other people were telling me not to listen to the first ten and Nick telling me not to listen to ANY of them, makes you want to put your hands over your ears, eyes and mouth in good monkey-like fashion.

Juno's continued advice was to find my own personal way of doing things and yet, passive aggressively, telling me not to fold the advos to get them into the small boxes, as I had been doing. There's a rat among us apparently!

Yet another Amazon Sunday came and I was told to be there at 8am. Of course, I was there at 7:55am. No one showed up. Samuel finally showed and he was just as perplexed as I that the place was locked up. I immediately had fantasies of just getting back into the car and going home and "having a day!". But, Samuel made some calls and it was decided that Enzo would come in and open the place. It really surprised me that for an organization that seemed to be obsessive about time, they seem to waste a lot of it.

Enzo arrived and opened the office and we all got sorted out. It was Tim's first Amazon Sunday and he was to ride shotgun as trainee as I had done a few weeks earlier. Perhaps with more manpower, we wouldn't need to be here every Sunday or, not as long on Sundays.

And what will become more evident in my future concerning scheduling, or, lack thereof, I was scheduled to start the following day at 10am but, texted at 7:50am to try to get there at 8am. I got there as soon as I could but hate that chasing yourself feeling. I cased and delivered an entire route but, was another 10 hour day.

The day after that, feeling even more run down by the respiratory infection, I found myself called into work that morning when I was supposed to have a day off. My dedication will look good on a headstone!

I still managed to case and deliver an entire route including businesses and got out by 5:45pm. During delivery that day, another retired Postal worker caught my ear and was exclaiming the virtues of a Postal career as he claimed his pension has been very good to him. We got on the subject of this new "bug" which has been creeping its way into the news lately. The Coronavirus was becoming an issue where it has been spreading almost out-of-control since it crept into the United States in January.

At that point, I expressed concern that my youngest son's school might have to shut down in-person classes due to this virus. He enquired about the location of the school and after I told him, he responded that it was a very good school and that, "Just don't let him be a postal worker!"

So, what I'm gathering from present and retired Postal workers is that, it's a great job, just don't anyone else do it because, you could probably do better! I didn't really understand the self-deprecation; the Groucho Marx adage that, "I wouldn't want to belong to a club that would have ME as a member!".

And speaking of the Coronavirus, when receiving a registered letter or a parcel where a signature is required, the carrier is supposed to turn over the scanner with the bungie chorded stylus attached to the recipient where they would need to sign the glass for the object.

Today, for the first time, a woman refused to handle the scanner for fear of germs. I can't say that I blame her.

Chapter 11 – COVID-19

On January 9, 2020, the World Health Organization (WHO) announced the existence of a virus with pneumonia-like symptoms, originating in Wuhan, China from a new coronavirus. There were 59 identified cases in China at the time and travel precautions were beginning to be taken into consideration.

On January 21, 2020, the U.S.'s Center for Disease Control (CDC) revealed that the first incident of COVID-19 in the United States had been identified in the state of Washington after the infected returned to the United States from Wuhan on January 15.

On January 31, 2020, the WHO issued a Global Health Emergency after the death of 200 infected and an exponential jump in cases to 10,000. Human-to-human transmission is quickly spreading and can now be found in the United States, Germany, Japan, Vietnam and Taiwan.

February 2, 2020, global air travel is restricted.

February 3, 2020, The United States declares a public health emergency.

February 25, 2020, the CDC claims that COVID-19 is heading toward pandemic status. Three criteria are needed for a pandemic to be classified where two of the three have already been met: illness resulting in death and sustained person-to-person spread. The third criteria, worldwide spread, has not been met at this time.

March 6, 2020, Twenty-one cruise ship passengers off the California coast test positive for COVID-19.

March 11, 2020, meeting the final criteria of worldwide spread, the WHO declares COVID-19 a Pandemic.

March 13, 2020, U.S. President Donald Trump declares COVID-19 to be a National Emergency and issued a travel ban on non-Americas who visited 26 European countries within 14 days of coming to the United States.

March 19, 2020, California issues a statewide Stay-At-Home order.

School grades from Kindergarten through college begin to move to a virtual learning environment. Restaurants, bars and entertainment venues close and there's a feeling of despair in the country. People are furloughed from their jobs and struggle with the loss of income. Wearing a mask when in public is highly encouraged and will eventually be mandated. Keeping a distance of at least six feet is thought to reduce the likelihood of becoming infected.

A Post Office sorting room is no place to try to keep one's distance. It's simply impossible. The casing stations themselves are separated by metal shelving a foot wide. Two mail carriers doing their sorting will stand no more than a mere five feet apart from each other for hours. Add twenty more carriers doing the same thing to a room and, there's bound to be a close contact problem.

During morning "meetings", where everyone is supposed to stop what they are doing and give attention to whomever needs to say something, usually the supervisor or Postmaster, it was suggested that the carriers take extra precautions in their daily activities to prevent the spread of this virus. Wash hands frequently, don't touch your face with your hands, disinfect the vehicles before and after using. Don't let the customer sign your scanner. You sign for them as an agent. They informed us that they have anti-bacterial sprays ordered and "on-the-way". Also, if anyone needs a mask, they should ask for one.

I saw an immediate problem with this instruction. Wash hands frequently? Where? I can't even find a restroom to use for biological needs. And, who's got the time for it. Washing hands properly is supposed to take two minutes. You do that five times a day and you just killed ten minutes, now you're in overtime and now we have to have a talk. Disinfect vehicles? How? And how much more time with THAT take?

I'm obviously overexaggerating here but, the point is, the time consideration for every little movement during the daily activities for a mail carrier can be compromised without much effort, and adding anything to the rituals can have devastating effects on overall delivery performance.

I tried wearing surgical gloves during delivery but, it was so hot that, sweat would literally pour out of the opening and onto the mail, soaking it. I reverted back to my Harbor Freight utility rubber coated gloves. At every chance, I washed my hand with the gloves on. Might as well wash the gloves too. At first, this extra effort in virus protecting cleanliness wasn't too much of a hardship as, I was mostly assigned to Century Village where, at every village, there was a pool with a pool house which contained a restroom. I took full advantage of the convenient location of these restrooms while on those routes. The problem arose when I was not within Century Village. There's just nowhere to go. Certainly, one could go the fast food route as Jeremy had shown during Shadow day but, I still couldn't see deviating from the route in which I was on to drive to a location to use the restroom and wash hands. In the area I was, the lights would be mind-numbingly long and the traffic choked to such a stop that I couldn't see how it could be accomplished without adding to the time stress of an already stressful time! At times I'd just poured some water out of my jug and onto my hands and rubbed them back and forth and hoped for the best. This was before I realized that I was on my own for self-providing antibacterial lotion but then, that couldn't be obtained either, due to the run on the stores.

After the meeting that morning, my neighboring casing carrier, Kate, said, "I won't let people touch my scanner. They're disgusting!" She meant the people.

Interesting; to the general public, the mail carrier is carrying potentially infected letters and parcels and, they themselves are travelling from place to place and are seen as an obvious source of infection and the ones to be avoided and to us, the letter carriers, the customers are disgusting!

I can certainly be sympathetic to both viewpoints. There's no safe harbor with this thing at this point in time.

Before heading out onto the street that day, I'd been called into the office to talk to Bill. In reference to the previous Amazon Sunday, you know, the one where I showed up at 8am and no one was there? The one where I'd finished delivering the packages I was sent out to do, only to be called back in to get more and be sent out again? Well, Bill wanted to know why ten parcels weren't delivered.

I was caught a little by surprise, I have to admit. I figured that he wanted me in the office so he could give me that $50 gift card to Chili's or something due to the extra efforts that I had been doing. I had no idea why ten packages weren't delivered. Why would I?

"Ten parcels came into the office that Saturday and weren't delivered until Monday!"

Again, am I the parcel coordinator? I'm given "X" amount of parcels to deliver, I deliver them. That's about the extent of my responsibilities, as I see it. I didn't care for the assertion.

I could have easily thrown it back with a "How come I was here at 8am on a Sunday and no one was here to facilitate the efficient use of my time?" Of course, all I said was, "I delivered what I had." And that was that. He then called Samuel into the office for further inquisition.

After no good information had been gathered, Bill said, "It's because there's no supervisor around to make sure this doesn't happen. I know what happened, a parcel bag fell off the truck and got lost!"

Frankly, I didn't know who the supervisor was, really. There are people who sit at the supervisor's desk and there seems to be some sort of rotating schedule as, one person can't be there all the time but, much like the rest of the scheduling around here, there doesn't seem to be a rock solid way of doing things.

So much for the $50 gift card.

Out on the street, I cased and delivered all of Enzo's route, who was on vacation. Was HE supposed to be the acting supervisor that Sunday where packages went missing? Who knows? Someone goes on vacation and all hell breaks loose? Doesn't seem very stream-lined to me.

Chapter 11

Enzo left for vacation on a cruise. The cruise lines had been hit hard by the pandemic, calling into question; why the hell would anyone voluntarily be cooped-up with thousands of people on a tin can with nowhere to go?

"I booked this last year! I'm going!"

"Ok but, keep your distance when you get back!" lol

On the next Amazon Sunday, I did deliveries mostly within Century Village but then was told to go to the East Side and find Samuel where, he was to dump off some of his parcels so that I could help him out. I hadn't been on the east side very much and, pretty much my main exposure to the area was as a "civilian" driving around the area up and down Federal Highway. Federal Highway is a traffic light laden roadway with two lanes going in either direction with various turn lanes thrown in indiscriminately as needed. The road is lined with the typical American menu of strip malls containing a variety of restaurants catering to every need; UPS stores, gas stations, Wal-marts, Targets and 7/11's, with only the occasional entrance to a marina, differentiating the area from anywhere else in the country.

I had to deliver a small parcel to an address which proved to be very difficult to locate. Driving the old bucket o' bolts in the right lane of Southbound Federal Highway, going slowly while looking for the address, I ignored the horn blows from behind me at the obvious obstruction I was causing. "Sorry people, you'll have to hurry up and get to that next 5 minute red light after I depart from the roadway". I turned off into a parking lot where I thought might have been close to the final destination. I found a safe area and pulled out the phone and did a search to find that I was in the general area. Just need to find the specific address. I still found it a little bizarre that I would be doing a map search on my phone to find an address to deliver a package processed through the United States Postal Service. Shouldn't they have some sort of beaconing device that you can program an address into and it tells you if you're getting warmer or colder? I'll bet FedEx has something like that!

I followed each storefront in the horse-shoe shaped office development which looked extremely weathered in its presentation. It was set back off the road a few hundred feet and had a feel of being forgotten. Vaguely decorated offices with no real signage made the area even more foreboding. The address that I had was 810B 8th Ave. I parked and dismounted with the parcel and thought I'd walk around as it had to be there somewhere. I walked around a VFW hall toward the back of some building and, tucked away in the back of another building was a grouping of "offices". Well, they had numbers and letters on the doors so, I assume that they were some sort of office but, it didn't look much like they were doing any real foot traffic business. Who could find them? I finally found the door labelled 810B and it was answered by a youngish black woman and I was hit in the face with the wafting smell of some sort of chemical. As I asked if this was the address on the package, I looked past the woman and could see another black woman reclined in a chair with her head back. The woman who answered the door acknowledged that I was in the right place and accepted the package I handed to her.

Apparently, this hole-in-the-wall was some sort of one-chair private hair salon. It made me consider that, there are actually people out there who create their own one-person businesses and do the best they can, even if it means setting up shop in the back of a building in a run-down tiny office where even the mail carrier has a hard time locating it. Is this a great country, or what?

The following Monday found the Deerfield Beach carriers with mountains of mail and parcels to be delivered. I cased and delivered four thousand DPS, plus Flats, plus SPRs, plus parcels. I did the best I could but had to call in at 3pm to say that I would be getting in late, probably 6pm or 6:30pm. Tina said that she knew that it was going to be a late day and to just keep going. I received a call from Tina's replacement as supervisor fill-in, Arnel, and he asked where I was.

I informed him that it was 5:50pm and I hadn't even gotten to The Lakes yet. He sent out someone to help me and I gave them half of The Lakes. I got back to the office at 7:30pm. 8am-7:30pm. "It's impossible", I thought.

The following day, the dreaded Tuesday, I found myself delivering a parcel that needed a signature. Due to the pandemic, people were instructed to keep distance from one another and, we had been directed to sign for parcels which required a signature. I could see that many head-strong carriers may have a problem with that. "You want ME to sign MY name saying that YOU received a package?!". "I don't think so....".

But, anything to get through this. And by "through this" I mean, through with this journalistic, almost social experiment that I had embarked on. The thought of bailing on this writing project surfaced many times during the experience and it depressed me a great deal to think that it was something that I wasn't going to see through.

But, I persevered and continued with the project under vehement objections from my body, my mind and, my wife. "Just quit already, you're clearly miserable? And, you're never home!"

The local streets were largely deserted due to the virus and it was very quiet and weird. As I approached the door to an address to which I was supposed to deliver the parcel, I heard very large dogs running amuck on the other side of the door. I figured that it wasn't even worth knocking and setting the dogs off even more so, I started to process the delivery of the package with the scanner when I heard a scared, female voice whisper from behind the door, "There's someone at the door!".

To put them at ease I decided to go ahead and knock and announce who I was. A male's voice then questioned, as he held back the dogs, "Can I help you?"

"Postal Service sir, I have a package here for you that needs a signature and…"

"Uhhh, we aren't allowing any contact with people right now due to the virus!"

"Understood sir, I'll just sign for you that you received the package and I'll leave it here by the side of the door."

"Ok, that'll be fine."

I scan and signed and placed the parcel on the concrete and to the side of the door so that the door can be opened. As I walk back to the vehicle, I hear the screen door open and I look back and, with the door only opened slightly, I see a hand come out with a finger on the trigger of a can of Lysol disinfectant spray. He then proceeded to spray the shit out of the parcel with the Lysol. And then, the hand retreated back through the crack in the door, the door slammed and the parcel stayed right where it was, perhaps, until all the kooties that I left on the box had died off.

The new world order.

The next day turned out to be pretty lite. I finished up and called in to see if anyone needed any help and no one did and so, I ended tour at 4:30pm, nice. On my way home I texted Tim and told him that I was done for the day and that I called in and asked if anyone needed help and they told me that no, no one had needed any further help. Tim said, "Fuck that, I need help! Come back out here and help me!!!" And I would have too, but, I had a super cold beer waiting for me at home that needed my attention.

The following day may have been a turning point for me. I may have just been over tired or still sucking wind trying to get over the bronchitis but, it all caught up with me on a lot of levels. Originally, I was supposed to report to work at 8am so, I prepped for that. Then, the starting time was changed to 10am. Then it was changed to 1pm. I finally received a text at 12:20pm saying to come in now as "the truck" just arrived. Whatever that means…

Why start the day at 1pm? Doesn't make sense. In my mind, whatever needs to be done after 1pm can be put off until the next day.

I was told that I should first deliver the express mail packages, as they are time sensitive and then to move on to do a piece of one route and then, after that, move to do a piece of another route. I didn't understand why I couldn't start at 8am and just get this stuff done early.

Delivering the express mail took way longer than expected as, they are not in alignment with any route and there is a lot of criss-crossing to different sections of the town.

I moved on to deliver the first "piece" of a route that I have never been on before and found it very difficult, as the locations of the addresses didn't flow in a cohesive way and it caused me massive delays. I received a call from Tina just as I had finished that first piece and was about to move to the second piece and she was surprised that I hadn't completed the second piece yet! This second piece was also on a route that I had never been exposed to. Trust me, it matters. She sent out a person to help me finish and to pick up my outgoing mail so that it can get back to the office and be loaded onto the outgoing tractor trailer by 6pm. I had trouble finding the entire apartment complex for the second piece and it took way longer than it should have and I was the last carrier to get back to the office. Major frustration took hold. That was six hours of work; why start me at 1pm? Because they THINK it should have taken only four hours! So, there's the problem. They think it should take a certain amount of time and plan for that. It takes longer than that and all hell breaks loose. My day is shot and, they had to pay someone else overtime for helping the new guy out on routes he had never been on before. Just plain old piss poor planning. (PPP).

At this point, I didn't think that I could continue with this. The disorganization, the unrealistic expectations, the insulting scheduling (EVERY Saturday and Sunday!?), maybe you get a day off a week and even then, you'll never know when it is! It'll just come out of the blue.

That night I spoke with Tim and he told me that he requested an upcoming Sunday to be off to spend time with his fourteen year old daughter on her birthday, and he was given a whole bunch of shit about it.

"You were hired to work Sundays. You should have been up front if you're not able to do that!"

Tim didn't call them out on it that this was NEVER a condition of employment and Bill had said that working on a Sunday would occur only about once a month. Combine those things with the original job description as "part time", this wasn't going well.

Apparently, requested a day off (one for which you won't get paid), is now a selfish problem and something that is frowned upon even after being taken advantage of with an unrealistic schedule.

Is this what is thought of when one considers becoming a mailman? I mean, it's just putting paper products into metal boxes, isn't it?

With taking the current climate into consideration, I didn't think that I would last much longer. Project aside, I've reached a point in my life where time, respect and a Zen-like existence is more valuable to me than money. Some things are just not worth the endeavor.

At this point, I'd been associated with the USPS for almost three months and I wasn't sure what my immediate actions would be. I told Tim that, "I want to quit this job every single day!" He laughed at that but, I saw that he understood exactly what I was talking about

Chapter 12 – Bronchitis Pt 2

My son's college in Tampa decided that they'd had enough and moved to a virtual environment in mid-march. He was currently in New York on spring break and had to fly down to Tampa and move out of the dorm in a hurry. I needed to meet him there but, how the hell was I going to get a day off at this point? I was still within my 90 working day probationary period and, I didn't want to rock the boat. Although, it may be sweet poetic justice that I be fired for tending to a family member. I had the same feeling concerning a trip I had planned for my wife and I to Paris in July. I booked the thing before any thought of working for, and writing about the Postal Service ever came up. I didn't need to get paid for the time off, I just needed the time. If I'm not being paid, what do they care? The trip had cost so much that, there was no way that I was going to take a hit on it. I was fully prepared to leave the job simply to go on the trip. It would be completely unreasonable on their part to hold it against me. Same with needing one day off to move my son Michael, out of school.

I looked at the schedule and tried to coordinate Mike's arrival in Tampa with my work schedule and went to Tina and asked, not for the day off but, to switch a working day with one that was scheduled for me to be off or (N/S) Not Scheduled. The Postal Service LOVES their acronyms; much in the same way the military does, FUBAR being one of my personal favorites, and sort of fits in here. The insult here is that, using a N/S as a bargaining chip really doesn't work too well because, while it says N/S on the schedule, it's not like it's OWED to you. If can be taken away, and does all the time, at any given moment, up to, and including the very morning of the day off. So, a person in that position doesn't really have a lot to work with. I figured that I'd start with a reasonable solution to a given problem and amp it up if it starts to go off the rails. If I was to be given a hard time and there was no other way to coordinate with Mike to move him out, I'd have no choice but to call out "sick" and deal with the consequences thereafter.

Luckily, Tina was very accommodating to my request and I was granted the switch. Still, the non-stop work schedule left me exhausted and drained and now, after getting home late on a Thursday night, I'd have to get up on the Friday morning, drive to Tampa (four-plus hours), pack up my son's dorm of all things dorm-like and, drive back across the state (another four-plus hours). Nine hours total driving and moving out a dorm, sandwiched in between brutally long and hot and stressful work days. Not my idea of fun.

When I arrived at the school in Tampa, they had confirmed that two cases of COVID-19 had been reported within the student body. The school was a maelstrom of activity and had the appearance of mild panic with concerned looks on everyone's face to try to get in, pack up, and get out! No one knew how long the campus was going to be shut down. Probably at least until the following fall semester so, it was clean-up and move out like you never existed type of moving out.

After packing up, I wanted to take him and his roommates out for lunch, as I would normally do but, there was nothing open. The whole campus and surrounding area was shut down completely. A four and a half hour car ride, a hour and a half dorm clean-up and pack-up, I gave him a hug and slap on the back and left for the four and a half car ride back across the state. Got back home at around 6pm and started unloading the car. I tried to unwind but, I think that ship had sailed for the foreseeable future. I was wound up like a clock and couldn't sleep well at all, no matter how tired I was. Never a good sleeper, the problem doesn't really come into play unless I'm called into "service" the following day. "Service", meaning, that I have to be "on my game", whether it's to do a presentation at work (past life) or climb in and out of a truck all day and try to make sense of where addresses are.

While Mike was in the air from Tampa to Newark Liberty airport on his way back to New York, the state of New Jersey went on full lock-down! Was he going to be able to leave the airport? I didn't know, I just had to keep delivering.

He actually did make it out of Newark Airport (an amazing feet, as anyone who's ever been there would attest to) and I managed to survive the gosling of emotions and physically during the recent day's activity and continued the grind. However, a few days after arriving back from Tampa, I started to feel horrible again, after semi-recovering from Bronchitis weeks earlier. The coughing was traumatic, almost passing out from it at times, as it was the nonstop, on-the-knees begging for just a little air, type of cough. The feeling of malaise and shortness of breath left me almost completely incapacitated. I needed to see a doctor but, how was I going to make a doctor's appointment in this situation? I just lucked out the last time with getting an appointment to see a doctor just when I wasn't working. I didn't think my luck could continue.

I never know when I'm working from one day to the next AND, I have NO WAY of knowing when I'd be finished for the day. It's not like I can make an appointment for 3:30pm and then, around 2:30pm, in the middle of delivery say, "Ok, that's enough, I gotta go!". It doesn't work that way. It did, sort of, make me yearn for that corporate life I had left a few years earlier where all you had to do was inform your boss that you had a doctor's appointment, and that you'd be back in a little while. Not that you'd have to do something like that considering the given situation. It's more a feeling of, "If you're sick, PLEASE stay home! We don't ALL want to get what you got!" Not with the Postal Service; if you're bleeding, rub some dirt on it and move your ass!

I kid, of course and, I am no stranger to the, "Quit 'yer bitchin' and keep moving!" work ethic but, when taken into context, sometimes one questions their existence and value. While gasping for air and sweat is dripping off of everything a person has that sweat can drip off of, and everything is swimming before your eyes and you're trying to determine if you're looking at a rubbed off 8 that looks like a 3 or, an upside down 9 or is it a 6 and, it's yet another Bed, Bath and Beyond advertisement that all this hubbub is about, it sort of makes you wonder what the hell you're doing.

Luckily, I was able to make an appointment with my doctor at the late hour of 6pm and I just hoped for the best that I would be able to run home to shower before keeping the appointment as, after a day of mail delivery, a person is in no position to get the old "feel-around". I was, in fact, able to end the day in time to freshen up and feel comfortable enough to make the appointment.

I decided to be forthcoming and informed the office that I had been diagnosed with Bronchitis for the 2nd time within a month and was sort of hoping that they'd tell me to go home and take a few days off to recover but, nah, wasn't going to happen. The doctor made no mention of COVID-19 as tests hadn't been available as of yet and, I didn't have the dreaded fever so… I asked for a mask at the office and Tina disappeared for a minute and came back with one. As she handed it to me she said, "Here, I stole this from my mother. We don't have any here!"

The office was still waiting for a shipment of masks and hand sanitizer weeks after the order was placed! I wonder who was delivering it? Heh!

I felt that I was getting sick because I'd been run down to the core with no rest to recover. The schedule that they had me on was brutal. It wasn't the overall hours that I was working that was so unreasonable as, I was only working 2 or 3 hours over forty at that point during a week; it was the combination of not knowing from day to day what was going on and the off-balance existence of having to do a piece of that route and then, do a piece of another route, then do express mail, etc. There's no cohesive workflow and it just never stops! I'd been doing it for three months with a couple of days off at this point and I'd say that I had ONE semi-easy day. One! The rest of the time was a gut wrenching exercise in an attempt at sustainability.

One of the benefits of this COVID-19 pandemic was that when people see a mailman wearing a mask and gloves, they tend to keep their distance. So, no idle banter to further delay me in my already delayed methods. No Justin Beiber yucking it up about being the original and no further advise on how great a job the Postal Service was but, just don't let your kids do it! So, I take lemons and make lemonade when I can. I'd decided that, should the pandemic suddenly end the following day, I'll continue donning a mask and gloves AND, perhaps I'll amp up the situation and put on a hazmat suit with an oxygen tank on my back. That should clear the field. I'd already taken to deep coughing or loud, fake sneezing when people approach. "Yea, you might want to drop that stuff you're about to give me into the outgoing..." Maybe I'll take it with me, maybe I won't!

I actually had a run of a couple of days in a row with no issues and relatively stress-free. The pandemic has reduced mail volume a great deal. The existence of the pandemic has helped me out greatly in this regard as, I'm not sure how fully up to speed I could have become with record volumes of mail during my acclimation period. I still don't know what I'm doing from one day to the next but, if put on a route that I'd done a few times previously, it seems to makes a big difference. The advos, however, are still a major pain in the ass and, occasionally, within the advos is an envelope of some sort, that prevents the overall advos from being rolled into a shape which enables it to be manipulated into a mail box of small stature. They're just an amazing drain on all aspects of the job.

And speaking of an amazing drain on the job, we are in a Presidential election year, among other offices, which are up for bid. If the odd dentist card or the advo was an exercise in futility, the political advertisement takes the cake. These things can vary in size from anywhere between 3" x 5" to 8.5" x 11" and all made of some glossy, heavily weighted stock that not only is difficult to manhandle from the bounded bundles but, adds to the almost impossible task of fitting into smaller cluster boxes (also known as "Knuckle Crushers).

And they keep coming and coming. Every day its someone different running for some type of office or another. And then you have the Presidential Candidates. One has to wonder if someone can be swayed to vote one way or another by a flyer shoved into a mail box, and if so, whether that person is stable enough to cast a vote in the first place. Just a pet peeve I suppose but, I seriously doubt that anyone would be sitting on a fence as to whom to vote for and then one day, they get their mail and in it is a slick, 8.5" x 11" heavily stocked flyer stated how wonderful that candidate is and bingo, the light bulb goes off and they are now confident of who it is they should vote.

The only solace came when tens of thousands of people were reported to be dying from complications from COVID-19, and then those who make such decisions decided that it would be in poor taste to send out "Vote for Me" flyers during the most sensitive of times. There was a lull but, like a herpe, they came back again.

The mask that Tina had given me had long lived out its usefulness and, not being able to obtain any, I'd taken to wearing a bandanna, like an outlaw. Just a little extra visual forbiddance. The office still did not have masks to give to its carriers. Safety doesn't seem to be of the greatest importance that it was made to be during training. Don't back up but, it's ok to contract a deadly virus!

I performed my very first "Postage Due". For this little gem, you deliver a piece of mail that requires extra postage due to the post office. The carrier is not to turn over the parcel or mail unless the postage due is conveyed to the carrier. No exceptions. If they don't have the money, they're told that they may go to the local Post Office to pick up the package and pay for it then, as the parcel will now have to be returned to it. And here's the skinny, the carrier can ONLY accept cash and it must be in an exact amount and it's the responsibility of the carrier to bring it back to the office and check it in with the clerk or else, the carrier is responsible for the payment. So, there I am in my bandanna and rubber gloves and here's a young college student, with the door open a crack due to fear of the masked stranger on the other side, calling to her roommates to see if anyone's got $3.29! They finally pooled their money and with three singles the various change (including pennies) was dropped into my hand one at a time with a clink.

Accepting multi-handled cash during a pandemic! How much am I getting paid for this?

Amazon Sundays have now started to begin at 7am! Now, on top of being exhausted all the time, I have to drag myself up at 5:30am on Sundays for this! On the one hand, the pandemic has helped with the reduction in mail volume, making it manageable for me but, because people in general are staying indoors, they're doing all of the shopping online and this has increased parcel delivery enormously.

I should say here that, while I say that the pandemic has helped me with the reduction of mail (if businesses are closed, there's no need for them to advertise), this seemed to have an opposing effect on the regular carriers, the office staff and the Post Office in general. Low volume means low revenue. The financially overextended service was already scuttle-butting about the need to shut down if the pandemic lasted until Labor day and beyond. Frankly, it was no skin off my apple as, I wasn't going to be around to witness it. And frankly, I was already cultivating my own opinions and plans for the Postal Service should anyone be interested in hearing.

So, with the increase in on-line shopping, the parcel delivery business was booming. While Amazon is the main culprit in the online shopping business and, they have their own delivery workforce, they are not able to keep up with the demand. And this is why they have contracted with the USPS for overflow delivery. Also, while Walmart (the nation's largest employer) doesn't have their own delivery workforce, they rely on others, including the USPS, for delivery of their wares. This, combined with the USPS's parcel delivery service, is giving First Class mail delivery a run for its money as the number one revenue source for the USPS.

For my part, I'm up at 5:30am on a Sunday to support this effort. Because of yet another 5 minute signal light, I pulled into the parking lot of the annex at 7:03am. Bill happened to be in the parking lot as I hurriedly locked-up the car and said, "Sleep in today?!" Passive aggressive not-withstanding, my thought was, "Why is he even here!?" Why is the Postmaster of an office on site at 7am on a Sunday? He did mention to me at our first face-to-face that he could retire if he wanted but, he trailed off. It did seem like the type of job that gets into your blood. Hard to walk away from, especially at that level where the money to work ratio leans heavily toward the former.

The suggestion of a 7am start was in an effort to not have the carriers out delivering all day. It didn't seem to work as, showing up at 7am instead of 8am just seemed to serve the sleep deprived even further and beat them up just a little more when showing up that next Monday morning.

Chapter 12

And there I was, the next morning. I was there three minutes early and yet, no one sang my praises. What DID happen that day was that Nick called me over to the desk and I was told to initial some paper in three places. I gave a cursory look and didn't see a downside and scribbled off a few T.S.'s. and was told, "You made it. You just need to make it a few more days without incident!".

Made what?, I thought. The end to the probation period? Not quite sure. I shrugged it off and just went to work. During the day's morning talk it was conveyed to the carriers to take the advos seriously. "The old folks love 'em and they constitute a good chunk of revenue. Don't even bother with the addresses, everyone gets one. EVERYONE GETS ONE!".

Well, frankly, I thought that made it easier. Just trying to read addresses and processing it all with sweat dripped stained eyeglasses made it challenging at times. It's actually a luxury to just take and jam these advos into a box regardless of who it's addressed to. No one is going to complain that they got their neighbors advos.

On many occasions I've seen signs taped onto resident's mail box's to not include advos or "junk mail". I've been asked by residents if they can opt out of receiving the advos and I conveyed to them that they're talking to the wrong person. It's given to me and I deliver it. Period. Further, the fact is, a business has paid the USPS postage to have something delivered, it MUST be delivered or the USPS is in breach of contract. The resident can then take it out of the box and light it on fire in front of me if they wish but, it's going in the box first.

I always look for ways of adding to a solution instead of adding to a problem and I thought that I actually came up with a good way to eliminate these advos and, perhaps have a good business venture. Why not set up a website and have the weekly coupons available for view and make them either downloadable to a phone or able to be printed by those who may find them valuable and thus, save many trees and, in my opinion, save the USPS money by not having to pay a carrier to deliver these things weekly?

I actually looked into it and guess what? It already exists! Yup, those advos that you get every week are already online in yet another example of redundancy.

While feeling more confident about setting myself up for the day's deliveries, the flurry of advice keeps coming. While casing, I hear someone from behind the case say, "Hey Frank, don't study it, just case it!". I didn't react or respond, of course. Then the person comes up to me and said, "You're Frank right?".

"No, Tom."

"Ohhhhh, riiiight!"

The continued name misidentification on me is mystifying. It's just three letters. How hard is it? Ya know, "Tom, Dick or Harry!" I dunno…

Mallory, a very pleasant career carrier originally from Massachusetts, often was helpful in breaking down the din of bullshit for me with a dismissive wave of her hand. "Don't listen to these people, they have no life!" It gave me faith that not all postal employees needed (as a former colleague used to say), with extra grace required.

Another told me that these "T-6's" have on a uniform, just like the rest of us and to not let them boss me around. They're just like everyone else.

I didn't know a "T-6" from a size "6" shoe and so, I didn't really know who, specifically, they were referring to but, I got the gist of what they were saying. You have to ride the line of listening to sage advice and deriving your own methods. Similar to that of a child evolving into adulthood. However, in keeping with that same analogy, I often feel that failing is one of the best teachers there is. You have to break things and then fix them in order to truly understand the inner workings. One should be left to discover and fail and move on to a fuller understanding and more well-rounded work ethic. The bombardment of "advice" sometimes gums up that effort.

For me, at this point, it meant forgoing my attempt at adhering to the training on vehicle safety. Gone was the headlight check. Gone was the flasher check. Gone was the break light check. And gone was the micro adjustments of the multitude of mirrors of the LLV. If the tires had some air in them, "Let's hit it!" Who's got time for anything more?

Gone was the delicate manipulation of an advo, positioning it so that I can make sure the address, ever so flimsily stamped on a hard to read section of it, makes its way nicely and safely into its new home of the resident's mail box. It's grab, roll n' cram, next… "Oh, you're not supposed to get one of these? Sorry, here ya go!"

Gone was the painstaking dissection of something if it's considered UBBM or, if there is some special treatment for this piece which is undeliverable. "It's UBBM!" Bam, into the tub!" No hesitation. Someone else can figure it out!

Almost gone was my pleasant demeanor. Eroded, for sure. But not gone completely. I have to be pretty well gone to give a rude interaction. It's just not my way.

Others, apparently don’t share my approach like that very much.

Chapter 13 – PrePaid Pension

Coming off of a two-day rest (I needed it badly) and something which I've come to realize is next to impossible to come by (so much for part-time or even full "reasonable" time). I was scheduled to go in at 10am that day and I actually had a few minutes to myself prior to that. I make the mistake of watching the news.

The Coronavirus COVID-19 is having a devastating impact on the world. I'd even gone so far as to stop joking about how, "I'm out of limes so, there's no way I can get the Corona Virus!" Heh!

Mail delivery volume has fallen off to a point where it's being reported that the Postal Service will be out of money by the coming June. It was April at the moment. The Postal Service had been losing money for the last fourteen years and this year is looking no different. It is widely known that the USPS has, as a source of revenue, UPS, Amazon and Walmart as a partner in delivery service. With the continued boom in online shopping (toilet paper is a big item these days and extremely cumbersome to delivery when in multiple units), the parcel delivery service seems to be a considerable goldmine for the Postal service. However, it's also considered that by general consensus that the USPS doesn't charge enough for its services.

At this writing, the cost of a first class stamp is $0.55. That's 55 cents to get a first class envelope to go from New York to San Diego, or Seattle to Miami, in a time frame of between three and seven days! Kinda silly, really. However, hint at the cost of first class postage will go up to say, $1, to offset the increasing cost of operating expenses (you know, to perhaps replace the vehicles that are catching fire for no apparent reason), and the public outcry would be tremendous. Or not, as, for the individual, to pay that type of increase may be palatable and, at the very least, leave the mailer with a sense of helping the USPS out by considering it a donation as they only process a first class piece of mail once or twice a month.

It's the businesses that end up taking the brunt of a Postal increase. If first class mail is increased, so too will all the other classes of mail postage. Businesses make up for the majority of volume, and therefore, revenue for the USPS. If mailing costs are increased to the business, they either scale back or pass on those costs to the middle, and final consumer. It's a bit of a "Catch-22" but, within the delivery ranks of the USPS, postage isn't thought of very much. Its above our paygrade (as most things probably are). We just satisfy the last mile of terrain to get the item from point A to point B.

During my previous Amazon Sunday, I delivered an Express mail package the size of a shoebox. It was marked that it was damaged and also that it had no contents. The postage read $50.21. I stopped the vehicle and took the package and processed it in proper procedure and left an empty package by the front door of the recipient. I delivered a box of air that someone paid $50.21 to have express delivered.

But, someone's got to pay me, pay for the gas in the vehicle, pay for the mechanics making the vehicle safe (enough) to deliver the package and the myriad of other costs involved in the action of me delivering a box of air. I'm sure that, at some point, the customer will file a case and ultimately, a replacement for the item will be sent from the mailer and the customer will finally receive the item for which they ordered at no further cost to them as Express Mail provides for that. Only a time factor is a source of concern for the customer at that point. If the item came from a retail source, the retail source needs to replace the original item at their cost, hurting their business. Even if the USPS reimburses the business for the replaced item (additional revenue drain on the USPS), the delivery machine still needs to make that delivery (for a second time) and the cost associated with it is exponential for the USPS.

When current Postmaster General, Megan Brennan, testified before Congress in April, 2020, she explained the Postal Services circumstances to Congress, not because the federal government funds the Postal Service (it does not), but because Congress controls the Postal Service. Congress set the postage rates, it regulates which services the agency can offer, and it legislates the rules on how it operates. Mail delivery is constitutionally mandated and, any time that a Post Office is closed or the cost of any service within the service is raised, the change requires congressional approval.

In 1970, President Richard Nixon changed the USPS from a Cabinet department to an independent government agency in an attempt to have the Postal Service run more like a corporation, with congressional oversight, but without taxpayer funding. At the same time, in exchange for collective bargaining rights, postal employees agreed never to go on strike!

By 1982, the USPS was operating completely independently and entirely without federal funding. However, in 2006, the Republican controlled Congress passed a law preventing the Postal Service from raising its rates for regular mail service by more than the Consumer Price Index. Consumers loved it but, this meant that, no matter how much the cost of fuel prices went up, leases for its cargo flights, health insurance for its career employees, or any other operating expenses incurred, the agency could not charge more than a few, almost symbolic, cents per year for its services. This is why first class stamps still only cost 55 cents to mail an envelope from Boston to Honolulu and why parcel shipping rates are less than private alternatives.

This is the same law that also mandated that the Postal Service pre-fund its employee-pension and retirement costs, including health care, not just for one year but for the next seventy-five years! The year that this mandate was passed, the USPS had nine hundred million dollars in profits. It has not had a profitable year since! The annual cost of the pre-funded retirement benefits is more than five billion dollars. Those opposed to the mandate are quick to point out that the Postal Service is the only employer who is forced to fund retirement accounts for employees who haven't yet been hired, or, who have yet to even been born!

Finally, after thirteen years of trying to repeal this mandate, Democrats got halfway there in February, 2020, when the House of Representatives voted to do so, but, the bill stalled in the Republican controlled Senate.

Postmaster Brennan's testimony came after this repeal effort and she pointed out to Congress the budgetary relief that would be realized by allowing the agency to return to standard pay-as-you-go retirement. Of course, just changing from a pre-funded retirement to a pay-as-you-go retirement alone would not be enough to make the agency profitable. Brennan advised Congress that the USPS was currently on track to run out of money by the end of September, 2020 and has the potential to shut down operations altogether.

She requested eighty-nine billion dollars from Congress to stop the services financial bleeding for the next few years. The eighty-nine billion includes twenty-five billion to cover the revenue lost most recently by the COVID-19 pandemic, another twenty-five billion to cover the cost of upgrading its infrastructure from antiquated sorting machine, dilapidated office and exploding vehicles. Fourteen billion was earmarked for paying off debts related to the pre-funded retirement mandate and yet another twenty-five billion for "unrestricted borrowing", should the Postal Service need it in the future.

This may sound like an extremely large ask of Congress but, to put it into perspective, Congress has already given the private airline industry fifty billion dollars, when only about half of the country ever takes a commercial flight in any given year. The Postal Service, by contrast, provides an invaluable service to every American every single day by a variety of factors: facilitating the constitutionally mandated national census questionnaires; distributing a hundred and thirty million copies of the CDC guidelines for COVID-19 prevention; handling vote-by-mail efforts for primaries around the country and, this year, the Presidential election; and, in additional to all the usual mail, delivering groceries, wipes, disinfectants, and prescriptions (including nearly all of the those shipped by the Veterans

Administration). It's true that, not everyone WANTS these things delivered to them if it isn't germane (that's up to the beholder), but, the service is performed nonetheless. And, the Postal Service performs these functions very well. The general consensus is that the Postal Service is well admired and has a higher approval rating of any other government agency.

The collective bargaining rights in which the majority of Postal employees realize is one of many aspects of the USPS that President Trump has proposed cutting. In 2018, President Trump convened a task force to assess the Postal Service's future. The task force recommended a reduction in wages for Postal Service employees as well as a reduction is benefits, closing Post Offices, eliminating delivery days and subcontracting mail processing as well as ending the service's universal delivery to all Americans no matter how remote their location (UPS and FedEx contract out their "last mile" delivery to many places in the US simply because it's not profitable.

But, it's worth remembering that, the original idea behind a "Postal Service", profitability was not the goal. Like public education and public libraries, self-sufficiency is not the measure of an entities success in America. However, this goes to one's political leanings and an individual's general stance toward the common good goal for the people ensconced within the guidelines of a given government.

The merits of the privatization of a national delivery service can be served and volleyed ad nauseum, and has been, but, suffice to say that, major financial adjustments are clearly in need of implementation in order for the service to continue its mission, or an incorporation of complete reorganization is evident.

All heady stuff. In the meantime, I mask-up with my bandanna (freshly cleaned of all potential COVID-19 and other nasty bits) and I put my game-face on for another day on my personal mission.

Masks are still “on-order” and so, everyone in the office is on their own to mask up. At this point, carriers are fearful of the general public and vice versa. The entire country is on lock-down until the end of April. It’s not known what will happen after that. It’s all very “Stephen King” and “The Walking Dead-like” out on the street.

Chapter 14 – Easter Sunday

April 12, 2020, Easter Sunday. I was a bit surprised that I was scheduled to work on this day. And yet, I wasn't. It didn't seem to me that the USPS pays much attention to, or gives any credence to any specific day on the calendar. It's just another day. And today, is just another Amazon Sunday.

Not being religious other than being respectful of an individual's beliefs, I was certainly aware of what day it was and that I knew that it held significant meaning for many Christians. No one asked for volunteers or asked if anyone had an ethical problem with working on what is general perceived as a major holiday. You're just scheduled. That's it. All I knew was that this was my 9th straight working Sunday in a row. Apparently this, "one Sunday per month" was at best inaccurate, at worst a bait n' switch. There doesn't seem to be an end to any of this.

I clock in for the day and see a person who I've never seen before at the supervisor desk. Larry sat in a reclined position with fingers interlaced on his stomach and waited for everyone to show up and clock in for the day.

With everyone clocked-in and standing in a semi -circle, Larry felt the need to make a speech about promptness. "Be on time! Don't be late!" He said it, "in that tone" that I don't care for. No "Good Morning!". No "Happy Easter for those to celebrate". No, "Thanks for coming in on a holiday". Nothing. Just, beratement with attitude right out of the gate.

And why, I wondered, was he sitting there, (god forbid he should actually have the decency to stand to address people) yammering on about being on time when, everyone who was standing there was on time and waiting to start to work? I know why; he was playing the part he felt he needed to play. He's a supervisor after all and, isn't this the way a supervisor is supposed to act?

The answer is no. You have adults standing there at 7am on an Easter Sunday looking to do work that they may or may not agree with doing but, do it anyway so that they can provide a better life for themselves and/or their families. They don't need some narcissistic play actor with a Napoleon complex berating them. Lead by example. Keep acting like a dick and let's see what attitudes are cultivated among the workforce.

Perhaps, however, I wasn't giving Larry a fair shake. Maybe it was just that I was on edge. This lingering illness and the scheduling thing had me completely disoriented and perhaps I was just a little reactive at this point. Larry was from the East side. I didn't know much about the East side, just that, "You don't want to go over there!"

Larry then started to berate the group further while consulting the computer on the desk. "Everyone clocked-in incorrectly. You shouldn't have clocked-in as "bla, bla, bla…"

Here we go again with the clocking situation. It's 7am on a holiday Sunday; just start paying me will ya? When I stop working, you can stop paying me, deal?

After doling out the various combinations of route assignments for everyone to follow concerning parcel delivery, he came to me and said, "You're Tony right?"

"Tom, nice to meet you!"

"Why did I think you were Tony?"

I have no fucking idea, I thought.

"Anyway, If (when) you make regular, you'll more than likely start on the east side. So, we have to get you trained on the east side. If you're not trained on both sides, you're useless to me!"

Fine, I thought, but, upon further analysis (which I'm want to always do), the fact that I need to go to the east side was not the source of my furrowed brow, rather, the interesting use of the word "me". This guy has the perception that any activity is there to accommodate him, not the company. Interesting. I'm aware of this odd personality trait and it's always fascinated me. Arguably, we currently have a leader of the free world with this type persona. In any case, I find it unbecoming and off-putting. I feigned mild acknowledgment of his comments and shrugged in a "whatever is needed for the cause" motion.

Toward the end of the day, my scanner made a noise that I hadn't heard as of yet. Apparently, a message was being sent through the scanners. I managed to poke my way through the various menus and see the incoming message from Larry asking the group of carriers that day to respond as to how many parcels they had left to deliver. I had a couple of parcels left and tried to relay this information via the scanners messaging system. No one ever mentioned the fact that messaging could be done with these scanner and I immediately thought, why is my personal phone being used if this is the case? I looked and couldn't find how to respond to the message. There was a "Message acknowledge" option and "Delete Message" but, I could see nowhere where it could be responded to. I actually never did figure it out. So, I grabbed my phone and sent Larry a message to the phone number he gave me on the way out that, I was almost done and I asked if anyone needed any further help.

There was no response. He later claimed that he never received the message. The whole communication system was broken. It was all very jerky movements with nothing being fluid.

Finishing for the day, you could tell that Larry was annoyed at how long it took everyone to deliver the parcels they went out with. He shouted to the group trying like hell to get out of the office and salvage some of the day, "You should be able to delivery twenty parcels per hour!"

As I left, I thought of this. There's no way in hell you can delivery twenty parcels per hour! Ok, maybe if the parcels were spaced just so, and you can bang out one right after the other. But, understand that, Amazon Sunday just isn't set up that way. I may have to look up an address on the phone, following those directions, get to the location, figure out how to enter the gated community, wait to get in, find the specific address within the community, make the delivery, then figure out what the next parcel for delivery should be, as there's no flow to it. The next address may be miles away. Look up the address again and repeat the whole process. Twenty parcels an hour would have you placing a parcel at the residences door every four to minutes! Impossible!

I have actually achieved the twenty parcel per hour rate that Larry promoted but, that's when three parcels went to the same address and two others were a couple doors down, etc. But, if left as individual deliveries, it's not very likely.

Of course, the main reason for this is because of the set-up. Or, lack of set-up. You see, trucks come into the various post offices and basically just dump out their contents. There needs to be a sorting of the parcels on Sundays, just as there is a sorting of first class and Flats mail every day. There may be a general sorting; for instance, Deerfield Beach is comprised of two zip codes (33442 and 33441) and, the parcels are first separated in that manner. And, they may be further separated into routes. If they are, they aren't done very well as there tends to be a lot of comingling of routes from what I've seen. And then, the parcels within the routes need to be put in some type of cohesive delivery order. Most of this is done by the carrier assigned to a grouping of parcels for that day. The problem, once again, is that most of the people who are there, working on a Sunday and Holiday, are CCA's or, very new and unexperienced, and they struggle to make efficient sense of where and how these parcels need to be arranged and ultimately, delivered.

It appears to me that, the overall efficient and timely delivery of these parcels rests in having them sorted and sequenced properly before the carrier even takes possession of them. But, that's apparently an additional job with additional financial implications associated with it. And so, it isn't at the top of the process improvement list.

Also, it may even be further efficient to get the regular carriers to come in to make these Sunday deliveries as they are experts in where everything should go and how everything should be sequenced. However, because they are veterans of the Postal Service with years under their belt, their pay rate is such that it puts a large financial drain on the operating budget of the individual Post Office. At some point, the local Postmaaster would have to answer as to why the operating costs of that office are so high for that month. Yet another Catch-22; have the low paid carriers do the work and have the work be done in an inefficient way that will cost more per hour (at the lower pay rate) or, have the work done more efficiently at the higher pay rate. It's a judgement call that's made monthly, weekly, daily and sometimes, hourly.

I must have officially overcome the probationary period as, with my latest paycheck, I noticed that I received the $0.50 rate increase that comes with satisfactorily completing the probation period. Three months in and I now make $17.79 per hour. From what I understand, that amount won't budge until, either Congress has something to say about it, or, at my one-year anniversary and I think it'll be another 50 cents per hour. There apparently is a larger pay increase when a carrier is made "regular". However, dependent on the size of the office a carrier works out of, becoming a "regular" may take years! It is mostly due to attrition. Carriers either retire or die, that's pretty much the only way to move up on the Postal Evolutionary ladder. Doing a great job won't do it; making cost savings suggestions won't do it. Someone's gotta die to get some sort of acknowledgment!

And, frankly, I didn't get what all the hub-bub was about with bridging the 90 day probationary period as, I didn't feel any different. I was still a scrub, subject to a disjointed schedule and working almost every day of the week with no Postal Service health benefit.

The next day, Monday, was one for the books; once again I'd been scheduled to do a certain route that I'd begun becoming familiar with and, as I get straight in my mind my plan of attack for it and show up that morning, I'm given the old switch-a-roo! And, lucky me, I was changed to a route with a heavy business population. I still wasn't sure how I felt about delivering to businesses as compared to private residents. On the one hand, there's heavy mail volume, coming and going with a business as opposed to a private residence. The parking for a business, depending on where it is, can be difficult for a mail truck, adding to the stress, and there's hardly any chance of a dog attack. However, businesses are usually within line-of-site and, as annoying as it may be to go inside each and every business, if you're at one location, you can be relatively certain that the next delivery location is pretty close. And, there's always the chance siting of some eye-candy in four inch heels, which is always a plus.

But, on this day, the route in which I was to delivery, had semi-industrial businesses on the route. A lot of heavy equipment rentals and cement mixing and semi-truck moving companies were in evidence. And, it appears, that they all were either on the same mailing list for a two-inch thick "tools & parts" catalog or, the business that manufactures this catalog just feels that it's in their best interesting to just mail out these two-pound catalogs to each and every business in the area. Either way, my face melted at the site of the mountain of catalogs standing before the casing station for the route.

I heard Nick from somewhere in the distance saying something to me but my mind and ears weren't focused on anything but what a disaster this day was going to be. But, apparently he was telling me to not deliver catalogs to certain sections of the route. Either he felt sorry for me (which I doubt) or, there was some other reason why some of the sections weren't getting the catalog that day. Too late, however, my attitude was shot. I had spent the night thinking about how I was going to try to be more efficient on the route in which I had be scheduled to work (park here, take "this" much mail at "that" point, etc.), that, upon being switched to a route that I've only ever done a small piece on and, it being a Monday (double the mail) and, having to dole out these massive catalogs, just put me in a funk.

The funk continued moments later when Juno went over to Bruna, who was standing near me and asked about why a package from the previous day's Amazon Sunday hadn't been delivered and why it was marked B/C (Business Closed).

Before Bruna could answer, I stepped in and told her that it was I who marked the package that way (which was true).

Yesterday, during the melee, Bruna saw that my pile of parcels was a mountain of mess and tried to help by doing a triage of sorts with the parcels. She would look, grab and throw a parcel into a separate hamper that I supposed meant something to her and threw parcels into another hamper and every once in a while would throw one to me and say, "Scan that as "Business Closed". I would do that, mark the parcel with a B/C as I'd be instructed to do and continue to watch her sort out the parcels in a method only known to her.

As I've stated, the parcels come into the station on a larger truck the night before or even during the early morning hours. Everything needs to be accounted for. If a business is closed, there needs to be an accounting as to why that parcel was not delivered to its intended address on the day that it arrived into the local Post Office. So, instead of just leaving the parcel for the next business day to be delivered when they are, again, open for business, the parcel needs to be scanned, and the menu system within the scanner answered to: Delivered? NO. Why? BUSINESS CLOSED. ACCEPT.

If there ever is a problem or delay in the delivery of the parcel, it can be traced with the scans which occurred at each step in the process. Checking the tracking flow of deliveries, these particular parcels were not delivered on this day due to the fact that the intended business was closed.

I never try to skate from anything I've done. Whatever I've done, it was for good reason. I'm happy to explain that reason to you should you wish to hear.

"I put that on there Juno.", I said, not feeling it necessary to inform her that it was done yesterday at Bruna's direction.

"This is a nursing home!" she said, as if to elicit some sort of response from me.

What response could I have? I assumed that Bruna knew what she was doing or else, why approach the parcel sorting with such commando vigor? If she wasn't sure, say, "I'm not sure!". And, giving benefit to the doubt to try to come up with a reasonable explanation, I figure that, perhaps the nursing home doesn't accept parcels on Sundays and that Bruna knew this. In any case, while these thoughts went through my mind I was sort of waiting for Bruna to pipe up with a "Oh, I told him to do that!" But, nay, there was no accountability. It was on me.

If memory serves, I actually did look at the mailing address of the parcel in question and, as I've said, we're to deliver to the address, not the name and I believe that the name said something like "The Forum". Not "The Forum Nursing Home" or some other variation. My mind didn't make the connection that "The Forum" meant that the delivery address was at a nursing home and, what if it did? My reasoning would have gone to what I've previously mentioned. And frankly, someone tells me NOT to delivery something, sheeeeit, I'm not questioning it!

And, of course, I didn't care for the tone at which the perceived job dereliction was being delivered to me. At first it was off-putting because I thought that she was simply complaining that, there was a parcel that had come into the office on the Sat/Sun overnight and wasn't delivered on Sunday as it was supposed to and here were are, on a Monday (double the mail) and this represented just one more parcel for the regular carrier to deliver, which should have been delivered the day before. But, at further thought, as it was in fact, a nursing home, this parcel could conceivably contain needed medication by a resident of the home. With that in mind, one can see Juno's concern.

However, not to make light of a situation; I'm not sure that relying on the Postal Service for life-altering medication might be the best business and medical practices. I mean, I'm sure there aren't infantry soldiers bleeding out on the battlefield calling for more morphine, only to be told by the medic, "Sure, no problem, we're just waiting for the delivery guy!"

What added to the frustration of the situation was that, not only didn't Bruna claim responsibility for directing me to mark the parcel as "Business Closed", she, almost apologetically to Juno said, "He's new". This infuriated me even further. Claim responsibility! What's so hard about that? Very off-behavior from people from all walks of life who, from the looks of things, have found a save harbor in the USPS in a world of rough employment seas.

Chapter 15 – The Dark Side

April 15, 2020, Tax Day. However, due to Covid-19, all filing deadlines have been altered. That's a good thing, for me. Less mail traffic, which would include any mail-in income tax filings, is always welcome, for me anyway. I understand that this mean less revenue for the USPS but, I can't really be concerned about that. I'm at a point of self-preservation, and today would be no different.

I was supposed to have the day off but, upon waking for the day was contacted to report by 9:30am, …gulp…to the east side! Not only am I working on my day off but, I must go to where people have gone, and have never been seen again! It was a Wednesday and I figured, the carrier on the previous day probably got out all of the advos. Surely, they wouldn't have me go to the east side (affectionately known as the "Dark Side"), where I'd never delivered to a route before and have advos added to the mix.

Getting to the east side from the west side took longer than I thought as, there are many traffic lights, railroad crossings, and Rte. 95 to circumnavigate, causing to me rush around a bit. Arriving already in a state of rush and not quite being sure where to park, I felt uneasy about the day already. Luckily, I made it inside with two minutes to spare and I reported to the local supervisor, Tangelo. Seriously. She introduced herself and asked if I'd been on a walking route before. Oh boy… I told her that I hadn't and she sort of rolled her eyes and said, "Well, today's your lucky day!" She brought me over to where a portion of the route had already been cased. That's good, no casing for me. I surveyed what I had and, being the seasoned expert by that point from the West Side, it didn't appear to be so bad. And the walking bit? It's about time. I was looking forward to pounding it out and, at least looking like a legitimate mailman.

Tangelo explained to me how to clock in with the proper route number, making sure that I enter the correct zip code for the east side. I saw that there was already an orange credit card looking electronic time card for me in the time card slots with all the other carriers. I swiped in (I think I did it correctly) and retrieved the proper scanner, vehicle key and arrow key.

I first took the parcels out to the truck and did the load truck feature and came back for all the rest of the mail. To my dismay, now, within the bin which had the DPS, Flats and SPRs, were bundles of advos. From across the room the regular carrier who had cased this for me said with a smirk, "Heh, I forgot to put them in before!"

Tangelo asked if I had a satchel. I hadn't. She brought me over to a casing station that didn't look like it was active, and dug out and old postal satchel for me to use. As I packed it away into the bin she said, "Here, better take this too!", as she handed me a canister of dog spray.

I packed up and put my best foot forward and "moved to street" from the office and got into the already boiling LLV Postal Vehicle. I was completely unfamiliar with the East Side except for having patronized a few restaurants there and I needed to Google Map where to go for the first stop. The first few stops were in apartment buildings and so, the process was pretty familiar to me. I didn't notice that the Flats were not comingled with the DPS and, while it wasn't too much of a dilemma for the apartments, I wondered how that would bode when on the street for the walking part.

I finished the apartments sections of the route and found my way to the beginning of the walking part of the route. However, I found myself looking at it in too much of a "focused" way. I was looking at it as, "There's the first home that I need to delivery to, so, let's go!". In fact, it should be viewed as "where does the "street" begin and where does it end?" And once you have a handle on that, you finger through all of the DPS that you need, all of the Flats that you need, all of the SPRs that you need and all of the parcels that go with that section, pack it up into your satchel and, off you go!

I simply couldn't get the hang of this. Not for this street anyway. I wasn't sure where I should park. In front of "this" house, or, the one across the street? I had no idea. I just parked, and, I had long since dispensed with locking the vehicle up every time I got out. It just took too much time. I'd deal with the consequences, if there ever were any.

But, there was already and immediate problem; there was no way that I could carry all that I needed to carry to cover the whole street. Covering the whole street means, you follow one side of the street until some end point, you cross the street and circle back to the vehicle. That's how it supposed to be done. That's not how I did it.

First of all, for this section of the route, there were about 6 or 7 parcels to be delivered and four of them didn't fit into the satchel. I stood there in the sweltering sun trying to figure it out and, if you've ever been bald, wear glasses, have no idea where you are or what you're doing and standing in 93 degree heat with the sun bearing down on you, you'd know that, "Fuck this shit!" was about to be uttered for the first of many times!

I grabbed a handful of DPS and an amount of Flats that I thought went with it. I grabbed the SPRs to go with that section of street and crammed three or four parcels that should go with that section of the street and was about to head down the sideway when, I realized that I forgot all about the advos. I find the bundle that should go with this section of the route and snip the plastic bands, freeing themselves to me. After every ten or so advos, the next group of addresses is turned 180 degrees in orientation so as to put the spine of the advos opposite to each other making them more stackable. I figured that I could reorient them so that I could read them more easily while on the run. Mistake. I also forgot at this point that I didn't even have to read the address from the advo that, basically, everyone gets one so, it didn't really matter to begin with.

I closed all the doors to the vehicle (windows down and unlocked). I positioned the very heavy satchel on my right shoulder as taught at the academy, piled the heavy pile of advos in the crook of my left arm, made sure I had the scanner in my belt holder and that the arrow key was on my belt and vehicle keys securely in my pocket. I gave a quick tug on the dog pepper spray attached to the satchel strap and with a step, I was walking my first mail route. Ten steps later, I was drenched in sweat!

I got to the first house and looked through the satchel to find the DPS but, found that there was none. However, there were a couple of Flats to be delivered and then, I pulled from the pile in my arm, the first advo of the bunch. And that was it. First house down. And off I went. We were told not to cross yards from home to home as, homeowners can get pretty irate at the prospect of a path warn in the yard. This is extremely easy to do in Florida as, if you simply step on grass, if you can find any, it immediately begins to die. Florida, apparently, is also Gods Waiting Room for grass!

I got a few homes down and realized that, after moving the parcels around in the bag, I'd forgotten to check on the addresses for the parcels themselves. I was too fixated on the juggle of fingering through the bag to find the correct DPS, the correct Flats and peeling off another advo from the pile that, I just screwed the pooch on the parcels. Sure enough, one of the parcels went to a residence three homes back. I stood in the street for a second trying to figure what to do. I could just continue, go to the end of the block, come back the other side and, when I got to the same area, cross the street and deliver the missed parcel or, forget about it and, when I get back to the vehicle, drive back to the house and make a special trip or, walk back to the house.

I walked back to the house. I later learned to NEVER do this! Oh well,… as Bruna had recently said, "I'm new!"

I made the delivery and, pounded out the steps to the place where I had left off and continued on with the route. By the time I got to the end of the street I was even more confused. The DPS and Flats alternating between whether or not there was a delivery, was screwing with my head. And trying to turn the advos around if they were 180 degrees in the opposite direction ended up causing more trouble than it was worth as, with the wind, it started blowing the open side of the advos like a sail, making then very cumbersome to manipulate. By the time I crossed the street and started coming back the other side, I realized that I was running out of mail. And then, after a few more homes I was completely out except for a bunch of advos still in my arm. I had to walk all the way back to the vehicle to get more mail! Unbelievable.

As I walk back to the vehicle to get more mail, perhaps a distance of a quarter mile or so, I figured that it really wouldn't make sense to get more mail, then walk all the way back to the spot at which I left off. I thought I'd just get in the vehicle and drive back and deal with it, however, by then.

I got back to the vehicle and opened the back door which slid up into the roof of the vehicle and to my horror, found that the wind had blown the unbound advos all over the back of the truck!

Mental note, "Don't clip the plastic bands that hold these things together!"

"Fuck this shit!" I threw the satchel down and climbed into the back of the vehicle and tried to put all the advos back together, one dumb advertisement at a time. Tick-tock…

I finally got them back to some reasonable semblance and I started to execute the plan that I hatched during my walk of shame that I had completed fifteen minutes earlier. I guzzled water when I got back behind the wheel and tried to dry off as best I could but, it was futile. I was losing 4lbs a day by that point. It was mostly water weight but, I had been keeping a weight-loss journal and almost every day I'd weigh 4lbs less than when I started that morning. The next morning, after regeneration, the scale showed that I had put back on 3.75lbs. And so it continued!

I drove to the spot where I left off and, as I felt "the wheels of the bus begin to fall off", I completed that side of the street, driving and stopping in front of each house. I should mention that, this was a walking route for the reason that, the mail boxes were mounted on the homes themselves. You couldn't just pull the truck up and open the box and shove the mail in there. You had to walk up the physical house itself and, sometimes the mailbox location wasn't always obvious. You had to root around for it at times. It could be on the side of the house, it could be a well disguised slot in the garage door.

Forget those soft accelerations and eased-into airplane landings I was talking about when Arnel was realigning every bone in my body during OJT. I was flooring it from the start and slamming on the breaks in front of every home. Shut down the engine, grab the appropriate DPS, Flats, SPRs, Advos, parcels if any, run to the front of the house, look for the box and deliver, run back, repeat. I say, "run" because, even as I was unfamiliar with the route and considering this was my first time on the Dark Side and my first attempt at a walking route, I felt that I was WAY behind!

I finally finished and was at least happy that I had gotten one damn street under my belt. Then, I realized that, I had forgotten to deliver those larger parcels that I had originally determined were too large to carry in the satchel. So, back down the street for the third time to deliver the larger parcels. Unbelievably frustrating.

The route is, in fact, designed where you should park the Postal vehicle in a given spot in a given direction, do the loop of delivery and return to the vehicle. You'd then usually continue in the direction that the vehicle is in. Usually you'd travel to the end of the street you'd just delivered to and either make a left or right and continue with the next parallel street to the one in which you were just on. Sometimes though, you'd get to the end of the street and have to continue to the other side of a crossroad and continue from there. These routes have painstakingly been cultivated and manipulated so that the delivery of mail may be done efficiently.

And this is what most people see on most days. They see their "mailman" coming down the street, one jerk-stop after the next with a giddy anticipation of what might have been put into their own mailbox. Maybe they see the veteran mailman parked later along the side of the road under a nice shade tree, eating lunch while thumbing their phone or, perhaps flipping pages of a book. All very Norman Rockwell shit!

What most don't realize is that, the CCA, or, replacement carrier for the day, doesn't really have much of a clue as to what's going on! Oh sure, it gets better if the fill-in has been on the route before and, within a reasonable time frame but, if they have never been on the route and, especially if the route is a "walking route", the CCA is huffing and puffing and cursing their mothers that they'd ever been born.

The main frustration that I've found is not actually performing the duties of the job, which, arguably is to simply bring properly addressed items to the location in which they are addressed, rather, it's just not knowing where to go! Looking at it from a managerial point of view, I suppose that it is felt that it isn't worth the time to really get the fill-in carrier used to a given route as, they won't be on it for very long.

In my experience, for a full casing and delivery for a given route, six full days (at that would include the unique characteristic of each delivery day) is needed to give the replacement carrier a fighting chance at delivering what is needed in a timely manner while also affording them their proper break and lunch times. But, that just doesn't happen.

The whole descriptor of the replacement carrier was something that took me a while to wrap my head around to begin with. I really didn't think that I was signing up for something like this. I thought that I'd be given a route and I'd take a week to get used to it and, there ya go! That's your route now for the foreseeable future.

That's just not how it is. You're hired to do whatever and whenever, is needed. The problem with that is that the worker is unable to cultivate a progressive work ethic. They're always made to feel that it just isn't good enough, fast enough or complete enough. And they can't feel that way when, every day they report to work, it feels like their first day on the job.

While many people claim that they don't like to get bored on their job (the day goes so slow…), the fact is, there's a certain amount of benefit that goes with getting to your job and almost mindlessly processing what needs to be done without stopping at every juncture and trying to figure out what each next step is. It's just, inefficient.

The adage is, "follow the mail" and that's all I could go on at this point. I looked at what was next up with the DPS and also with the Flats and was relieved to see that it was the same address. So, at least there's that. I pump that address into Google Maps and it takes me around the corner to the first house on the next street.

I remember Arnel telling me that, yes, looking up an address can get you where you're going but, it's so much faster if you can get there by memory. Well, of course! But to have a memory, you need to experience something first, am I right? I'd never been in this location before and have no idea how the street runs or how the numbers run within those streets.

Chapter 15

I probably make the general mistake of thinking that every town works like New York City. NYC is a simple, understandable grid pattern. It's hard to get lost. Except in the West Village, all bets are off when you're in the West Village!

When you're on West 23rd street and you go South one block, take a guess at what street you'll be on? Right, 22nd. And it's considered west because you're west of 5th Ave which runs North and South. Where I was didn't really work that way. What added to the confusion was the additional compass rose heading. North East 8th St runs parallel to North East 8th Place which runs parallel to North East 8th Way, then the next street runs parallel to North East 8 Ave, then, to finally connect the dots in my mind, North East 7th St. But, for some reason, the next street would be called North East 6th Place. What happened to all the rest of them? AND, while we're at it, North East of WHAT? What am I North East of? Somehow it mattered to me. If I was standing on West 21 Street in Manhattan, all I know is that if I head east, I'll eventually be on East 21 Street and if I continue, I'll reach the East River. Makes sense to me.

Here, I was scratching my head a lot. But, again, I put my best foot forward and tried to calm down and make sense of what it was I was doing. I decided that I would dispense with delivering the parcels altogether. It was just too much, carrying everything on foot. I figured that, if all went well, I could do the loop on foot and deliver the DPS, Flats, SPRs and advos and then, since I would already have to drive down the street to get to the next street, I'd then do the Amazon Sunday thing and get rid of the parcels. While that's not the way it's supposed to be done, it actually worked on the street that I was on that time.

What also adds to confusion is the fact that, on a park n' loop, the DPS sequence of mail, if sorted properly goes up chronologically and then down. The house numbers don't just keep going up. If you're parked at the end of a street to begin to deliver across the street at number 1, you'll continue down that street, delivering to odd numbered homes and then, you'll cross the street to the even numbers and work your way back to number 2. Mathematically understandable but, when in a steaming hot truck with sweat dripping off every appendage, trying to grasp this numbering sequence from a variety of sources tends to be confusing for the uninitiated.

I was dragging in posture as well as in time and after a few streets I received a call from the office asking where I was. I tried to explain my location but I guess it was pretty vague. When I was asked how much I had left to do, all I could do was explain how many trays of mail and about how many parcels I had left to delivery. This was met with obvious dismay and I was told that someone would be out to help me.

While at about halfway down a street I see a mail truck coming up the street in the other direction. I waved and the truck headed toward where I had parked my vehicle. As I had left the sliding doors unlocked, I figured that the person could get in and take whatever it is they wanted in order to help out but, the rear door, which slides up, is always locked when it latches closed which would prevent the person from getting back there to take any parcels. So, I tried to speed up to meet them so I could open the back and they could help me out.

There was no pride left at this point. I just wanted it to be over. I was going house to house, got to the end of the street, crossed it and started to work my way back toward the truck and, sure enough, found mail in the bag that should go to residences back where I just was and so, high-tailed it back and delivered.

I finally got back to my vehicle and greeted the mail carrier who was parked behind me looking not all pleased. I honestly didn't know what he was doing that he had to be interrupted to come to my location to help me but, I guess, it didn't really matter; he was there and that wasn't good.

The first thing that I noticed on this guy was that he was dressed head to toe in long sleeved clothing. I didn't get it. I had on a golf shirt and shorts and I was dyin'! He had on those long Lycra-type leggings that runners wear with shorts over those and long socks that went half-way up the calf and the same type of long sleeved shirt with the postal uniform shirt on top of that.

He was clearly Jamaican and the heat didn't have much of an effect on him. Made me wonder if certain nationalities and racial make-ups might actually have a better aptitude for the requirements of the job. Much like what is commonly thought of the Native American who are purported to not be afraid of heights and is why many Native American Mohawks were used as laborers in construction of skyscrapers. However, the reality is, they're just as afraid as any other but, it's their culture that promoted that they never show the fear.

He came at me right out of the gate; "I've been waiting and waiting for you! It should take fifteen minutes to do a full street!! First of all, you left the windows down in the LLV, AND, you left it unlocked! That's no good! That's a fireable offense! AND, you don't have your flashers on! Let me show you…"

He then went through the motions of showing me how I should leave the windows closed except for an inch or two so that air could get in but an arm couldn't reach down to unlock the door and, to lock the doors every time I exit and to always put the flashers on when stopped and locked.

The fact was, I was aware of all that. But, at this point in my short "Postal Career", my "Give A Damn" had been busted, as Jeff, my childhood friend is often heard to say. Fireable offense? Let's go baby. Bring it on! Put me out of my misery. It might actually add an interesting dimension to the book. It's been over three months and this walking bit may have just put the final nail in my Postal coffin.

I asked his name and he responded but, I didn't catch it. He ended up taking a good majority of what I had left and delivered it himself leaving me with another street or two. He told me that this was his route. Well, of course it would take HIM fifteen minutes to do a street! Double it for me. But, again, I was unsure of how things worked even after months on the job. This was HIS route that I was doing. And he's here. I didn't understand. If he's working today and this is his route, why is he not doing the whole damn thing? AND, if he's here and they want me to get trained on the route and be introduced to the world of walking while delivering mail, why not let me go out with him on a training day and he can show me where to park, how much mail to grab, show me the idiosyncrasies of the route itself? The whole method of operation left me in wonder.

I have completed what was left of the remainder of the route but, by the end of the day, I was a used up, wet rag. I was sweating so much that I was making sweaty handprints on the mail as I put it into the box. And then, there were the advos; as I carry the bundle of the newspaper-type material in the crook of my left arm, the dripping sweat actually soaked through five or six bottom advos. Everyone knows what happens when newspapers get wet. They were so wet that I actually had to peel them apart and mush them into the mail box. Yes, if you find your mail a little damp in your mailbox, it's not necessarily rain!

Chapter 16 – Going Postal

Back on the west side the following day, I was greeted with smirks, as most had known I had gone to the dark side the day earlier and wanted to see how I fared. I probably looked better than I felt. Greg was right, it sure as hell is a young man's game. I was 58 years old. Doing some research, I discovered that the average age of retirement for a Postal Employee was 56. I started doing this two years AFTER most people retired! And it felt like it.

The actual walking that I did yesterday wasn't really the source of the challenge; it was the juggle in the heat and overall stress that added to aches and pains. I had walked a little over eleven miles while on the walking route and, from what I'm told, "That's nothin'!" Some carriers cover a good twenty miles a day, every day! I'd been averaging seven to eight miles a day lately and that's when not on a walking route. You end up putting in the miles simply going from the vehicle to wherever it is you need to go to deliver whatever it is you're delivering. Those high rises within Century Village will put on the mileage real fast if you need to deliver a parcel at one end of the top floor and at the complete opposite end of another floor, and so on.

I had lost about twelve pounds at this point and there was no reason to see how it could stop. I was a little intrigued as to why there were still many carriers with extra weight on their bodies. It seemed to me that you'd have to try to put the calories back on that you've lost that day just to maintain the necessary energy to keep going.

On this day I was to case and deliver all of route 26. I liked route 26 (as long as it wasn't on a Monday, or Tuesday). It had just a manageable business stretch on the front end (an Anheiser Busch distributor being the first stop which, there was nothing wrong with, as far as I was concerned) and then it went straight into Century Village that mainly stayed within one of the villages (Durham) within the Village and only had a few additional buildings tacked on at the end of the route. Each building flowed with one coming right after the next. Even I had a hard time mucking it up. The only drawback to the route was that it contained those smaller mailboxes that made it hard to fit everything if the resident didn't empty it out on a daily bases.

As is typical of human beings who are faced with hardship, anything less than that hardship feels easy. And today, in comparison to the day before, even though I was doing the full route today with casing, felt like it was being done properly and at a pace that made sense. I even stopped and had lunch. Not under a nice shady tree because, well, those unicorns don't exist in South Florida. But, I stopped non-the-less, and took a twenty minute lunch break while I threw down my sandwich and grapes.

I was back in the office at 4:15pm and about to punch out at 4:30pm when Enzo asked a favor.

This was April 22, 2020 (Earth Day), and Broward County was still technically on "Lock-Down". Meaning, no business should be open to the public and people should stay at home so as to not further spread the Corona virus. People and businesses were getting extremely antsy as people and businesses have been struggling due to the social distance dilemma as it was taking a toll on personal and business income. Protests had begun springing up throughout the county with calls to "open up" so businesses could get back on a paying basis.

The debate on the merits of mask wearing began to appear and there were some within the Postal Office while the milling about took place in the morning that simply refused to wear one. I'd heard rumors that some who refused to wear a mask when it was mandated would be asked to go home.

Enzo asked me if I could do the piece of Juno's route that contained The Forum Nursing Home. Apparently, because it was a nursing home, they were taking extra precautions in who they were allowing onto the premises. Firstly, no visitors were being allowed as, obviously the occupants are very old people with medical complications and fragile immunes systems and, for essential personnel (of which the USPS is to be included), it was required that the carriers wear a mask and that the temperature of the carrier be taken upon entry by way of a forehead scan.

The regular carrier who's route this was had a personal problem with being subject to the temperature check and refused to do the delivery to the address. Enter, the new guy.

I had my own reservations about going into a place like that and frankly, I wasn't concerned about getting THEM sick, but just the opposite.

I arrive at the Home and haul everything I had via hand truck into the lobby where I had my temperature taken (97° as usual, even though I always felt hot as balls!). I wheel everything to the little alcove of mail boxes and pull the movie theatre retractable ribbon across so no one can come in and interfere with delivery and spread whatever it is was floating around that place. Once you walk through the door it just seemed, ill. It had that feeling you have deep inside you if you're honest when you have a cold that, you may be functional but, deep down, you still ain't right!

I finished up as fast as I could while touching the least as I could and I got the hell outta there toot-sweet!

As I got back to the office after a long, what I felt was, a successful day, I see Mallory in the parking lot doing a walk-around for the vehicle that she just parked and was taking video. She sees me and says, "It's called "Covering your ass!"

I asked, "Do you do that every day!"

"No", she replied, "Only when I suspect something is going to happen!"

The following day found me ironically on Mallory's route. I tried not to be paranoid about what I had witnessed the day earlier and why it was that I was on a route for which the regular carrier was taking video of the vehicle that I was about to drive, and just muscled through.

I found this heavy industrial business route to be a bit of a challenge in that, many times with industrial businesses, you don't really know where the mail should go. Mallory was nice enough to create a very accurate map that helped me immensely. Again, why this isn't a standard thing, I just don't know. On the rare occasions where I had a spare few minutes at home, I actually started created my own maps using Google Maps and marking where all the stops of a given route should be. I never got anywhere with it though because, I was just never on one route long enough to document all the nuances of that route.

As I said, some storefront businesses were taking it upon themselves to open to try to reclaim whatever business they may have lost in the previous month and, in Florida, it's sometimes hard to tell if a business is actually open or closed as, they tend to black tint the sun facing windows to reduce the heat inside the store.

I came up on one particular storefront that sold mattresses where, the only way to know if it was open was to walk up to the door and try it to see if it opened. I was surprised to see that this particular store was, in fact open as, the selling of mattresses didn't seem to fit into the "essential" moniker which had become the word of the day lately. But, I had mail for it and so, I entered.

A guy in a suit stands from his desk situated all the way in the back of the store (another feeble marketing ploy to get you to walk to the back of the store and harder to just leave without bouncing up and down on a few mattresses) and asked, "What's going on?"

"Postal Service sir, I have some mail for you!"

He takes a few steps forward, but I have already closed the gap and circumnavigated my way to him through the sea of mattresses.

I hand him his 3" x 5" advertisement for a muffler special and he said, "That's it!?"

"Yes, that's it!"

"Next time, don't bother!"

"Alrighty!" And back out of the store I went, causing more wonderment of what it is that I'm actually doing.

I'd gotten back to the office and was sent out again to help out Dino.

Dino was actually newer than I and we had first met weeks earlier during an Amazon Sunday. Dino was a medically discharged Marine of about twenty seven or twenty eight years old who was discharged due to a back injury who told me that he loved the Marines and would still be in if it weren't for the injury.

I found Dino on the other side of town on a curbside route. It was late in the day and he looked like I had looked like at the end of my Dark Side day. Before I even got to him he was punching at the air in frustration. "This route is too damn long! It doesn't end! This is impossible!!!!"

And, what made it actually harder was that it was a curbside route. To the unfamiliar, riding in that Postal Vehicle from curbside mailbox to curbside mailbox is actually a form of torture! Waterboard survivors stand back in awe at someone who's spent a day in one of those things. And if you have any malady at all, doing this will surely magnify the intensity of the discomfort.

For me, the hardest vehicle was the ProMaster as, you literally had to climb into the vehicle from every entry. Too many years and miles of running on roads have all but made my ankles and knees useless. I can walk, I can ride a bike. But climb a ladder or stairs or twist into a tight opening to a seat and, Houston, we have a problem! At the end of some days at home, my wife would offer up a needed rejuvenating massage that, at times, I'd actually had to refuse because, it would just hurt too much!

Anyway, Dino's back was screaming. He said, and I agree, "I'd rather walk all damn day than sit inside this vehicle!" But, we don't get to choose. That actually becomes a problem in the path to becoming a career carrier; you may wait three years of being on a different route every day, working every Sunday and then, finally, someone retires and you come up on the list to become "regular", and in order to do so, you are to go on a route that generally disagrees with how your body works optimally. It can be a very long process to where a carrier feels comfortable at all.

Speaking of feeling uncomfortable, the following day found me in that apartment complex that I loved so much, the Waterford Courtyards. You know, the rat apartments?

I was having a hell of the time finding these damn buildings and the apartments to which they belong. I was late on the day already due to it being one of those days where everything went wrong. The scanner, the time clock, the vehicle, the scanner again, the gas station, I kept dropping my pen…

It was a mess. I couldn't get out of my own way. And then, I get to one of those cluster boxes that I had described where rats had been seen in the area.

The cluster boxes within this apartment complex were an older type where there must be a coordinated effort in getting them unlocked and opened in a similar way that there needs to be two separate keys to unlock, arm and fire the intercontinental ballistic missiles from a submerged submarine. Thinking about it, launching those missiles might, in fact, be easier to accomplish.

I was struggling with it then and all day when, just when things couldn't get worse, I inserting a key in a box, twisted, shimmied up, twisted, shimmied down, opened the box and, I couldn't get the key out. I couldn't deliver the mail as, only one door could be opened because the key was stuck and it didn't allow for both doors to be opened. I've heard of not being able to get a key in but, not being able to get a key OUT, was another new one on me.

You must understand that, for anyone to succeed in the mail delivery game, there needs to be a coordinated, almost choreographed dance that takes place between the carrier and the various paraphernalia, which is the mail receptacle. There can be no herkie jerky movements or stumbling's or missteps of any kind, or else, you're done for the day. And while it is generally accepted that when new to the game, there is bound to be those types of missteps but, as more and more time goes by, there is little sympathetic acceptance concerning missteps such as these.

However, once again, the carrier who is exposed to the very same route daily is also exposed to the idiosyncrasies of the various sticky points along the route and can combat them more readily.

I jingled, I jangled, I twisted back and forth, it was no use. It was stuck.

As mentioned, the arrow key is attached to a brass chain that is to be threaded through a belt loop on the pants and then back again through the unbroken end, making it almost impossible to lose. It also makes it almost impossible to become untethered from, unless you simply rip your belt loop off your pants or, as I wanted to do, take my pants off completely!

Dripping sweat from my head, down my arms, inside my gloved hands, made everything slick, making it more difficult to gain a proper purchase. This is silly, I thought, take a breath…, relax…, retrace your step…

Slowly, I massaged each moving part of this cluster fuck, I mean, cluster box and, I slowly manipulated the key within the lock as if cracking a safe. I quieted my breathing, I slowed the world down around me and I listened for that faint click of the tumblers within the lock. Slowly…slowly…quietly…

Just then, a rat ran up my leg and bit me right on the dick!

Not really, but that's what I was envisioning.

Nothing doing with the key. Then, I started to feel the rage boil up from deep within. I couldn't believe that I was stuck here tethered to this cluster box and unable to move. I tried to calm myself again, waiting a minute or two and started the process all over again. There was no hope. Now I was coming close to snapping off the key inside the lock and shaking the cluster box so violently, to the point where, if I wanted to, I could've probably broke it free from its bolted concrete foundation.

I ended up doing what I hate doing above all else in this world; I asked for help. I called into the office and I started out ok but, soon after Enzo answered, something in me snapped and, I went off!

"I can't fuckin' do this shit! I can't! This is dumb, this is stupid! I just can't do it!"

"Calm down, yes you can. Tell me what's wrong!"

"I'M CHAINED TO THE FUCKIN' CLUSTER BOX ENZO! I CAN'T DO ANYTHING! THE KEY IS STUCK AND THERE'S NOTHING I CAN DO!"

"Did you jiggle it!"

"AHHHH, FUCK THIS SHIT! OF COURSE I JIGGLED THE MOTHER FUCKER!"

"Alright, calm down. I'll send someone out there to help!"

He asked where I was located specifically and I explained it as best as I could while in that white hot, make no sense, stupid anger talk that comes out at times when in a rage.

And I stood there…for twenty minutes.

As I waited, and calmed down slightly. I felt bad at raising my voice to Enzo. He was a nice guy and it wasn't his fault and I had no business taking it out on him. He was just in my sites as I had a loaded mouthful. While standing there, I was thinking of Enzo and, I found out that he was originally from New York and a fellow Mets fan and we had some mild discussions on the tainted spring training and impending delayed baseball schedule due to the pandemic.

A bit baffling though, after New York, Enzo Guaraldi is reported to be from…North Dakota! What kind of Gumba comes from North Dakota, I thought? Especially if you were originally from New York. How could someone from NY….. ohhhhhhhhhhhhh, I get it. I suppose children in the witness protection program have to grow up somewhere! Ok, we'll leave it at that.

Finally Robinson shows up. Robinson is the most senior CCA and is about to be a made man or rather, made a career employee after three years on the list. He parks his LLV behind mine and walks to me and asks what's wrong. I tell and show him how I'm chained to this thing and I can't move. He comes around and I was happy that the rats had another target other than myself, and he twists and pulls in one motion and just like that, the key comes out and I was free.

I felt like an idiot. Actually, I was an idiot, I not only felt that way. The feelings of despair, inferiority and uselessness were overwhelming. And now, add guilt to them as I felt horrible about spouting off at Enzo. These feelings are foreign to me. I never ask for help, mainly because, I never need help. But not with this job. They say that it's not for everyone and, it certainly wasn't my intention to make this a life's career at this point but, I try to succeed at everything I put my mind to. That's what both my parents always claimed that I could do anyway.

Robinson helped me yet again by taking a lot of what I had left in the truck and I finished the rest. I managed to limp back to the office and once back there, I apologized to Enzo for going off on him and of course, I probably felt worse than he did, if that's any consolation. And, who knew how "connected" he really was?

I went home that night and when my wife saw the beaten shell of a man before her, she reaffirmed her convictions and care for my well-being and said as sweetly as can be, "That's it, I'm going out and being a prostitute so you can quit this job!"

She's good that way.

Chapter 17 – The 5th Floor

I managed to recover from the previous day's stress and outbursts and, was back at it the next day. But I was surely feeling that I was up against the ropes at this point. I wondered how much longer I could take it before going down for the count.

As per usual, reporting to work, I was scheduled to yet again be put on a route I had never been on before. It's just exhausting. I got the impression from those around me that people were a little concerned about me doing this one specific route for some reason. I showed up a little early to try to get a bead on the route so that it wasn't completely foreign. That didn't work. Nick, I think may have caught wind of my "breakdown" the day before and may have taken a little pity on me by removing a piece of the route so that it would be a little bit more manageable for me.

At the end of the day, it didn't turn out to be so bad. I got turned around a bit within corporate parks and witnessed temporary COVID-19 test sites being erected in the odd parking lot here and there. I forced myself to slow down as, I was at the point where this job may allow me to write about it, and it may allow me to experience new things and meet new people but, I can't allow it to kill me. I'd reached the point where, if I get it done, I get it done. If I don't and it's not good enough, well then, I guess they'll have to once again advertise the "Part-time" job opening with Indeed.

Chapter 17

I was actually done by 3:30pm. I was concerned that, if I went back to the office now, I'd just be sent back out to do more. But, I couldn't just sit there. The beaconing GPS scanner will surely send out a signal to Big Brother reporting that I am stationary or, not moving along the route in which I was supposed to.

I decided that I had no choice but to go back to the office. As luck would have it, I wasn't sent back out and I finished the end of day sort and was clocked out by 4pm. Unheard of. But, I wasn't complaining.

But it speaks to the dilemma I had previously touched on where, the incentive should be to want to get the day's work done early and the reward for that would be to allow the worker to then secure for the day and feel fulfilled that they succeeded in their job responsibilities. What is the incentive to complete your work early, only to be given more work from someone who hasn't completed their responsibilities?

Once comfortable enough, I began to get a better feeling of how long things will take me and, at times, I throttled-up and throttled-back so that I could "be done" and back to the office at a time where, after careful assessment of what day of the week it was, whether there'd be a good chance to be sent back out or to just, finish up. 5:00pm seemed a good target time to return to the office as, it gave me a half hour over time on most days and, depending on the day of the week, might be considered too late in the day to be sent back out. So, I tried to target 5pm on most days. But, if I had my way, I'd like to get done as fast as possible and bang out at 3pm and go home.

The next day I was on Jeremy's route. This is the route that I had done my Shadow day on and I figured, even though it had been three months since I'd been on that route, there'd at least be some familiarity of the flow. Jeremy was off that day and I was tagged as the fill-in. It would have been ok, I thought, except that, whoever cased the mail somehow screwed it all up. When I got out on the street, I was immediately messed up because of the erratic way that everything was cased.

Once out on the street, I couldn't make the connection to what we did on Shadow day. At that point, I was just in it for the ride-along and wasn't observing with the "mail carriers" eye that I probably should have been. I passed-over an entire apartment complex. I was, in fact, following the mail but, as I said, it was cased improperly and I followed the mail to the other side of town. When Tina called to ask how I was doing and where I was, she was shocked that I was at a point on the route at a time that I shouldn't be.

"You did the 8th street apartments already?"

"What 8th street apartments?"

"The apartments you were supposed to do after the bla, bla, bla…!?"

Again, without trying to rat someone out, I tried to convey that the mail casing was all messed up and, I guess that the 8th street apartment were there somewhere in the truck but, no I hadn't gotten to them yet.

"Ok, I'm sending someone out to help!"

Here we go again, I thought.

I had been at another apartment complex that again had very odd number sequences but, within that complex was a high rise complex comprising of 6 flours that had a large cluster box within the wall in an alcove of the building's lobby.

Chapter 17

I like these types of deliveries, sort of like that of the Nursing Home, where you can cordon off the area and just, “do your thing” without interruption or contamination.

The arrow key was needed to gain access to the lobby and that presented its own obstacle as, in similar fashion to opening a gate, there is a time factor to when the key triggers the door tumblers to unlock and, when they reengage to lock back up again.

The intercom box, and therefore, the arrow key slot seemed to me to be a good distance from the entry door and when I twisted the arrow key, and, hearing the buzzer sound that triggers the door lock to release, by the time I removed the arrow key and walked to the door, the buzzer had stopped and, therefore the door had relocked. And the mail carrier dance continued.

The arrow key is fastened to a chain approximately three feet long. I positioned the tubs of mail just in front of the door and moved back into position in front of the intercom box. I twisted the key, buzzer sounds, and shuffled to the right with the key still in the keyhole, swung the door open with one outstretched arm and soccer-balled the tubs of mail into position to hold the doors open using a sweet shuffle pass the likes of which Pele’ would have been impressed. Of course, I think I pulled something in my groin doing it but, the ball’s in the back of the net so, it was worth it!

I remove the key and grab the tubs of mail and I’m in. I do the deliveries at the boxes without a hitch and only have three parcels to deliver at the front doors of the residences as, they were all too big to fit in the boxes.

I was thrilled to see that all three parcels were on the 5th floor. I squirreled the empty tubs of mail in the corner of the lobby to be picked up on my way out and I enter the elevator and stab at the 5th floor button.

Once on the 5th floor, I exit the elevator, which is positioned at the center of the building's expanse, and I pick a direction and walk along the outer hallway with one side exposed to the open air. The three packages were to be delivered to apartments, 519, 523, and 532. I continued walking, looking for these numbers. I couldn't find the numbers to the apartments. Learning my lesson about trying to make sense of the numbering sequence schemes around these parts, I just dismissed it and figured that they must be in the other direction from the elevator and I backtracked.

Nope, none of the apartments were there! I stood there, again, in that all too familiar "lost stance" that I had come to adopt on this job, trying to figure it out. I'm pretty certain that there was only one entrance and exit door to the elevators as I'm aware that, especially in hotels, there may be apposing doors within the elevator to allow access to the other side of a building and I wondered if I missed it somehow. Perhaps there's another side of this building and the needed apartments are on that side.

I go back to the elevator and get in but, I confirm that there is only one way in and one way out. I thought to go back down to the lobby and perhaps there is some sort of directory present where I could ascertain where these apartments might be located. But again, I was dumbfounded at the effort needed in simply finding an address, much less deliver something to it.

On my way down to the lobby I just now take notice of a hand-written sign taped to the control bank of the elevator which reads, "Delivery personnel, please be advised that ALL of the apartments in our building begin with the number 5! You may find the appropriate apartment number by referring to the second number for the floor and the third number for the specific apartment. Thank you".

Huh???? Why the hell would someone do that?

So, I have packages for 519, 523, and 532; the normal delivery method is to work from top to bottom and I guess I had to go to the third floor for 532! Ya follow? I get to the third floor and do the walk around again and there it is, 532! I deliver and, seeing that I now had to go the second floor to delivery 523, I take the stairs. 523 now delivered. 519, first floor, I again take the stairs. But, upon exiting the stair well on the first floor, I find myself on the outside of the building's secure perimeter. And, of course, I'm all the way at the end of the building and I now must walk back to the center span where the locked doors were and elevator is, inside.

As I reach the front doors of the building, I see that Robinson is there, leaning up against his LLV, thumbing his phone, waiting for me. He had been sent to help me out again. As he looked at me, he didn't say anything but I could tell he was wondering where the hell I was coming from. He sees the lone package in my hand and, not looking up from his phone said, "Oh, by the way, all of the apartments in this building start with a 5!".

Really?

I arrow key back in, take the elevator to the first floor, deliver the parcel and come back down with my head spinning again.

Robinson takes all of the 8th street apartments that I hadn't done and left me with the last bit of the route; another nursing home. I pull up to the nursing home with a massive amount of mail and parcels to be delivered. I have a ProMaster and so, I slide open the side door. I retrieve the U-boat cart from inside the lobby after having my temperature taken and I'm now back in front of the home and I position the U-boat just so I can haul out of the ProMaster all of the tubs of smaller parcels, the trays of mail and the larger parcels stacked on top of the whole mess.

An old woman zips up to me on one of those scooters and said, "Excuse me, do you have anything for Brooks? B…R…O…O…."

I said, motioning to the mountain of mess before me, "Ma'am I wouldn't know until I delivery it!"

This is a repeated question that I always found entertaining during my travels; "Anything for me?"

Who the hell are you?

Again, the regular carrier who's been doing the same route for years probably does have a handle and good memory of actual names on a route and, they may even have absorbed the fact that today, during casing, they may have seen something that goes to a certain name and has somehow retained that information, should anyone ask. But, for the fill-in who is barely keeping their head above water just finding an address and who probably didn't even case the mail, this question becomes humorous as, we have no idea who YOU are and we certainly have no idea if you have any mail whatsoever! And even if we did, its packed away so deep within the trays of mail, there's no retrieving it unless it's done in a systematic way in which it is supposed to be delivered.

I felt bad that I sort of snapped at the lady. Everyone has seen YouTube videos or news reports of delivery people approaching a home in a huff and delivering a package or a piece of mail in ways that give people pause but, you need to understand that at any given time during a delivery route, the carrier may just have had enough and is one ridiculous question away from losing it. Of course, no different than any other customer service job. And, it's not an excuse, just an explanation. It's the dynamic range that puts a magnifying glass on this situation where, most people think that the job is really just driving around and bringing a box to a residence with a smile. How could anyone have a pissy attitude while performing those duties? Well, you could say that about any job, couldn't you?

I've had to remind myself that people would like to perceive the delivery of an item as something which is cared for by an individual who is mindful of the importance of the item to the recipient and is single-handedly transporting it from its point of origination to the customer with eager hands. In fact, it all just becomes a fish frenzy blur as you try to get the truck empty as fast as you can. And sometimes, patience is stretched to the point of being a tad rude.

I delivered to the Nursing Home as fast as I could. Was there something for Brooks? I have no idea! And I got out of there without taking a full, deep breath.

To further report on my state of mind at this point, I needed to return a personal package for something that had been ordered online weeks earlier and I had printed the return shipping label provided to me. Easy, I though, I'm not to report to work until 10am the next day, I'll just go over to the Post Office customer service desk a little earlier, which was located in the strip mall adjacent to the annex, and send it out and then go to work.

I'd been around for a while at this point and, while my name probably wasn't on the tip of people's tongues, I was identifiable.

The clerks see me enter the Post Office customer area and kiddingly say, "You're in the wrong place!"

I said, "Oh no, I'm here on official personal business! I just need to mail this out. I have the prepaid return mailing label affixed and all ready to go."

"Not here you're not!"

What did I do now? I wondered.

"Why not?"

Pointing at my package the clerk said, "That's a UPS label, not USPS!"

Sighh… You'd think I would have picked up on something like that by now!?

What is causing my mind to be disjointed beyond the rigors of the job itself, is the inconsistent work schedule. I can't stress enough how much of an ill affect it has on me. Perhaps I'm an creature of habit or that my military training had such a lasting effect of being so highly regimented, that I need to move in laser guided precision ways or, as my wife might suggest, I'm just an old man who can't adapt. Either way, I need to know what I'm doing in the immediate and near future in order to be productive.

For this upcoming week, I was scheduled to have off the Wednesday and Thursday. Two days back to back! They're not Saturday and Sunday but, I'll take it. Great, I can already plan the things that I need to do personally and around the house for those two days. That's how I have to do things.

I was to report on that Monday at 8am for a normal day. I show up and was told to deliver parcel's for route 33 (for which there were many) and then go back to the office to pick up the mail, which will be cased for me by then.

Chapter 17

I completed the delivery of the parcels and was back to the office by 10:30am. I was surprised that no one had called me prior to that to tell me to come back and pick up the mail as they normally would by say, 9:30am or the latest, 10:00am but, I was happy that I was actually able to complete something by delivering all of the parcels.

When I returned to the office, I was told to take the rest of the day off! Not being very confident with myself lately, I surely thought it was because I had done something so offensive that I was relieved of my duties. Was this the first salvo in being let go? A girl can dream!

It turned out that, there was a schedule conflict and, I wasn't needed for the day. But, as I was counting on having that Wednesday and Thursday off to do things that I scheduled, I was told to come in the next day (Tuesday), off on Wednesday and then, come in on the Thursday. There goes two days in a row and everything I had planned for Thursday.

Tuesday and Wednesday come and go and there I am, making ready to go to work on Thursday when I receive the text to take the day off and to come in the next day (Friday)! The USPS is inconsistent in its employee scheduling that one wonders how anything gets from point A to point B at all!

I wondered what was the source of the inconsistency. I'm sure that there are many, many things to be considered when scheduling in the way that they have the employees designated. And, perhaps, this is what was meant by "Part-time" when the job was advertised. In other words, the employee will work some of "this" time and some of "that" time but, "we just don't know when that'll be, until we know. And then we'll let you know."

I considered that COVID-19 is having a major financial impact on the Postal Service. It's been reported that the Postal Service will run out of money soon and I've heard different times for when this might occur. Of course, I also heard that it was going to shut down in April and I guess that didn't happen. I wondered if they are now beginning to cut hours because of the pandemic and the low hanging fruit (me being one of them) are the first to feel the pinch. Pinch or no pinch, it would be nice to get a couple of days off in a row.

I also considered the fact that, having surpassed the three month probationary period, I was due to receive a uniform stipend of $535. Things being so tight, I wondered if they were aware that I was to receive the $535 and to make the balancing of finances looked a little better, to short some hours in an effort to borrow from Paul to pay Peter.

If that was the case, since no one can remember my name anyway, I'll gladly be Peter in this scenario.

Chapter 18 – Cadaver Inc.

In 1994, Jeff Bezos left his job as a vice-president at a Wall St. firm and moved to Seattle, Washington to rethink his future and to try to forge a plan which might take advantage of the impending internet boom. After reading a report that projected internet sales growth of 2,300%, he created a list of what he thought would sell the best via the internet and soon narrowed the list down to five; CDs, computer hardware, computer software, videos and books. However, he decided that the company's initial offering would be books exclusively because of the large worldwide demand for literature, the low unit price for, and the huge number of titles available in print.

Bezos decided on the name for his company as Amazon after initially rejecting his original name of "Cadabra" (as in Abra Cadabra), after a lawyer he consulted with misinterpreted the name to be "Cadaver"!

He considered that Amazon sounded exotic and different, just as he had envisioned his internet company to be. The Amazon River, he reasoned, was the biggest river in the world and, he planned to make his online store the biggest bookstore in the world.

In 1997, Barnes & Nobles (a mainstay in the brick & mortar book resale world), sued Amazon, alleging that its claim to be "the world's largest bookstore" was false because Barnes & Noble claimed that Amazon wasn't really a bookstore at all, rather, it was a book broker. The suit was settled out of court and Amazon continued to make the claim.

On June 19, 2000, Amazon's logo was updated to the present curved arrow leading from the "A" to the "Z" in the word "Amazon" to represent that the company had now carried every product from A to Z, with the arrow shaped like a smile.

As I enter the office today, my fourteenth straight Amazon Sunday, I was gob smacked with the amount of parcels in need of delivery. They were piled high and stretched across the entire office floor. I guess there's no easy Sunday. I was already feeling almost completely drained like a cell phone with one bar left. After seeing what was in store for me for the day, my battery bar dipped into "Shutdown" mode.

I almost walked off the job. I fantasized that I would simply unharness the scanner from the belt, undo the arrow key tethered to the belt loop, dig the vehicle's keys from my pocket, take my postal ID from around my neck and place them gently down somewhere and walk out without saying a word to anyone!

I heard from the regular carrier that it was equivalent to the Holiday Season, and we were only in May. The amount of parcels that were piled up from Amazon, UPS, FedEx and all of the regular USPS parcels (which included the giant, Walmart) was monumental!

It's not hard to cultivate a poor attitude over this situation as, USPS has made contractual agreements with these companies to deliver to the "last mile" of the delivery journey. Most of these delivery companies don't provide Sunday delivery services, except in special circumstances such as Amazon's Prime Delivery service. The COVID-19 pandemic has stretched out available manpower to its thinnest as employees are either out of the office due to being exposed to the virus and needing to quarantine for two weeks or, actually have the virus itself. My paranoia also tells me that these delivery services know that the USPS is there to pick up their pieces that don't get delivered during the week, and may, "dog it", knowing that, what they don't get done, the USPS will.

Oddly, as I write this, I just received a news blast on my phone reporting that NY Representative Alexandria Ocasio-Cortez called Amazon jobs a "scam" because some workers have struggled to pay bills. She makes this claim because she feels that Amazon's jobs are not creating financial security for its workers. "A job that leaves you homeless and on food stamps isn't a job. It's a scam.!", she said. Ocasio-Cortez was referencing a "Bloomberg News" report that detailed the many Amazon warehouse workers who were struggling to pay bills, with as many as 4,000 employees on food stamps. The report said that Amazon has turned logistics work from a professional career option to "entry-level" work for many and that safety conditions in its warehouses have failed to keep pace with its growing business.

In March of 2020, some workers in the Staten Island, NY warehouse staged a "walkout" in protest of the poor health situation at their workplace amidst the pandemic. One of the organizers was first put on quarantine without anyone else being quarantined at that time and later, dismissed from the company altogether.

This added to the dilemma of increasing the amount of parcels to be delivered by the USPS. The extra business is certainly good for the USPS as a business, as it does make up for the lost revenue of the continually declining First Class postage but, because of it, its stretching the USPS workforce to the point of snapping.

The further problem with this is that the pandemic has also had the same effect on the USPS and the amount of carriers available to work on a Sunday. And to further my personal frustration was the fact that, once again, I was left with the lion's share of the bunch. While everyone huffed and puffed at the amount of parcels to be delivered that day, while doing the load truck feature out in the parking lot, I'd hear various carriers shout their load for the day; "65 going out!", "Another 80 parcel day!", "I've got it easy, only 53!". And there I sit with a count of 152! It was the same deal for the last two weeks. Am I doing such a bang-up job that they feel that I can handle the extra load? That can't be it because, every time I go out with this much, invariably, they have to send one (or two or three) carriers out to help me out.

I actually began to think that it was better to be loaded down initially with the very most parcels to be delivered because, there's just no way that one person was going to deliver that many and, after a certain period of time, help would be sent to take away the bulk of what I had. If I went out with a small number of parcels, I'd get that done and get back to the office and I'D be the one to be sent out to help someone else with the large number of parcels.

There's no real incentive to get the bulk of the job done. Perhaps if they paid a carrier per piece delivered on top of a salary, there'd be more of an incentive to get things done faster. But, there's no way to make this sort of suggestion either. If there is a suggestion box ("And if used, you'll get a $100 gift card to the Outback restaurant"), I'm certainly under no knowledge of where it is or how to go about making such suggestions.

And, to add insult to injury, while trying to load all of these parcels into the truck, just about everyone who passes by feels the need to suggest on the best way to handle it. “You should start “here” and then move to “there”. Here, let me show you”! or “If I were you I’d mark the parcels like this; here let me show you!” And none of them realize that they are literally undoing what the last “expert” had just suggested that I do. What ended up happening is that the entire load-in was FUBAR!

At a certain point in the delivery day, where it was time to check up on the status of everyone, and it gets to me, and I’ve only delivered a certain amount, chalk it up to the “help” that I received at the load-in. If you protest to those offering their advice and claim that, the only way that you could digest a better of way executing this procedure is to do it your own way and make small adjustments along the way in improvement, all you’ll get is a hands up “Hey, I’m just trying to help!”.

If you want to help me, take 25 parcels from me!

Still, the situation was “killing” everyone and Amazon’s original name might have been more appropriate at this point as “Cadaver”!

Speaking once again to that overall feeling of disorientation, I wasn’t supposed to go into work the next day until 10am. And I planned for it once again in my own personal way. Due to my poor sleeping habits, it’s always been a struggle to live with that constant feeling of tiredness during the day due to lack of sleep. I actually had a sleep study done and, after all the probes have been removed, the official medical diagnosis is, “You’re a light sleeper. Stop thinking so much!”

Chapter 18

Thanks Doc, how much do I owe you for that life altering advise?

I'd been prescribed a variety of medication to help get my sleep schedule on a track where the body's internal clock might want to decide to mimic it but, I never liked taking any medication for this purpose in the long term. A lot of it causes a headache the next day so bad that, not sleeping might be the better alternative.

So, if and when I decide to take a sleep aid, I try to forecast what is in store for the following day and if I didn't have to be up and at it early or, not operating heavy machinery, I might go ahead and help myself get a once per week decent sleep (albeit drug induced) and take something for the cause.

I slept "ok" (It's never great) and sat holding my head over my cup of coffee when the phone beacons. "Come in as soon as you can!" It was 7:45am.

So much for nursing my drug induced sleep hangover! I ready myself for the day as best I can and head to the office, always feeling like I'm back on my heels.

Upon showing up to work I was told that I had to case and delivery a whole route that I had not been on yet. Of course, I didn't get there until about 8:30am and so, I was already behind and the day hadn't even begun yet. My head pounded behind my eyes and every little noise sent my whole nervous system into a panic. This is going to be one for the books, I thought.

I was casing the mail and, almost done, needed to then case in the DPS (Delivery Point Sequence) with the "regular" mail, which is only generally sorted per the local district at the upstream postal distribution center. Tina came to me and asked, "Did you move to street yet?".

I thought, of course I hadn't; or I wouldn't be standing here. But apparently, during the morning, a supervisor gives you a "leave time" where, based on the amount of DPS, you are expected to leave the office to begin delivery. This NEVER happens. At least, I never saw it happen while I was there.

The "leave time" is the time calculated without sorting in the DPS with the "regular" mail. I'm still not sure how they can determine a time if the Flats aren't sorted per route, but, I guess they have their ways.

Tina tells me that I'm supposed to move to street on the time clock by the time given, regardless of if you are actually ready to go out on the street, or else it is reflected in job performance. I wasn't really concerned with a record of my job performance at this point as I was just trying to survive. She further explained that, "We let you case the DPS as a courtesy so you can go faster but, you have to be sure that the regular mail is cased first and you are swiped to the street at the time you're given."

So, I stopped what I was doing and went over to the clock and programmed it to read that I was now moving from the office to the street and I slid my electronic card across, capturing the data. I then went back to the desk and continued sorting the DPS in with the regular mail, something that I witnessed every carrier in the building doing.

I found it odd that it would be considered a "courtesy" to allow a carrier to sort the DPS in with the regular mail if, in fact, it provides for a faster delivery. If it does, then the courtesy goes to the USPS and not the carrier. The carrier completes the route faster, spend less time on the payroll, thereby saving the USPS money. It seemed to smack of contradiction. It would appear to me that, if, casing-in DPS with the regular mail allows the carrier to go faster, casing in DPS should be mandatory, not a courtesy!

But, it would appear that this is just another incident of the USPS operating in certain ways because, "That's the way it's always been done!"

Finally on the street and with a little fresh air, the head started to clear. As with many occasions, today had me come across yet another retired Postal worker. This one, Gus, was a nice guy from Cape Cod. He asked how long I was on the job and I conveyed to him that I had only been on for four months. He said that he retired after 26 years on the job and I could see that he could barely walk. His legs were all banged up to the point where he could barely stand still and straight, much less walk.

He asked how much I was making and when I told him "17 and change" he made the face where you take your lower lip and drive it up into your upper lip as if to say, "Not bad!". I still was having a hard time getting used to the financial skewing of Florida salaries compared with up north. I felt like I was hardly making anything at all. And frankly, I felt that I have never worked so hard while earning so little before in my life. And that includes a stint of dish washing at a Chinese restaurant while in High School.

As with the others, Gus had a default stance of bashing the USPS. "They're so fucked up these days. Didn't used to be. In the 80's I was making 50K a year! Mostly due to double overtime and that was because (he lowers his voice and leans in…) these fucking women are so fucking lazy. I had to pick up their slack!"

He went on and on about how the USPS is all kinds of messed up, when I interjected that I was only planning on staying with the job for a short while. He jumped in and said, "Ohhhh.....you should stick with it. It's good benefits!"

I found it amusing again, that most of the ex-Postal employees are quick to bash the establishment but, want YOU to stick with it. As in, misery-loves-company type of thing.

But, true enough, when you are a regular carrier, you do have the options to choose a health care plan that may benefit the individual as they see fit but, the new carrier has no such benefits other than what is cost prohibitive. It's just odd that the dynamic of the job's responsibilities, being so physical, is not compensated in any way as a new employee. If someone should go down, like a death in Disneyworld, they just hose it down and keep it moving!

The financial agreements that the USPS has with Amazon, UPS, FedEx etc., doesn't seem to merit compensating the very people who are carrying out the job responsibilities to garnish said finances. It's forever the working man's argument.

Chapter 19 - Penalty

While casing a route on a particular day, the clerk rolled her cart by and stopped at me to assigned to me "accountables". Accountables are anything that, well, needs to be accountable for. Priority Mail Express, special service mail such as Certified Mail or, anything that needs a cash collection on delivery, is an accountable.

The carrier needs to take possession of the item in need of delivery and sign for it. So that when returning to the office, should anything negative happen with the delivery, the carrier is then identified as the person who was in possession of it last.

On this day, there was no parcel to deliver but, it was determined that a parcel had been previously delivered to an address where there was postage due. I was tasked with going to the address and collecting the money.

This particular address wasn't even part of the route that I was on for that day and so, I had to deviate from the route to get to the address. I've explained how just putting gas into the vehicle can cause a major delay in the day's delivery so, deviating from a route to find an address to collect money can be quite a time drain.

I find the address and was concerned because, the area didn't look inhabited. I drove around the small circular building and, while I did see a couple of cars in the parking lot, it still didn't look like the place had clientele coming and going. Again, all the windows and doors were all reflective mirrored to deflect the sun so, I couldn't see anything inside.

This was definitely the address so, I parked and went to investigate. The front door was open and it was dark in the lobby. There were two "businesses" at either end of the hall way which clearly looked vacant. Doors were locked, lights out and not much of furniture or anything within the offices. There was a lone bench in the lobby and I sat down to call the office to see if I could get further information. Tick-Tock…

I decided a text might be the better way to go since I could barely hear anything from the other end when calling into the office, and I sent Nick a text explaining the situation. While I waited for a reply, a door opens (that didn't even look like it was a door) and a guy walks by and asks if he could help me. I described the address that I was looking for and he confirmed that I was in the right place. I explained that I was there to collect $0.62 on a previously delivery parcel for postage due.

He rolled his eyes and told me to go with him. Up the stairs we went and he explained that they had recently moved from the lower level to the upper level of the building, that's why things looks all disheveled. He brings me to a girl who seemed to be working some sort of reception (and anything else he needs done) job and instructed her to give me $0.62. Meanwhile, in my mind, this was taking wayyyy to long. As I've said, this whole mail delivery deal has to feel like a finely tuned choreographed dance where each partner is moving in the right direction at the exact right time. What I'm doing is like watching two elephants mate; just slow and sloppy!

While the girl was rooting around in her desk, in her purse, then the middle drawer of the desk where everyone keeps change, the guy was huffing and puffing and asked me, "How much do you get paid to come here to collect $0.62?" "Not much", I replied. He continued, "The money spent to collect a little bit of money is unbelievable! The effort and time, the vehicle, the gas…to get $0.62!? That's why the Post Office should be shut down! And they keep asking the government for money!"

Not that I was in a position to argue, he was the customer after all and, you know what they say about customers? And aside from the unnecessary beratement, I couldn't argue. He had a point. I'm sure like many, I've received checks in the mail for $0.02 for something or other and wondered about all the effort made to get that 2 cents to me. Primarily, $0.55 had to be paid for postage to send me $0.02! Not to mention how many bits and pieces of an administrative team were involved in identifying and processing that 2 cents. One has to wonder about such inefficiencies. Certainly, "the books need to be closed" on certain financial transactions but still…

The girl wasn't able to come up with the $0.62 and the guy, now full of piss and vinegar said, "Alright, come with me!" Tick-tock…

He takes me back down the stairs and out to his car in the parking lot. It was then that I had another epiphany and saw my place within the universe. I'm 58 years old and I'm standing in an almost vacant parking lot in the South Florida sun burning a hole through me like I used to do to ants with a magnifying glass, watching the crack of some guys ass as he's bent over his center console of his car, looking for 62 cents!

Chapter 19

Well, I thought, THIS wasn't really what I had in mind when I signed up for this shit! My parents would have been so proud.

He unravels himself from the car and almost sarcastically drops coins of varying denominations into my hand one at a time, clink…clink…clink…clink…to add up to $0.62.

"Alright?", he says.

"Thank you", I reply. And we both parted company, each shaking our heads for our own personal reasons. After that, I moved to the original route to begin to deliver what was assigned to me.

The following day the office manager addressed the masses of carriers in the morning before they went out for the day. He was addressing the issue of some who are taking advantage of over time. He was asking that people try to be reasonable in their requests for overtime.

I thought, really? They're asking US to be reasonable? Doesn't it work both ways? This coming Sunday will be my 15th straight working Sunday. Let's talk about being reasonable some more, shall we?

The issue here is one that I've always been aware of but was one that was really driven home while working for the USPS. This "overtime syndrome" is a fascinating one. Time is money, that's for sure. But it works on a couple of very different levels. On the one hand, the business wants their employees and machinery to work in the most efficient way so that the most work is completed in the shortest amount of time, saving money for the company. This isn't meant for USPS exclusively of course, it's just common sense. However, from the workers point of view, some might want the task at hand to extend to a point where the completion of the task is delayed, increasing the financial compensation based on time served.

I've run across this a few times in my life, when first working as an hourly worker and coming to that anxious point where I felt that I should be compensated more for the work that I was accomplishing. I was told in no uncertain terms that it's not going to happen but, there's overtime available "if you need money".

"If I need money?" What does that mean? Did he think that I was there because I had nothing better to do? However, the trade in time for money wasn't ringing true to me in that instance. Of course, I thought, I could work MORE to get MORE money! I mean, I could work twenty four hours a day and I'd be making more money, wouldn't I? That's not what the ask is. I'm seeking a higher level of compensation based on the higher level of work in which I am giving back. Sounded simple to me but, as with most relationships, you reach an impasse in garnishing what you perceive as a proper level of respectful satisfaction for your efforts and, you part company for greener pastures.

It appeared to me that, on the one hand, there were carriers who, once they've reached a more solid foundation as a career carrier, must actually be put on a physical list of NO overtime. It appeared to be a reverse (and negative) methodology to me. It reminded me of when, there used to be in existence these very large books called "Telephone Books". They were big and very heavy. I know, I used to deliver them door to door. In these books were listed everyone's name and phone number that had an account with the telephone company. If you had an account, you were listed in the book for all to see. If you didn't want to be listed, you had to pay to have your name and number removed from being listed in the book!

Wouldn't it make more sense that you would have to pay to have a printing press stamp your name and phone number into tens of thousands of heavy books rather than have it left off? I mean, if I wanted my name tattooed onto skin, I have to pay someone for that! Imagine having to pay a tattoo artist NOT to tattoo your name somewhere?

And further, wouldn't it make more sense that everyone in the Postal Service be OFF the overtime list and if you wanted overtime, you must have to be physically put on THAT list?

Again, it's probably just my odd ways of looking at things.

There definitely seemed to me to be a general consensus that overtime was good and something that most were looking to do, to "Get that money!". Still, perhaps if the USPS were to play a little hardball with Amazon and push back and increase the compensation that Amazon pays the USPS for being bailed out for delivering its packages, general starting wage for a Postal worker might be a little more north of seventeen bucks and there wouldn't be such a rush and "unreasonability" in asking for more overtime.

Perhaps I'm wrong. Perhaps the "overtime syndrome" has no bounds and, no matter how much a person makes, they'd be apt to trade even more of their time for more money.

What I found interesting and, frankly, a bit insulting, is when being forced to work more than 10 hours per day, it is paid at double time the base salary but, on your paystub, it breaks down your hours worked and it will itemize to the minute just how many straight hours you've worked, how many overtime hours you've work and for those minutes and hours in which you've worked over ten hours in a day, it lists it as "Penalty" overtime.

It's such a negative way of displaying ones effort. You're tired, you're beaten to a pulp, your wife's about to leave you because you're never home, even the dog sees you come home and gives you a "whatever..." look and, to the USPS, you've work so much that, you need to be penalized!

I just assume they list the hours worked over ten per day as, "Amazing" overtime or, "Going The Extra Mile for the Last Mile" overtime. Something a little more positive!

During COVID-19, the government has approved a stimulus package to be distributed to its citizens. Twelve hundred dollars were to be distributed to those making a base salary of less than $99,000. Those who've electronically filed their income taxes in the past received a government check in this amount faster than those who may have filed their taxes in other, slower ways.

While on my route for the day, a woman stopped me and asked if I knew where her stimulus check was. She was confused because her pension check was automatically deposited into her account and noticed that she hadn't seen the stimulus money deposited into her account as of yet and wondered if I might have further information. She wondered if they (the government) were, by default, sending out paper checks regardless of how income taxes were filed or how her pension was distributed. And clearly, since I control the mail, I must have her check.

I actually had a reasonable answer for her in that I was able to ascertain the proper website to go to and have the ability to check on the status (with proper identification) of their distribution and also offered that, should a paper check be targeted for her, she might want to see where it might be going based on her cyclical living arrangements as she was a snowbird and lived at different residences at different times of the year.

And, of course, I couldn't just leave this alone in my mind. As I continued with the route, in my mind, I questioned the morality if someone who is retired and on a fixed income and receiving a pension should even qualify to receive a stimulus check? They weren't out anything. They weren't put on furlough, they didn't lose a job. It's as if nothing happened. Perhaps she wasn't eligible and that explains why she hadn't gotten one at that point.

Ending the day, I was finishing up with distributing the returned mail from the route and settling up, returning all the paraphernalia that belonged to the office. I tried to give the filthy $0.62 that I so heroically salvaged for the USPS, to the supervisor on duty and he backed away like I was about to throw acid on him and said, "Don't give to me. I don't want it! Give it to the clerk!". I seek out the clerk and give her the money and close the storied cycle of the missing $0.62. You're welcome America!

As I went to clock out for the day, the acting supervisor sees and tells me to hurry up and swipe out because I'm coming up on overtime. I didn't see the big deal. I was still at work. It takes me whatever it takes me to process my exiting and whatever it ends up saying on the clock is whatever, and, that's what I expect to be paid for. I clocked out and it a yielded a one minute overtime result. That's an extra $0.44 in my pocket! Pretax, of course. If the red lights in South Florida were four minutes instead of five, I could've saved the Postal Service some money that day.

With the upcoming Memorial Day weekend, I asked what time I should show up. Enzo didn't know and was told to ask Larry. I asked Larry and he smugly said, "I don't know, I'll be home watching TV!".

Ok, no one has the answer. It's a major holiday after yet another Amazon Sunday, I'll assume we'll start at 8am, like normal.

At 7:50am while driving to the office I get a call asking where I am. "I'm driving to work!".

"We start at 7am!"

"I tried finding out from supervisors what time to start on Memorial Day and no one knew. So, I assumed 8am."

"It's 7am! Get here as soon as you can. Everyone has left the office already."

And so, not only am I working yet another holiday, I'm already behind in the process. A minute later I receive a call from Bruna asking where I am.

What's it to her?, I thought. Oh, right, because if I don't show up, she'll be saddled with more. But, it's odd that there's no cohesive pecking order in this situation. There was a disconnect in informing the work force on what time we are starting that day and, when the confusion is apparent, there should be a point of contact to investigate the situation. Everyone feels that they can get involved.

I was at the point of being done with this mission anyway and just wanted to turn around and go home.

And then there's the day after a holiday again. Memorial Day is observed on a Monday. So, no mail is delivered on Sunday or Monday and the perfect storm occurs on that Tuesday where three days' worth of regular mail needs to be delivered plus, it's advo day and, if that wasn't enough, I'm put on a route that I had only been on once.

It was truly a disaster of a day. The worst yet. Almost five months into the job and it would appear that this situation is set up to fail. I'm convinced that, if you have a decent day where everything goes smoothly and there's little stress, it's an anomaly. Just wait, there'll be a disastrous day soon enough. As I've said, everyone at any job has bad days, that's not the point, it's the buildup of stress on little sleep or no down time to cultivate one's personal agenda.

And, again, if the perfect storm occurs literally in a storm, it makes for an extremely trying situation.

The tropical storm blew in that morning and didn't let up at all. Everything was soaking wet, including myself. On top of three days' worth of mail having to be delivered, the storm was slowing things down even more.

While opening one particular cluster box, a gust of wind took the door and threw it open with a violent bang. After pushing the balls of wet mail into the individual slots I tried closing the doors only to find that the metal hinge holding the door was bent out of shape by the aggressive opening by the wind and it prevented me from closing the door.

The rain was torrential and everything inside the cluster box was getting wet. I called into the office to explain but I could hardly hear from the sounds of the rain and the thunder. Because I was so late, I was told to keep going and that they'd send someone out to look at the box and to also help me with what I had left.

I just left the cluster box open and unlocked with rain pouring into it and moved on with the route. Between the overcast clouds and the fact that it was getting late in the day, it turned black as night. There's a little dome light in the cargo area of the ProMaster but, it is little help when it gets that dark and I could barely read addresses from the labels.

Finally, two carriers show up like the cavalry and we divvy up what I had left and we all went in our separate directions. We got it done but, it wasn't pretty by any stretch of the imagination. Word tends to get around about the prior days antic and I think it was commonly known that I had a day that makes a person really question the value of things.

I saw Jeremy the next day and I said, "Sorry, I really fucked up your route yesterday!"

He just shrugged and said, "It happens."

Others, I think, saw how much of a beaten man I was at that point and tried to offer solace in their own way; "It's gets better." or, my favorite, "Only thirty more years to go!"

How old do these people think I am? You think I'm doing this at 88 years old!?

I'm lucky if I make it another thirty days!

But I'm sure it's not seen that way. They tend not to look at things through YOUR eyes, but theirs. In their mind, they've been chipping away at that thirty year goal and, to them, everyone is on that same track and I'm viewed at being at the starting line, regardless of age.

Chapter 20 – 2-Ton Red Onion

I was finally scheduled to take 2-Ton training. This was almost done at my original drivers training as I had completed the LLV and ProMaster training so quickly. That didn't happen then and it's taken five months to get to the point of being trained on it now.

The 2-ton truck is a UPS looking truck which is mainly used for business parcel pickup. Tim was smart enough to mention, pretty much right out of the gate, that he needed a schedule that was more…accommodating…and, it was suggested that he get trained on the 2-Ton so that he can primarily take over its operation as, being assigned 2-ton duty means a more "business hours" type of operation.

He received the obstacle course training and then received the on-the-job training and then, became the main go-to guy for 2-ton operation. This was something that I was originally interested in but, by this time in the process, I really didn't care. I wasn't really looking forward to having to adapt to any more procedures based on the specialties of a given sub occupation. I was more looking forward to basically having a day off if I was to be assigned 2-ton training than, receiving the training and being put into operation itself.

The joke was on me again as, I was scheduled to go to West Palm Beach and report there for training at 7am and once the training was done, report back to Deerfield Beach for the normal day's work. I'm already behind and I haven't even left for the day.

What I found funny was that, I was given the wrong address. I'm expected to know every little stop on every route but, I can't count on getting the correct address on where to report for something. Pretty ironic.

I found where I needed to go and I met the trainer for the 2-ton vehicle and she was a very pleasant older lady. She, like Maggie during my training for the LLV and ProMaster, was very patient and safety minded. She went through each and every operation and safety feature for the 2-ton truck. And with this, there was no caveat about not backing up. You had to backup. You needed to back into loading docks in order to perform the bulk of business pickups. However, the beauty of these trucks was that they had a rear-facing camera to help with the process.

I'm pretty confident that I can pretty much drive anything on wheels and I wasn't really concerned about this as I have driven non-articulating trucks before. And my feelings were confirmed as, after the routine instructional presentation, I was throwing that 2-ton all over the obstacle course with little problem.

The whole morning was pretty uneventful and I wish that that was all there was to the day but, I had to still settle up in West Palm Beach and then make the 40 minute trip down to Deerfield Beach to start the day.

I got to the office at around 9:45am and I was given a piece of a route as they weren't sure at what time I'd be arriving, they had doled out everything to be sure it could be completed that day.

I did the small piece of the route and, chalking it up to "Murphy's Law" that there'll always be something to go wrong, mixed in with the mail that day were these little post-card looking types of things that had to go to everyone. They were the size of about 4" by 5.5" and they were imprinted on the front with a handwritten message which read:

"I was trying to reach you about the possible sale of your business.

If you have ever considered selling, please contact me at:"

They were sized just so as to be annoying to be picked up and, together with the DPS and Flats to be delivered, it was maddening. The cards gave contact information with a telephone number and website and I had half a mind to reach out to them and complain. Once again, when you consider the job of mail delivery, this was not what was primarily on my mind. It just seemed like a gigantic waste of time and energy. But, as it was presorted First Class mail, the USPS was making money off of it so, deliver we must.

As with the advos themselves, I've had people ask me if it was possible to opt out of delivery for them. I had supposed that it was possible to have the persons address removed from the list of having one printed, but the fact is, the carriers just end up throwing one into every mail box. It's just easier. And, like those annoying cards, it has to be appreciated that a business has paid the USPS postage for delivery of such things and, we'd be remis in agreement of contract had we just not delivered them.

Back to the office early from this short piece, I was told to go with Tim for the rest of the day and shadow him on the 2-Ton duties. That's a relief, I thought.

It was mid-afternoon and we still had to go out for pickups at certain times for certain locations. I didn't mind at all. I just sat in the hard jump seat in the front of the 2-ton and road along while Tim explained the process.

The main problem with being assigned 2-ton responsibilities is that, yes, while the 2-ton caters to that of normal business hours, that sort of creates a problem because, the first pick up from businesses might be at say, 10am and the carrier begins the day at 8am. They fill that time with something like, doing a piece of a route or going out to do deliveries for a regular route. The problem there is, once you go out, you never know what's going to happen by way of delay. And then, if you get back to the office late, you're then late to make your first 2-ton pick-up and the rest of the day, you're chasing yourself.

Same with in-between 2-ton pickup times; if you've made a pickup and returned back to the office with plenty of time to spare in between pickups, might as well send the carrier out to do a small piece of a route.

I knew that it was at a time of the day where Tim and I didn't have to worry about any of that and he just needed to show me the ropes on how to perform 2-ton duty. He had a clipboard with handwritten short-hand names of businesses. He was explaining the order in which we should go but, there always seemed to be some sort of exception ("We have to go here but, we can't because…" or "We should be doing a pickup there but, not today because…") again, just like with the various routes themselves, there always seems to be some sort of asterisk in the way, altering the way that things should normally be done for that specific day.

We got on our way but Tim said that, he hadn't had lunch yet (it was 2:30pm) and we're going to stop first so he can get a bite.

We pulled into a nearby Wawa in town. What's a Wawa? Well, let me tell ya…

Wawa, Inc., is a privately held company (much to my chagrin as, if it were public, I'd be all in!) that began in 1803 as an iron foundry in New Jersey. Toward the end of the 19th Century, owner George Wood took an interest in dairy farming and the family began a small processing plant in Wawa, Pennsylvania in 1902. The milk business was a huge success, due to its quality, cleanliness and "certified" process. As home delivery of milk began to decline in the early 1960s, Grahame Wood, George's grandson, opened the first Wawa Food Market in 1964 as an outlet for their dairy products.

Today, Wawa is an all day, every day, stop for fresh, built-to-order foods, beverages, coffee, fuel services, and surcharge-free ATMs. With a chain of more than 750 convenience retail stores (over 500 offering gasoline), Wawa stores started primarily in Pennsylvania and New Jersey (especially along the shore) and moved to neighboring Mid-Atlantic states of Delaware, Maryland, Virginia and now, Florida.

The stores offer a large fresh food service selection, including Wawa brands such as built-to-order hoagies, freshly brewed coffee, hot breakfast sandwiches, built-to-order specialty beverages, and an assortment of soups, sides and snacks.

The Wawa logo is a Native American word for the Canada Goose that was found in the Delaware Valley over 100 years ago. The original Dairy farm was built on land located in a rural section of Pennsylvania called Wawa. That is why they use the goose as the Wawa corporate logo.

Sounds like most run-of-the-mill service stations that sells "stuff for the road" but, not so. Wawa takes pride in it's cleanliness factor which was grandfathered from its Daily farm practices. And this is apparent when one walks into a Wawa. You don't feel this sense of disgust that you usually get when walking into a roadside service station mini-mart. Wawa is revered by most in New Jersey as it was a staple, the way 7/11's are for most of the country, only better! I, for one, am thrilled that the company followed me to Florida, primarily due to its "Delicatessen" existence.

I'm somewhat of a connoisseur of the sandwich arts. I've often said that my favorite meal is, the sandwich. Any sandwich, really but, it's the famed "Italian Combo" in which I seek the holy grail of sandwich perfection. This is something not the be taken lightly with a dismissive hand. Procuring the correct (fresh) ingredients and proper distribution in the correct ratios of meat to cheese to vegetable with proper vinegar and oil, herbs and spices, is paramount and similar to how I view the works of Michelangelo.

Since relocating to South Florida I am sadly disappointed in what I've found to be offered in this light. Wawa, at least, offers a wide variety of clean and fresh ingredients that lets a customer feel that they at least have a little say in what's going on. I've searched far and wide seeking a presentable "Italian Combo" and, I'm sad to report that, I've all but given up my search.

It's said that the bread is a major factor when it comes to sandwich building and I must say that it is a major contributor to the overall experience of the proper sandwich and also, here in South Florida, we have a problem with that to begin with. I won't even get on the whole bagel thing! Let's just say, it's just not right. I'm no baker and I can't speak intelligently on the proper chemical compounds that go toward the making of properly made hero bread, all I know is what's right. And the mark is sorely being missed here.

The ingredients, to me, aren't as important as how the thing is put together in total. Surely, there must be some sort of ham (smoked? No thank you!), salami (I prefer genoa), provolone cheese (again, not smoked. Please…), shredded iceberg lettuce, thinly sliced tomatoes (that have some taste.) and thinly sliced red onion.

Hold on, let's talk about THIS for a second! What…is…the…deal with red onions in South Florida? Can someone tell me?

I can't get anyone to put sliced red onion on a sandwich. It's very difficult to find it at all. What happened here? I'm to try and choke down these chunks of white or Spanish onion plopped indiscriminately onto my sandwich? Really? What am I, an animal?

I was in what appeared to be a very promising deli with a line of people queued out of the door. Not one for waiting in lines anymore but, I was on a mission. I took my place in line and observed. The line was moving pretty quickly for the amount of people crowded into this small area and, I was a little dismayed to witness that you are to place your order with one person, it is handed off to another person whose job it is to slice whatever protein is to go into your sandwich and is then, literally thrown to the next person in line in Seattle fish-market throwing style where, the construction of the sandwich would then take place.

I wasn't thrilled with how many people were involved in the construction of my sandwich but, I went with it. And then I witnessed once again the droppings of non-red onions on my multi-manhandled sandwich. I could take no more of this insanity. I asked, "Can I get sliced red onion on that instead?"

The server flat out refused my request. "We don't have any red onion!" He saw the disappointment and bewilderment on my face and offered, "Hey, I agree with you, I think red onion tastes better but.....that's not how they do it in Philly!"

Huh? What do I give a rats ass about how they do it Philadelphia?

I later found out that I was in some sort of chain deli originating in Philadelphia and, apparently, they don't deviate from the way that "they" do it. Fine but, I won't tell you how to make a cheesesteak, don't tell me how to make an "Italian Combo", deal?

I took my $15 sandwich and left and was already disappointed before I took one bite.

And if, when ordering an "Italian Combo", one more person asks if I want mayo on that.....I have very simple requests and yet, they can't seem to be met.

Back in the Postal Service's 2-ton vehicle;

...remember the Postal Service?...

...this is a book about the Postal Service...

...Tim tore open his plastic sealed, half triangle of a sandwich, choosing that route as, we didn't have time to even place a custom order and cramming it in as fast as you please as, there is also no time for savoring anything.

Luckily for me, that day I able to enjoy a nice leisurely lunch of about 4 four minutes while stopped at a typical South Florida red light. I watched as each lane took it's turn going through the intersection one at a time, affording enough time to cram down my own sandwich brought from home.

Finished with yet another gas station lunch, we were off on our route to pick up parcels from the various businesses in town. After a few stops of picking up bag after bag of prepackaged and prepaid postage of USPS boxes of a variety of sizes, it appeared to me that this was the way to go. Forget First Class mail, this bulk business mail seemed to be the money maker. We pulled into businesses of all types; hair products catering to African America Woman to a tassel manufacturing. No kidding, tassels! You know, the thing you move from one side of the hat to the other upon graduation. That's a business. No shit.

I'm no businessman but, all I know is, I'll bet that if I walked into a lending institution and asked for a business loan to start a business and I was asked what kind of business it was, and I replied, "I'm going to make tassels!", I'm pretty sure I'd be laughed right out of the office.

But, there is was, in full operation. As Tim handed box after box to me and I stacked them nicely within the 2-ton, I glanced down at the mailing labels attached to the boxes. These things were going to every corner of the country! Well, I guess tassels have to come from somewhere I supposed. If anything were to be thought to be made in China, you'd think that was a prime candidate? Nope, right there in Deerfield Beach, Florida, a major tassel manufacturer. Shows you what I know?

We continued going business to business and to my amazement, we filled the entire 2-ton truck to the brim. And that was the second round for Tim that day. We got back to the annex and unloaded our bounty and sorted as we did so. We had to sort the incoming parcels based on their destination and postage paid. We set up the corresponding bins and upon removal of the parcels from the truck, tried to stack neatly each box in the corresponding bin. At 6pm, a USPS tracker trailer backed into the annex and hauled all those bins away, along with all the mail that the carriers had brought back with them during the day.

Everything's in constant movement. When I hear talk of delays in the mail I have to say that, as first hand witness, if there is any delay whatsoever, it has zero to do with the local mail carrier or even the local Post Office. If there's a delay, there's some anomaly happening upstream or downstream of the local Post Office.

Chapter 21 – Dogs of War

On the sixteenth straight working Sunday, I questioned Larry, the supervisor in charge of uniforms, on how it was that I should obtain my uniforms? I'd been on the job for over five months at that point and, I apparently "made the cut" having completed my probationary period and therefore, been eligible to receive the $535 to be used for uniforms but, I'd heard nothing about it, nor had I received an additional $535 in my paycheck. The clothes that I had been wearing were basically falling off my body and, no matter how much you wash them, the generated sweat from the average day's offering altered the molecular make-up of the fibers, rendering it impossible to ever restore any semblance of pleasant odor.

"Hey Larry, got a question for ya!"

"Denied!"

(Dick…) "I guess that I'm supposed to get some sort of uniform allowance and be able to obtain uniforms at this point but, I have no idea how that's supposed to be done. Nick told me to ask you about it.

"I don't know, ask one of the regulars!"

Typical blow-hard of a supervisor. Just likes to yap, and when it comes time to actually do something, he retreats to all-to-familiar stance of "I can't be bothered".

Eh, as I've said, it's no-never mind to me. Frankly, these uniforms that I see people wearing look horrible. They just hang there with no thought of catering to an individual's body type. They'll all just boxy things that, when a little sweat is added to it, drape down on a body like a sack of potatoes. I'm not a fan of the colors either. Certainly, Blue and Gray harkens back to the wonderful Civil War era of our country but, along with the business model itself, can't the uniforms be updated as times goes by. Powder blue? White would be better. At least you could bleach the hell out it! So, frankly, I was in no rush to even get the uniforms but, I was occasionally prodded by some when they see me coming in at the end of a day with my salt-stained clothes looking like I'd just crawled across Death Valley on my stomach.

I wasn't about to go buy new clothes for the effort so, I figured that, if they want me in new clothes; they'd better come up with the uniform allowance. My stinky, sweaty line in the sand was drawn.

But the bottom line was, another Amazon Sunday had come and gone and this was my only opportunity to speak with the person who was in charge of uniforms and, he chose to sidestep the issue at this point.

The following day I was put on Mallory's route which I'd done portions of a couple of times at this point and was semi comfortable. However, this was a Monday and she felt that I needed some additional instruction. While she was describing special instructions for various addresses, Jarod was shouting something somewhere within the office. Jarod and Nick were engaged in some sort of heated argument. Nick turned to me (because I'm a sympathetic ear) and said, "Tom, did you ever see a man complain so much!". Jarod never stopped. He was going on about something or other that I couldn't quite pick up on. I just shrugged. Mallory, in reference to Jarod said, "…And he wonders why he's alone!".

A small window of social interaction that I found pleasing. There wasn't enough of that in my opinion. Not that I want to get into anyone's business, nor they in mine. But, what I felt was lacking at this work place was any show of personal empathy. Even in the military you find ways of stopping and asking about a person's life. Nothing too probing of course but, there can certainly be some sort of pleasant and jocular banter that delves slightly under the surface of "How many hours did you work last week?" or, "How many parcels did you deliver today?"

I had been out on Mallory's route before but, only on a Saturday when most businesses were closed. And this route had a lot of businesses. She did a very thorough job of explaining the finer points of the route and anything that was out of the ordinary that I should watch out for.

While casing the route, the morning clerk, Melinda, approached me with her cart of arrow keys and accountables at the ready to be distributed, asked me about Tim.

"Have you seen, uh, Claudio lately?

"Sorry, I don't know a Claudio."

"The guy…the tall guy…he started around the time you started?"

"Tim?"

"That's it! Tim. I can never remember his name."

Truly bizarre. Around here, they have first names that are slightly outside the realm of commonplace with Arnel, Juno, Enzo…Tangelo!, and yet, there seems to be a hard time remembering, Tom and Tim! I'm not sure about Tim or Timothy as it translates to Spanish but, since moving to Florida, I have picked up on the odd occurrence which happens when I introduce myself to someone who is of Spanish origin, I get an odd look, like a dog tilting its head to the side. Upon further investigation, I realized that "Tom" isn't really part of any dialect, other than English. Sure, there's "Thomas" which translates nicely to "Tomas" but "Tom?", just doesn't make sense I guess. What doesn't make sense to ME is, why is there an "H" in "Thomas"? But, that's a whole other discussion I suppose. I just find it very interesting that multisyllabic names roll off the tongues around here with no problem but, the three letter names find themselves caught in a first name twilight zone of sorts. I'm not sure how much easier I can make it. I've been known to answer simply too "T", which I'm fine with but, if T.O.M. causes the tilted head stare, I don't know if I want to go that far out on a limb with the one letter name. How would they spell it, "Teigh"?, "T'Eae", "Thei"? No, it's just, "T".

Before heading out for the day, Juno stopped me and whispered, "I'm going to fill it out and you just sign it!"

I had no idea what she was referring to but I later found out that, in consulting with the calendar, which was displayed for all to see, she saw that a regular carrier was going on vacation for two weeks and was trying to help me "Opt-In" for the route.

"Opting-In" for a route means, when a regular carrier goes on vacation for anything longer than five days, a CCA can Opt-in to the route and if approved, that CCA can have that route for that amount of time that the regular is on vacation. This is desired by the CCA, in most cases, because of the constant lack of any semblance of schedule in the life of a CCA and, getting this, at least provides a daily routine, albeit for a short period of time, where the CCA can have a predictable schedule including the same route every day. This makes it easier for the CCA to gain a better foothold of the route and of the day to day requirements. They get a reprieve from the roulette wheel of the daily obligations of never knowing until the last second what the responsibilities are. I also heard a rumor that, while on an "Opt-In", because this was also a full schedule of hours, you didn't have to work an Amazon Sunday during that time and, you get the days off that the regular carrier would get.

She came back to me with a mostly blank piece of paper with only written in basic terms that "Tome Spallone is requesting to opt-in for Route 25 during a period of June 1 to June 14."

She said, "Sign it and give it to the desk."

Sure, I thought, that would be great. I've been looking for redundancy and this might be a nice little reprieve from the madness. I took the paper and decided that I couldn't let it go like that; ya know, with the name and all, and chose to rewrite. In another example of ironic happenstance, in a roomful of paper products, I couldn't find a blank sheet of paper. I quickly dug into my backpack for my notepad and relieved it of a page and rewrote Juno's note and after dropping the final "e" from my name, I signed and submitted. No one said anything. I just placed it on the desk and went about my business of delivering Mallory's route.

The first sign of trouble that day was within a corporate park. I shoved a bunch of mail into a slot of a business that was vacant. I just screwed the pooch on that one. I thought it was the correct address. I didn't realize it until I got next door when I was fingering through the mail and couldn't find any for that address, which was odd and I went, "Ohhhhh…"

I doubled back and tried to see if I could gain access to the vacant business but, it was a no go. Locked up tighter than a drum. I tried calling the management company listed on the front of the building but, no one answered. I went to the intended address and, it being closed, I wrote a note describing that their mail is next door, should they know a way of accessing the business, and I shoved it through their slot. I later fest up to Mallory and she told me not to worry about it.

While on this route in the past, at a certain points in the route, the scanner would start to vibrate and an alert would sound with a text message stating that "Warning – Violent dogs have been reported to exist in the area!". I kept seeing these alerts and I acknowledged the messages as they came up to quell the chirps and buzzing of the scanner but, I never saw any dogs. Except for one time, out on the median of the road I saw a guy throwing a Frisbee to a dog and having it fetch.

The pooch was in his own world chasing the plastic disc and I didn't really feel any concern was merited. However, as I went from building slot to building slot, I kept looking behind me in anticipation of charging paws. But, he never deviated from game time with his owner. So, after seeing so many alerts come through, always at the same point in the route, I began to sort of take a "cry wolf" approach. Perhaps the dog(s) were removed and are no longer a threat after many complaints? Who knew?

I reached that point yet again where the scanner began it alerts and I gave the cursory look around and didn't see anything to be concerned about so, I just went about my business. As I've said, if a business is open, you open the door and go in and hand deliver the mail. If it's closed, and there exists a slot, you put the mail through the slot. Now that this was a weekday, the business was open and I tried the door and it was unlocked. I took one step in and that's a far as I got.

The largest, loudest, deepest sounding "dog" charged from somewhere within the offices. I say "dog" because, I'm assuming that's what it was. However, it was the size of a small pony!

I backed out and, sizing up the situation, knew that just letting the door close wasn't going to be enough. This damn thing could have pushed it open with its momentum with no problem. I braced my foot up against the bottom and held the door closed by putting all my weight behind it. The dog hit the glass with a thud and showed obvious frustration by biting at the air.

What to do? If I let up on the door, the dog would have surely pushed it open and come through and there was no way I was going to get back to the "safety" of the vehicle. We stood there for a seemingly long time in our own battle when a couple of people strolled out from where the dog had come as casual as you please, placating the animal; "That's a good boy…be nice now…move out of the way."

She grabs hold of the animal's collar and with the other hand, reaches up to begin to open the door. I thought, this isn't gonna cut it. There's no way that lady was going to be able to hold back that dog should it not want to be held back. I stood my ground. I said, "How 'bout I just put the mail through the slot?" "Oh, I got him." She opens the door a crack and said, "Oh, you must be new. He never behaves this way when Mallory is here. It must be the hat!"

I surrendered the mail to her and gave a wave and beat it out of there. I got back to the LLV and thought, at least the alerts on the scanner were accurate. I finally had a face-to-face with Cujo! And survived.

I pull up to the very next adjoining business in the corporate park and the scanner is beaconing again and I silence it as, I'm sure it was notification of the dog that I just engaged with. I go through the same motions with the open door delivery, and to my surprise, exactly the same thing happened, with the same type of dog of a slightly different color. The businesses must have been connected in some way and the dogs had to have been related.

I go through my same foot prop and weight-on-door as before and, a woman comes to the door smiling and said, "Oh, you're new. You must have met Bruno next door. They're brother and sister! Can you push the mail through the slot please?"

I hold the door closed and managed to put the mail through the slot and the "sister" immediate chops down on the bundle as I push it through. When I was convinced that it was safe to remove myself from barracking the door, I eased up. While walking back to the vehicle I hear a muffled "Thank you" from the women behind the door. I just did a backward wave without turning around.

Two close calls. I had heard of another carrier getting bit on the thigh a few weeks earlier and it was a whole paper trail of reporting which had to be done. I wanted no part of an attack or the paperwork. Again, it's something that isn't given much thought when first accepting the job responsibilities as, all you have to do is put the mail into a box and go to the next one. You really didn't think you'd be in any danger from attacks by animals, or people.

At least I didn't. And then it becomes real and you find yourself always scanning, head on a swivel, always looking for the next danger zone.

I remember when I first went out with Arnel on our first Amazon Sunday, he was explaining to me how we were going to "Attack" the first section for delivery. It occurred to me that this gig was every bit a type of military mission that you go out on in the morning and, maybe you come back, maybe you don't. And maybe you come back with a war story to tell or a scar from a rabies ridden bite from some animal.

I continued on the route, now hypersensitive to the whereabouts of our canine friends and I got to a section of the route which was very seedy. It was near the town dump or, landfill, if you will. There were open lot storage facilities where people might keep RV's or boats on trailers that weren't being used now or in the near future. It all looked very, Junkyard-Dog ish. And then, the scanner buzzed, making me jump a little. It was alerting me of another dog danger zone. Of course. At least it makes sense that an angry dog would be in the Junkyard Dog zone.

I approach a gate with a curbside mail box and waited and listened. Nothin'! I got out and quickly jammed the mail into the box, closed the door and got back into the LLV. I moved onto the next address. I stopped, waited and listened. Nothin'! Delivered and moved on. I did this for the entire section, waiting to be attacked and it never came. I never even heard a bark.

I'm not sure what's worse, getting attacked, or expecting to be attacked? The best practical joke is the one that keeps you on edge waiting for it but, never comes.

Chapter 22 - BLM

On February 26, 2012, in Sanford, Fl, Trayvon Martin, a 17 year old black teenager, was fatally shot by George Michael Zimmerman, a 29 year old white man. After Zimmerman was acquitted on all charges on July 13, 2013, the Black Lives Matter social movement was created by Alicia Garza, Patrisse Cullors and Opal Tometi advocating for non-violet civil disobedience in protest against incidents of police brutality and all racially motivated violence against black people.

The movement gained national recognition for street demonstrations following the 2014 deaths of Michael Brown Jr, an 18-year-old black man, after being shot by a white, Ferguson, Missouri Police Officer, and Eric Garner, after dying by way of suffocation from a choke hold while being arrested by a white New York City Police Officer after both officers were criminally exonerated in their respective cases.

The movement gained further national, as well as international attention, after the death of George Floyd at the hands of a white Minneapolis police officer, after Floyd was arrested for allegedly trying to pass a counterfeit $20 bill at a grocery store. The police officer was relieved of his duties and fired from the force the next day and, as of this writing, the trial is pending.

The Washington Post newspaper reports that approximately 1,000 people were killed at the hands of police officers in the United States in 2019. About half of those killed were white, and one quarter were black. This puts the death rate for black Americans in the United States at 31 fatal shootings per million which is more than twice the death rate for white Americans at 13 fatal shootings per million.

The protestors of these incidents sought to bring attention to the imbalances of police shootings and other forms of brutality and, at times, brought with it their own imbalances of action against the innocent. During the course of some demonstrations, store fronts were compromised and stores were looted of their contents, innocent bystanders caught in the melee of street closures and occupied neighborhoods were hurt and/or arrested, either wrongfully or rightfully. Combined with the fact that COVID-19 was reeking its own havoc with the mortality of society at large, the Presidential election had degrading to an almost embarrassing point to the disenfranchisement of its citizens; the summer of 2020 was a shit-storm out on the street.

While it seemed to me that the vast majority of Postal Employees in my purview were black, I never really felt a sense of discourse within the racial divide at the workplace of the USPS. If anything, it was an “us” vs “them” feeling that I perceived. “Us”, meaning those who are carriers of mail within the USPS and “them”, meaning the rest of the world! The racial divide was never a “thing” in my opinion, Although, at the height of the protesting in the area, I did catch a bit of an empathetic few point from some of the carriers whereas, from others, there was no empathy at all. But, I think that pretty much summarizes the attitude of the country as a whole and is not so much a microcosmically internal stance.

At the morning meeting today, it was conveyed to us that the pandemic had blossomed to the point where we were now mandated to wear a mask while in the office at all times. Some carriers still refused and I am not aware of how that situation was handled. We were also spoken with about the potential for protestors popping up within the area and instructed to not stop for anyone who might interfere with our duties.

It brought back imagery from the 1992 Los Angeles riots where truck driver Reginal Denny was pulled from his truck at an intersection in L.A. by protestors and beaten to within an inch of his life. The protestors took to the streets in outrage at the initial verdicts handed down to four, white, Los Angeles Police Officers, who were charged with using excessive force against Rodney Glen King after he was apprehended while trying to evade police in a high-speed chase during his arrest for drunk driving.

At a press conference, then Los Angeles Police Chief Daryl Gates said that, "We believe the officers used excessive force taking him into custody. In our review, we find that officers struck him with batons between fifty-three and fifty-six times." He said that, "…the officers involved would be disciplined and that three would face criminal charges."

The LAPD initially charged King with "felony evading", but later dropped the charge. The four officers were eventually tried on the charges of excessive use of force. Three were acquitted and the jury failed to reach a verdict on the one charge for the fourth.

The city erupted at the perceived injustice. The 1992 Los Angeles riots started, sparked by outrage among racial minorities over the trial's verdict and related longstanding social issues. The rioting lasted six days and killed 63 people, injuring 2,383 and ended only after the California Army National Guard, the United States Army and the United States Marine Corps provided reinforcements to re-establish control in the city and surrounding areas.

The federal government prosecuted a separate civil rights case and obtained four grand jury indictments against the officers for violation of King's civil rights. The results of the trials held in federal district court was that two of the officers were found guilty and sentenced to prison terms and the other two were acquitted of the charges. In a separate civil lawsuit in 1994, a jury found the city of Los Angeles liable and awarded Rodney King with $3.8 million in damages.

The images of Reginal Denny, while driving a truck for a living, as he was pulled from the cab of his truck at the intersection of Florence and Normandie Avenues in East Los Angeles were burned into my mind. He was pulled from his cab and beaten with fists, kicked, beat with a hammer as his long hair splayed out when the final blow landed from a cinder block. He suffered a fractured skull and impairment of his speech and ability to walk for which he underwent years of rehabilitative therapy. Soon after Denny was taken to the hospital he suffered a seizure. His skull was fractured in 91 places and pushed into his brain. His left eye was so badly dislocated that it would have fallen into his sinus cavity had the surgeons not replaced the crushed bone with a piece of plastic. A permanent crater remains in his forehead despite efforts to correct it. After unsuccessfully suing the City of Los Angeles, Denny moved to Arizona where he worked as an independent boat mechanic and has mostly avoided media contact.

Rodney King spoke to reporters from his wheelchair after the arrest with his injuries evident: a broken right leg in a cast, his face badly cut and swollen, bruises on his body, and a burn area to his chest where he had been jolted with a 50,000-volt stun gun. He described how he had knelt, spread his hands out, and slowly tried to move without making any "stupid moves", while being hit across the face by a "Billy Club" and shocked with tasers.

Rodney King was found dead in his swimming pool in 2012, two months after publishing his memoir. The coroner found evidence of alcohol and other drugs in his system and ruled that based on his history of heart problems, he had likely experience a cardiac arrhythmia which resulted in his accidental drowning.

During the summer of 2020, it was almost a daily event that during a normal day of delivery, there'd be a warning that would beacon from the scanner that there were rumors that protestors were going to be present in a given area and it was highly advised to avoid those areas. I did the best I could but, sometimes there was just no way to avoid certain streets while navigating a given route. At times I was forced to be at an intersection that was warned about at the exact time that the warning advised to avoid. But, I never witnessed any gatherings or protestors while on my own.

I was out with Tim for another 2-ton training excursion during a point at which the protesting was at its height. The night before, protestors had shut down I-95 North and Southbound near Okeechobee Blvd in West Palm Beach and the situation in the area was tense. There was a report of a mail carrier in nearby Miami having been shot while delivering that day.

We got through most of day without incident and then we received the warning on the scanners. We came on the intersection at just the exact time and there was no way to avoid the area. The police and sheriff's department were out in force and the traffic lights were switched to blinking red while an officer manually directed traffic.

It sure looked like something was going to happen and, as we were stopped at the intersection waiting to be given the ok to proceed, Tim and I gave a wave to the police along the side of the road as a sort of, "If anything goes down, don't forget your friendly mailman in the truck over here!" There was the semi conceited notation that, "we're Federal Employees in a Federal vehicle, surely we're untouchable, right?"

I was in the jumper seat and, I actually was wearing my seatbelt and, I think that my sliding door needed to be released from inside in order to be opened but, the vision I had of Reginald Denny being dragged from his truck and pummeled on the pavement was ever present.

The heat, the stress, the lack of sleep, the dogs; and now, I'm going to have my eye sockets bashed in! All for 17 bucks an hour while I deliver toilet paper to people who don't want to leave the house!

We made it through without incident and shared our experience with the supervisor on duty. He enforced what he had been saying all this time; "I'm serious, if you get stuck in a protest crowd, lock the door and don't stop for ANYONE! Just plow through the crowd! And if you take out one or two or TWENTY, so be it! And if, after the fact, someone questions you, you just say that "I feared for my life", and that's that!"

I certainly hoped that it wouldn't come to that and, while I was with the USPS, no racial protest and interruption of service ever became so inflamed that I was seriously concerned. We had heard of a carrier who just up and went home after she tried to make a delivery and was met at the door with the resident holding a gun on her, clearly in paranoid fear. Dangers on the job lurk in every corner and tensions during the summer of 2020 didn't help to diminish any.

Chapter 23 – Big Mama

I finally received my uniform voucher from Larry. I needed to reach out to some third party representative to get the uniform ordering started. I had asked the salesperson if there was some sort of storefront I could go to so that I may try on some things so I'd be sure they would fit properly but, she said that, due to COVID, the storefront had to be shut down and to do the best I could do with ordering online. As I've seen the result of how these uniforms look on some people, I didn't have much faith in a flattering fit for me.

After a few bumbled tries I was able to submit a shopping list of items after being given much advise about what is most important to have and what can be safely sidestepped.

I submitted my order:

- Shirts (4) = $156
- Shorts (3) = $204
- Belt = $19
- Hats (4, included the coveted Pith helmet) = $129
- Gloves = $18
- Socks = $16

For a total of $542. I was over by $7. But there was nothing of value for $7 and, I didn't want to leave anything on the table, if you know what I mean. So, I figured that I'd either pay the difference somehow or, I had heard that if I ordered a certain amount, I get some sort of discount and I would imagine it would offset the difference.

I was advised by the weathered veterans to not purchase shoes from the uniform supply company. They were way overpriced and was I given shoe advice that spanned a wide spectrum of choices. I had foreseen this ahead of time and, during training, purchased the ever popular Nike Air Monarchs for $85. They weren't really to my fashion satisfaction but, they fit the criteria that the Postal Service required and, they seemed like they'd last a bit.

Rain gear was very high on the list of must haves but, I already had a pretty good rain jacket and rain hat that directed the gathering rain on the hat to flow behind me and down my back, like a fireman's hat.

I didn't see the point in ordering long pants. I didn't work inside and, the heat just didn't allow for it outside. However, I did question one young lady as to why she was wearing long pants as an outdoor carrier and she stated in no uncertain terms, "Are you kidding? And mess up my tan lines?" So, I guess everyone has their own criteria to cater to.

After submitting the order, it started a whole jockeying of emails and text messages between the uniform person and Larry. The uniform person needed the voucher in order to pay for the order that I submitted. I sent it to them but, they needed to come from Larry as he is the authorizing supervisor. I conveyed this information to Larry and, after a couple of days, received notice that he had sent it to them. Then I received notice from the uniform company that they were still waiting for the voucher. And so it went for weeks.

I finally got the uniform purchase processed with no extra charge due, and no remaining balance until the next year. But, once ordered, I received a message that, due to COVID, some items may be delayed in receiving. I was in no rush.

Due to COVID, carriers starting calling out sick or, that they'd been exposed to the virus and therefore, had to quarantine for two weeks. The workforce was being depleted just when the volume of parcels were exploding. The east side took the brunt of the first hit and I was relegated there for an unknown period of time.

It had to happen sooner or later. But, just like with any dirty job, you make it harder on yourself if you try to stay clean. Best to get dirty, and stay dirty, until the job is done.

I'd had previous exposure to the east side with a piece of that walking route and, I supposed that I'd be subject to more of the same. But, that wasn't the case, really. A carrier was out with COVID who was normally assigned to a route that I hadn't been exposed to as of yet and, I was getting it.

I hadn't cultivated any associations with anyone on the east side and it made it that much more difficult to get a grasp of things. But, the carriers who had been asked to help me with casing were very nice and offered as much advice as they could. I was at least grateful that I didn't have to case the new route initially as, that would have taken way too much time and I'd never get the route done by the end of the day.

I'd been given the appropriate arrow key, the scanner, the vehicle keys and, the satchel with the dog spray. The configuration of the office on the east side was completely different than that of the west. After exiting the swinging double doors which led to the loading dock, you had to make a sharp left turn with your pumpkins in order to go down the ramp which then made a ninety degree turn to the right, finally exiting to the parking lot.

I pushed my loaded up pumpkin through the double doors and turned left and all of the mail and parcels stacked above the rim of the pumpkin shifted and fell to the ground.

I'm not making a good impression with the Dark Siders right off the bat. As I pick everything up, which of course has messed up any casing order, and try to pack everything on top of the pumpkin so that it doesn't fall again, someone passed by and said, "It happens to everyone!". That made me feel a little better but still, a lot of mail has been "de-cased" on a route that I have no idea about and, I was already screwed!

I finally packed the LLV with very disorganized trays of DPS, Flats, SPRs and parcels. I also had advos, of course, and normally this would have been a disaster right out of the gate but, this route comprised of just about half business, and they didn't get one, so, at least I had that going for me.

I sat in the parking lot and realized that I hadn't scanned out to the street. I had to lock everything up and, here on the east side, the parking lot is a pretty good distance from the building itself and I had to walk back to the building, up the stairs, go inside, scan the bar code and then walk back to the vehicle. Tick-tock…

Back in the vehicle, I knew enough to just take the first piece of mail in the DPS tray (hoping that it was the very first piece and that the drop didn't mess me up from the start) and I plugged the address into my phone's map app. It was now June and if I thought it was hot in March, it didn't compare.

Funny enough, I'd picked up on a verbal tick in the Postal community when addressing new people. The fact is, "You ain't seen nothing yet!" It doesn't matter how hard you've worked, it doesn't matter how long you've work, it doesn't matter how hot it is or how cold or wet or slippery; "You ain't seen nothin' yet!"

I would come back at the end of day literally soaking wet with salt stains on my shirt and shorts and hat and I'd be met with comments like, "What's goin' on with you? Are ya hot?" "Ehhh, you ain't seen nothing yet. Wait 'til August!"

Or, if I delivered 150 parcels on a Sunday morning; "Ehhh, that's nothin', wait until Christmas!"

As a new person, you're just not impressing anyone! Don't even think that you are. And when you get home like a beaten wet dog, looking for a little sympathy and your wife says, "What's the big deal, aren't you just putting letters into the boxes?", don't be surprised.

It was 10:45am and I was already soaked with sweat sitting in the LLV with the hot wind of the fan blowing on me. I headed out. East on Hillsborough Ave, South on Federal Highway.

Federal Highway is a busy roadway in Southeast Florida which runs from West Palm Beach to Ft. Lauderdale. It has its mix of drivers who think they are in a NASCAR race and with those who can't seem to comprehend the fact that if they are not sure where they are going, that they should be as far right as possible so as to be able to exit at the last moment without causing too much turmoil with surrounding traffic. It's difficult getting around the area. If you miss the turn-off for your destination, in order to get back to that spot can seem like an eternity, especially if you need to contend with four or five traffic lights during that maneuver.

Chapter 23

This was something that I just couldn't afford. No one likes to get behind a mail truck but, it didn't bother me to go as slow as possible while in the right lane so that I didn't pass my first turn off. If you want to get behind me, be my guest. You'll just have to wait.

I found my first turn-off but, I was immediately confused. There were multiple addresses within this courtyard type of environment. There was a small hotel-type looking building on one side but, there were no markings.

I just pulled to the side and tried to figure things out. Thankfully, someone came out of a small office and said, "This is the door you're looking for." I pull the vehicle up to the door and was immediately swamped by people who came from seemingly nowhere. One guy asked if he had anything. He was waiting for new sneakers, you see. Someone else put their head through the open side window looking for anything addressed to them.

I didn't know what to make of it. All I knew so far was that, from the looks of what was in the DPS tray and the SPRs, they got a lot of mail here. I gathered up as much of it as I could and almost dropped everything as I tried to open the door with my arms full. Someone sort of opened the door a couple of inches so that I could toe the door open enough so that I could worm the rest of my body through.

It was a nice, sort-of temporary looking office, with a pleasant young lady behind the desk. I said, "I'm new and I'm not even sure if I'm in the right place." She rattled off a whole bunch of addresses for mail that I should deliver right there to that office. Great, one stop and I can dump off a whole bunch of stuff, I thought. The problem was, the original dropping of the mail back at the office had interfered with the ease that it could have been. I had brought in the very first bunch of mail for the first address but, for the three or four other addresses, well, they were back in the truck somewhere. I had to go rummage through everything. I jotted down the addresses she mentioned and went back out there. This time, more people were sort of shuffling toward the vehicle dressed in a mix of "I just woke up" and "I'm ready for the concert", garb.

I finished going through everything and I believe that I retrieved all mail and parcels for those addresses mentioned and brought them in. I was relieved that I was done with that stop and thanked the young lady and went to leave when she said, "Oh, don't forget about those!"

I looked to where she was pointing and there was about three tubs of outgoing mail and parcels. Ugh. I had to scan each parcel as accepted and bring back out to the truck and pack in such a way so as not to comingle with what was already in there. And it was already a mess and I just got started. I wasn't familiar with this route but I already knew that I was way behind.

As I saddled up and got ready to pull away, the guy questioning the arrival of his sneakers approached again. "They didn't come? They were supposed to arrive today!"

"I didn't see anything that looked like a shoe box but, everything I had I brought inside the office."

He looked very disappointed and I felt rather sad.

I pulled away and moved along the route in a very tentative way, pulling onto and off of Federal Highway. I found myself back in the very odd Palm Plaza that looked like a hastily thrown-together alcove of business buildings. But, at least now I knew where that single chair hair salon was located. The businesses on this route seemed to me to be very hard to deliver to as it wasn't simply a matter of; pull up, get out, walk in, deliver and walk away. Everyone had something difference about them. One had a mailbox directly on the front of the building, another had a slot, another had nothing at all and then, the next group of six had a cluster box somewhere and on the next building you had to go in and upstairs to deliver to what look liked vacant offices and down again to delivery to the first floor and then to the tattoo studio that seemed always closed, then to the pawn shop where you had to be buzzed-in; it was dizzying to me.

I somehow managed to finish with the business section but, it was about 2pm by the time I had completed it. I was probably two hours behind by that point. But I reached apartment buildings and I'd come to rather like delivering to them because, you basically stand in one relative spot to do what I imagined I'd be doing; shove paper products into metal boxes.

The problem here was that this complex was divided into two building and each building was further dividing into two sections. And, in keeping with a naming convention that is completely lost on me, Apt 1 was in the first section of the first building, Apt 2 was in the second section of the first building, Apt 3 was in the first section of the second building and Apt 4 was in the second section of the second building!

Fingering along the DPS, I find mail for Apt 439. Where could that go!? Talk about being slowed down even further. I later figured out, and semi absorbed the number scheme for these particular apartments but, that's just one incident. The next apartment buildings are on a completely different numbering scheme.

I finished with the first and second apartment buildings and now, I had to go to a section that was neither apartment building, nor business, nor park and loop, nor curbside. This was an anomaly. Lucky me. For a stretch of one street, I had to drive the vehicle and stop at each private home, shut the vehicle down, gather the mail and bring to the front door of each home. Go back to the vehicle, start it, pull up to the next house and repeat. And repeat, and repeat. Perhaps it sounds easy but, have I mentioned the heat?

Having spent most of my life living in New Jersey and New York and now living in Florida, here's what I know to be true; do you know what works well in extreme cold and extreme heat? NOTHING!!!!

Nothing works well! It's just that simply. Everything is harder, everything takes longer and is more arduous!

And the stopping and starting in these vehicles is just brutal. If you are unfortunate enough to be cursed with any occasion of hemorrhoids, not to worry, the springs in the driver's seat will take care of that situation fast enough!

I managed to finish with that stretch of hell and had to work my way back to some predetermined point where I would finally start the dreaded park and loop where, as I've explained, you park at one end of a street, pack up all the mail in your bag and walk down one side of the street, delivering as you go, cross the street and work your way back to the vehicle.

It's normally a difficult routine but, for the newbie, it's next to impossible to do with anything resembling grace. And, I'm already hours late and there's nothing I could do about it yet. It wasn't yet 3pm, the time at which carriers are supposed to call in to ask for help. The problem is, since I wasn't familiar with the route, I didn't how much longer everything would take so, should I ask for help or just keep pushing through? This is another aspect of the mail delivery game that I didn't quite understand. I didn't really mind if it took me until say, 7pm to finish the route. It's on me. I'm new to the route and it takes me longer to finish the job at hand. If I had to do the route every day, I'd become more familiar with it and complete it at a faster rate with each occurrence. Sure, I have to be paid for it but, if you put me on yet another unfamiliar route tomorrow, the same delays will occur. And then there's the sense of accomplishment felt when left to be able to finish a job. I get nowhere if I'm bailed out and have mail taken from me and delivered by someone else.

I decide to just push through and keep going and play dumb. So, I park at the appropriate spot at the beginning of the first park and loop and I begin gathering all the DPS, SPRs, Flats, advos and parcels and then I see a box the shape of a shoe box. I read the address. Sure enough, it goes back to the first business address where that guy was expecting his new sneakers.

I later learned that this "business" was a Drug and Alcohol Rehabilitation center. That would explain the milling about and hyper attraction to anything coming in from the outside world.

Now I really felt bad that I had disappointed the guy who was waiting for his sneakers. Never go back, they said. That's one thing you never do. Especially when you're late on your route for the day, never go back.

So, I headed back to the rehab center with the shoebox at the ready to be delivered. It was around 3pm and about a mile away. I'm doing everything that I shouldn't do. But, I'm adlibbing here.

Regardless of Postal procedure, I feel that this is the right thing to do.

I pulled up to the office and was happy to see that it was still open. I didn't see the guy roaming around but I explained to the young lady inside that I think the recipient of this package was really set on receiving it today and, unfortunately, it got jumbled up in the truck and I just found it among all the other things. She thanked me and said that she'd make sure that he got it.

I felt good about doing that but, I'm was so deep in the shit now that I was very far behind on the day. By the time I got back to where I was to start the park and loop it was about 3:20pm. I packed up and started out down the street. I crossed over and started working my way back when the phone rang.

"Where are you?"

I tried to explain my location.

"That's it!?

"Well, I…"

"Alright, I'm sending someone out to help!"

I knew it was coming and I guess there's no way around it. I was able to finish with that first park and loop and I moved the vehicle into position for the beginning of the second park and loop when, not one, but two Postal vehicles pull up behind me.

One asked, "How much do you have left?"

I just slid open the rear door of the LLV and presented with a wave of my hand like, Tuh-dahh!

The look on their faces told me that humor wasn't going to ease the situation. They swarmed onto what was still a messy situation from the very beginning of the day when I dropped everything and they picked through it and took whatever they felt was necessary for all of us to get done within some acceptable time period. As they drove off, one of them said, before trailing off; "Just follow 8th Ave and then come back around to.....". And they were gone.

I looked at the remains of what was picked through and tried to put everything into some recognizable format, and I continued with the route. I was getting it done and then, came across another package that should've gone to one of the businesses at the start of the route. I found it so frustrating that I couldn't keep everything in a certain order to make the delivery go smoothly. And this is five months into the job!

I finished the route and went as fast as I could to deliver that last parcel. Luckily, it was a business that was still open and I was able to get rid of it.

I got back to the office at 6:30pm and saw the carrier who had cased all the mail for me that morning. She said, "What happened? I cased all that stuff so nicely, you should've been back here by 3pm!"

All I could manage at that point was, "I dunno…"

I was told to come back to the east side the next day and so, I did. As luck would have it, I was put on the same route. But this time, I was to case the entire thing. Having done the route the day before made it more easy to visualize the route as I looked at the slots of shelves standing before me. I actually got the whole casing done and was able to pack up and move to street without too much of an issue. Ok, I was the last person out of the office but, I think that that's pretty much to be expected.

I managed to navigated my way out the double doors, turn left, down the ramp, turn right and out to the vehicle to load up without dropping anything.

As I did the load truck feature on the scanner, another carrier came running out to me with a small, soft package in his hand. "Here, this goes to you."

Before handing it over to me, he felt up the package. "You know what this is?" He hands it to me.

"Feels like a shot glass!", I said.

Laughing, he said, "Yea, look where it's going!"

Yup, to the rehab center. We shared a small chuckle over that one and off I went to tackle this monster of a route yet again.

Down Federal Highway, up Federal Highway, around to the first and second group of apartments, to the stop/get out/walk to front door/walk back/start and repeat area and then to the park and loop. Still couldn't get this whole walking thing down. There's just too much to carry. Now being semi familiar with the layout of the streets that made up the Park and Loops, I decided to just forego delivery of the parcels while walking. I'm parked at the head of the street and I have to walk to the end of the street, cross, and return and then drive down the street to the end anyway, so, I'll just stop a few times at the homes that have parcels to be delivered to them. And that's what I did. It's not the correct way to do it but, it's how I found that I could manage.

Soon after I started the park and loop, I was met in a driveway by the most beautiful cat. A mixed color of white, orange and brown, the feline greeted me pleasantly. I bend over and had a quick conversational greeting with her and I moved onto the next house.

Chapter 23

After a few houses, I had the unmistakable feeling of being followed. I looked back, and there was kitty. She stopped when I stop to look around. I said, “You have to go home. You don’t want to go where I’m going!” She stared.

I continued to the next house and turned around and saw that the cat had advanced an equal distance as I had gone. We continued our game of “Red-light, Green-light 1-2-3” until I got to the turnaround point.

“You better not cross that street!”, I warned, with a finger wag. She stopped and stared. I continued on the route working my way back to the vehicle a half mile away. As I delivered mail to one side of the street, the cat mirrored my movements on the other side of the street until I got back to the vehicle. As I packed up to leave the area I gave the kitty a pat on her head and said, “Maybe I’ll see you tomorrow, ok?” And we parted company. It may have been the most pleasant encounter I had so far while on the job.

I was late getting back to the office but, I didn’t care; I did the whole route (on the Dark Side) by myself and, as a bonus, I made a new friend.

I was told to go back to the east side again the following day and was again assigned to the same route as the past couple of days. I was hoping for that as I had a bit of granola bar waiting for my new friend when I reached that point of the route.

During the morning briefing, the Postmaster of the office spoke with the carriers before going out for the day. We were reminded to wear masks, don’t let anyone touch our scanners, wash down steering wheels and wash hands frequently.

We were advised that a “Carl Higgins” would be coming back to the office tomorrow and that, everyone should behave maturely and appropriately. He said that Carl wasn't able to retire after the incident and so, they're letting him come back.

After the gathering had dispersed, I went over and asked John what that was all about. John was a fellow CCA hired around the same time that I had been only, we had just recently met due to the fact that he'd been relegated to the Dark Side almost from inception. He probably did something really bad in a previous life.

The running joke among those of us most recently hired as CCA's was that John, who could easily be mistaken for a famous jockey (due to his stature) was unable to help Tim and I with 2-ton duty because, "He can't reach the peddles!". That jibing came from John himself so…

If you can't laugh at yourself…

John informed me that part of the reason why they were so shorthanded on the east side was due to the fact that this guy, Carl, had walked out after having an argument with the manager. Apparently, this guy, who was a U.S. Marine veteran from New York, got into a heated argument with the manager and, after the typical political disagreements (that's what the current political landscape seemed to trigger) he claimed that he was going to blow the place up or something like that. He left in a huff and after the Postal Service tried to determine what to do with the him, he figured that he would just retire and disappear. The problem was, he didn't have enough time served to retire so, they came to some agreement and, he's coming back tomorrow.

Really?, I thought. I might be privy to a bone vide incident of a guy actually "Going Postal" while at a Postal Office? This was too good to be true! I was giddy with anticipation and now, was actually hoping that I'd be assigned again to the east side just so I can be there!

While thinking about this, I cased, pulled down and packed up without incident and, just before rolling out to the street, Larry called out to me; "Don't forget those." He pointed to two boxes in the center of the office. I go over to the boxes and each was about four feet long by two foot square and I tested their weight. I could barely pick them up. I tried to determine where, in the route they should be delivered but, it didn't really matter. They were so big and heavy, they had to be put in first and everything else piled on top of them. The problem was, getting them out of the truck without making of mess out of everything else.

I rolled out to the parking lot and was immediately hit with the blast of heat from the hottest day yet. It was 10:45 am and about 95 degrees already. I had already gotten used to being just normally sweated up by the time I got to the office at 8am but now, after loading everything into the vehicle, especially with a tremendous amount of parcels due to COVID-19 and these two exceptionally large and heavy parcels, I was soaked through and through and I hadn't really begun the route yet.

This, being the third day in a row that I was doing the same route, I was confident that I'd get through it with little incident. But, it was just one of the those days where everything was going wrong. The vehicle was acting up, advos were flying all over the truck, packages were shifting all over the place, the traffic was abysmal and there always seemed to be a problem with parking. The mail just didn't feel right in my hands that day. And I was blinded with sweat. It was like delivering mail and packages under water.

I got through the businesses and I kept being offered water at almost every stop as I probably looked like someone who could use it. I came to the apartment buildings that were split into two buildings. I discovered that the two heavy parcels should go to these buildings; one to each tower. One went to the second floor of the first tower and the other one went to the fourth floor of the second tower. I figured that I should just get rid of these things first so I can make room in the truck and not be so confined. But, in order to do that, I pretty much had to take out everything that was stacked on top of the parcels. This added to time and exhaustion. I wrangled the first heavy package out of the truck, locked everything up and heaved the package onto my right shoulder. My back cried out in agony. The stairs were much closer than the elevator and so, I figured that, it only being on the second floor, that it might be better if I took the stairs. Every step was agony and when I got to the second floor, I realized that in order to get to the apartment in question, I had to pass the elevator anyway so, there went that great idea!

I tried to place the package down at the front door as gently as a 50lb box of that shape would let me and I limped back to the truck. Instead of moving the truck to the second tower I decided to deliver all the mail for the first tower and that gave me some recovery time between heavy parcels.

While trying to deliver advos at this apartment complex, the cluster boxes were in an outside lobby and situation just so that it made for a powerful wind tunnel. It made delivering flimsy paper products, like the advos, challenging. Everything was flying all over the place. More than a few coupons broke free and were lost to the wind and, I wasn’t about to give chase.

This goes to the point where, you have to experience a given route on each day of the week as, because it was advo day, it made it harder and took longer than had it not been advo day.

Heavily drained and beat up at this point, I moved the truck to the next tower. I repeat all that I had done in order to free the second heavy package from the truck. I lock up and heave the package onto my shoulder with a crunch sound that I'm pretty sure the body isn't supposed to make. Forget that plan with stairs this time, I head straight for the elevator while trying to balance the heavy load just so, so it would at least seem lighter. I get to the elevator and I see a hand written sign apologizing that the elevator is out of order and to please be careful when using the stairway.

I leaned forward a little and let the cool metal elevator door sizzle against my dripping forehead and let out a slow muffled moan.

I readied myself and stepped off. I mustered all I had to lift each leg at a time and climb each stair, stopping only slight at each level so as to not inhibit any momentum I had stored. I made it to the top and managed to get to the apartment and do the delivery. While dragging myself back down the stairs and to the truck, I thought, "This might be it. This old(ish) body may have reached its limit for this type of thing. I'm not old, but I'm not young either. The years that I have left, I'd rather like to not spend with the help of some apparatus or to have to be heavily sedated to quell the pain. My days on the job were numbered.

The next stretch of the route, where you had to stop, get out, walk to the house, walk back, get in, startup, really put the nail in the coffin for me. "It's a young man's game!" said the very wise Greg. That's for goddamn sure!

I finally got to the Park and Loop point and was at least pleased to see that my time was looking pretty good, considering. Just a couple more hours to go and then I could go home and try to mend until the next day.

I geared up and got to the house where I had met my new friend a day earlier. It would have been nice to see the pleasant disposition of the kitty that would help calm my stress ridden body but, she was nowhere to be found. I kept my senses up while continuing down the street in the hopes that she'd want to play again but, she never showed and it kind of brought me even further down. I checked my pocket for the granola bar but, it was a disintegrated mass of mush from my sweat and, it wasn't good for anyone.

I finished the route and as I headed back to the office, I seriously thought about it being my very last day. Or, at least, perhaps this was the beginning of the end for me. I could continue and try to gain a better grasp on the whole thing but, I wonder what kind of saying could be put on my headstone; "At least he finished the route!" or "He hardly went into penalty time!".

I pulled back into the parking lot and, as hot as it was, I sat there for a minute. I had to catch my breath. I was completely used up. Everything hurt, everything was wet and chaffed and I was light-headed from not eating. I pushed through the route, not wanting to take a lunch just so I could get it done. I cleaned up the LLV, locked it up and put all the empty bins and trays into a pumpkin and with my last efforts, I pushed that thing across the parking lot, up the ramp, turn left and up another ramp, through the doors, scanned the vehicle back in with its proper end mileage and entered the cool Post office at 5:30pm.

Chapter 23

Larry sees me and says, "Oh, you think you're done!?"

Mother fucker!

"I have about six parcels that need to go out. It shouldn't take you more than 30 minutes!"

I just walked into the men's room and splashed cold water all over me. I took a minute to gather myself and went back out and finished putting everything away from that day's route and took the six packages back out with me without saying a word.

They either can't read the state that a person appears to be in or, they just don't care. Or, perhaps that's the wrong choice of pronoun and I should replace "they" with "he". Regardless, the job just needs to get done. There's no tomorrow apparently.

The six parcels were scattered in a section of town that I had yet to be in. I first did a quick drop off at townhouse and then found myself just a few blocks away in what can only be describe as a "shanty town". Crude shacks set back from the road with their corresponding mailboxes lined up 4 in a row on a hastily put together, rickety 2 x 4 frames, each about to fall from its one nail fastener. No doors on the mail boxes, just metal, Quonset hut shaped voids with a number scratched into it. I shoved a soft package into one of them wondering what anyone in these shacks could be ordering online. Two down.

I get back to the LLV and ease down the dilapidated street, looking for the address of the next parcel. I find it and it's for a house which is a little better in appearance to the shanty town ones I just left but, not by much.

I park the vehicle almost in the middle of the street and exit the right side and walk around to the other side of the vehicle with the soft package in my arm and that's when I witnessed the largest dog known to exist. The brother and sister tag team that almost had me for lunch were huge, but this thing dwarfed them. He stood in the neighbor's yard while his owner worked under his jacked up car. It would have been easy to let my imagination run away with me and think all kinds of bad intentions of the dog but, the fact was, I was so pissed off at that point, the dog had better not fuck with me if he knew what was good for him! I'd tear his goddamn throat out with my bare hands! And then, I'd walk over and throw the entrails at the owner before kicking out the jack stands and letting the car crush that fucker to shit!

Turns out, as dogs tend to sense this sort of stuff, he took one look at me and, did nothing. I frisbeed the soft Amazon package at the door after scanning it and I was gone. Three down.

The next parcel was another easy townhouse delivery with no issues. Four down.

The fourth and fifth parcels were on the same street, it looked like. It was only a few blocks away and in a better area in which I had come but, could not necessarily be described as "nice" by most people. As I neared the area, I had to slow the vehicle because, a rooster was crossing the road. You could probably tell by now that, I'm not kidding in the slightest. A damn rooster…crossing the road, in South Florida, at 6pm, and it wasn't crowing. Do roosters crow at any other time than, well, the most inconvenient ones? I'm from the Bronx, I surely didn't know. I was just sort of, mystified that I was stopped in the road and was watching a rooster cross in front of me. I looked around at the run down homes with broken lawn mowers in the yard and just up ahead, on the side of the road, was a broken jet ski, just sitting in the dirt road. Was the rooster someone's pet? Or was it dinner? I snapped out of it and continued.

Chapter 23

I picked up one of the two parcels I had left as I drove and looked at the address and came to a stop at where I thought it was located but, there was no number on the house or on the mailbox at the curb. I got out of the LLV and looked around. Next door, on the stoop in front of the house sat a very large black woman in a sun dress. The dress was pulled up above the knees with legs akimbo. I called to her motioning to the house in front of me, "Ma'am, do you know if this is 480?"

Referring to the parcel in my hands, "Is that for me baby!?"

"Uh, no, it's for 480."

"Uhhh, I don't know. Yea, probly!"

"Ok, thank you!"

I walked to the house and delivered it. Only one to go and I think this day might just be done!

I get back to the LLV and pick up the last parcel and the address says, 378. I look around and sure enough, it goes to Big Mama! But, she'd already gone inside by this point.

I walk up to the screen door and I can see her in the kitchen of the shotgun-style house in the back. I gently knock and she sees me at the door and gets all exited.

"Mmm-Mmm. Hellllooooooo!"

"Package for you ma'am."

"Ooooooo, COME INSIDE BABY!!!!"

"Uhh, I'll just leave it here by the front door."

As I hightailed it back to the vehicle, I could hear her from inside the house, "Oh you can come and bring that package to me right now baby! Mmmm-mmmm! Yes you can!"

Chapter 24 – End Tour

The following day, I was told to report to the annex on the west side and I was both relieved and a little disappointed as, I wasn't going to be on the east side today to be witness a Postal employee potentially "Going Postal" at the work place but, relieved in that, anything on the west side was better than anything on the east side and, after the past few days, I could use a break, even if the break consisted of a hard day on the west side.

The previous night I made my decision that I had had enough with the immersion part of this project. It was time to fall back, digest what I had just been through, and determine how I was to process the literate part of the project. My intention was to experience the Full Monty of being a Postal worker during the holiday season but, I didn't see how I was going to last to that point. I got the gist of it. I know that postal workers, past and present, who read this will be of the opinion that, "If you haven't delivered during the holiday season, then you haven't really experienced the full thrust of the job!" Fair enough, but, I'll have to leave that part to someone else to immerse themselves into. I had to now come up with an exit strategy.

I'd only been on the east side for about a week and I feel like I'd gone to the front lines and have now been given a small reprieve by falling back to the rear. I'm still in the fight, I just don't feel like I have a sniper's cross-hairs trained on me.

And, upon arrival, the looks I received from the regular crowd on the west side, were those similar to what would be on someone who's gone to hell and back! That's not such an exaggeration and it's not to diminish the grind that exists on the west side. And for my sins, I was given Route 73, the marathon. But, at least it was contained within Century Village. What I once thought as a major disaster of an area to deliver, I now found to be some sort of safe haven. I think that was so, mainly because I really didn't have to research addresses as I went along. Once you were there and just a little familiar with the area, you just had to grind it out. With other areas, especially the Dark Side, I found myself looking up almost every address on every street. And doing that with your phone is just another thing to juggle along with the mail and parcels.

This was the beginning of July in South Florida and, it was so that, "People were going up to cops and begging them to shoot!"[2]. Ha, that's always good one.

But seriously, the heat was no joke. By that time, it was not only hot in temperature but, the country was on "the balls of its ass", to coin a colorful phrase, where racial tensions, in my opinion, hadn't been this high since the 60's. The pandemic, which was approaching one million deaths in the United States at that point, and showing no signs of slowing down, was causing yet another divide amongst the populous. But this time, the divide wasn't racial but of that between pro science types and the conspiracy theorists.

In consideration of this current pandemic of COVID-19 specifically, there are those who feel that having to be vaccinated

---

[2] Glengarry Glen Ross, 1992, Zupnik Enterprises, New Line Cinema

(once a vaccine becomes available), in order to quell the disease, is an infringement on their human rights. The general consensus among those who believe this typically deny the existence or validity of the science supporting their use in the general population and feel that it is unsafe.

The anti-vaxxer movement began in the 18th century in the U.S. with religious leaders describing them (vaccines) as the "devil's work." This belief grew in the 19th and 20th centuries as a matter of human rights.

In 1998, Andrew Wakefield, a former medical doctor, suggested a possible link between the MMR vaccination and autism in children. A respected scientific journal, The Lancet, published Wakefield's research but withdrew his article in 2004 after an investigation found major flaws in his study.

A "British Medical Journal" investigation found that Wakefield didn't disclose several conflicts of interest in his research, including involvement in a lawsuit for claiming links between MMR and autism. The BMJ also found that Wakefield was guilty of deliberate fraud and deemed that he and his research team had cherry-picked specific data that suited and supported their case and falsifying facts in his report.

The United Kingdom's "General Medical Council" revoked Mr. Wakefield's medical license, declaring that he abused a position of trust and acted unethically to provoke a dishonest and callous controversy.

Despite this, the scandal that created the conspiracy theory, led to a drop in MMR vaccinations that remains to this day. There is still no scientific study showing a link between MMR and autism.

The World Health Organization (WHO) highlights six common misconceptions about vaccines:

- Diseases were already declining before the invention of vaccines due to improvements in hygiene and sanitation.
- Most people who get diseases are already vaccinated.
- Some batches of vaccines are safer than others.
- Vaccines cause many harmful side effects and illnesses.
- The diseases that vaccines prevent are no longer prevalent, so there is no need for vaccines.
- Giving children multiple vaccines at once increases the risk of harmful side effects.

The WHO have given responses to these misconceptions, providing evidence to the contrary.

Vaccines are second only to the provision of clean water in reducing infections worldwide.

Before the invention of vaccines, many infectious diseases were widespread and had a significant impact on well-being and regularly led to death.

Vaccines are now one of the safest health interventions, saving millions of lives each year. They are safer than many other common medications or healthcare procedures.

According to the Department of Health & Human Services, there are five reasons to vaccinate a child:

- Vaccines save lives from deceases that can otherwise cause injury or death.
- They are safe and effective.

- Immunization protects others, including family members or friends.
- Some Schools or childcare facilities require vaccinations for admission.
- They protect future generations from diseases.

All of this is well and good but, anti-vaxxers don't give credence to the WHO or Department of Health & Human Services, or agencies like them, and dismiss anything these organizations purport as being politically manipulated and/or propagating a pharmaceutical agenda.

The Anti-vaxxer movement can influence people's decision to vaccinate themselves or their children. This not only effects their health and well-being, but also the health and well-being of others. For example, they could pass a disease to other children who are unable to receive vaccines due to allergies, age, or medical conditions.

Likewise, the Anti-masker movement has been an outcrop of the Anti-vaccine movement. The wearing of masks has become a heated point of contention during the Covid-19 outbreak with people having meltdowns because of it, and it isn't uncommon for strangers to confront each other in public places on the issue. The reasons for being anti-mask are varied, including those who simply believe that they are cumbersome and have no benefit and those who choose to go down the conspiracy rabbit-hole involving Big Pharma, Government take-overs, YouTube and Bill Gates.

But there are also commonalities; many people pointed to government official's confusing messaging on masks in the pandemic's early stages. They don't feel that they are conspiracy theorists and don't necessarily believe that the coronavirus is a hoax, but many expressed doubts about the growing body of scientific knowledge around the virus and choose the cherry-picked approach from unverified sources of information found on social media rather than traditional news sources.

These are people who claim not to know anyone who had contracted Covid-19 or died from it, and, if pointed out evidence contrary, the responses seem to be the same; Did they have a preexisting conditions? How old were they?, etc. minimizing the fact that, had these people not contracted the Covid-19 virus, they'd still be alive!

The mask debate is a complex one. As much as it is about science, health, and the risk, it's also about empathy. Are older and immunocompromised people disposable? See the movie *Soylent Green*.

Surely, the empathy question also works the other way; attacking people for not wearing a mask doesn't change minds. As the coronavirus pandemic continues to spin out of control in the United States, many states, localities and businesses have turned to requiring people to wear masks in the hope that the measure will slow the spread of infection. Most people generally seem not to be so much anti-mask rather, anti-mandate. The concern is government overreach, not necessarily the masks themselves. They just don't like being told what to do.

You could almost revise the old argument against wearing a seat belt. People claim that it's a violation of their freedom. Many will site the 14th Amendment of the U.S. Constitution, "No states are allowed to make laws that take our freedoms away". Wow, where do you draw the line on that one before taking up arms?

Obviously, the issue of the freedom argument is that wearing a mask is about more than protecting yourself. Does a surgeon wear a mask to protect himself from exposure to some airborne agent or, is it to protect the open wound from anything that the surgeon might spew? Or both?

It would seem that masks are acting as a proxy for not believing in science, poo-pooing the experts in the field. Certainly, masks aren't a panacea, but that doesn't mean they're not worthwhile. Some would claim that, in a one-to-one encounter, if one person wears a mask, wouldn't that then protect both of them? Freeing one to be unencumbered.

"My body, my choice!" appears to be the pedestal on which anti-maskers stand. Interestingly, those who would align themselves with this stance, seem to fall within the same group who are in opposition to the other, "My body, my choice" stance on the subject of abortion.

Add this indecision in healthy practices to combat Covid-19 to the well-divided political landscape and, the general landscape of social attitude in the country is a sour one. It's difficult to go anywhere without observing the strain on the faces, body English and especially voices of the people in an attempt to overcome these trying times.

During a stop at a large cluster box within Century Village, a very nice old man approached me. He had concerns of his own, you see. He said that he was ninety three years old and was worried that the ladies were not interested anymore!

He began to talk politics and because he knew he had a captive audience (I was arrow-keyed tethered to the box and wasn't going nowhere), felt that he could expound on what he felt was a disastrous current administration. He went on and on while I continued delivering and broached the subject of how President Donald Trump wants to dismantle the United States Postal Service and was seeking my own opinion.

Never wanting to engage in any dialogue concerning anything more than a cursory discussion on the weather or, how the customer felt that there's "nothing but junk in their box", I sidestepped the issue.

However, the old man was so charming in his approach, with his yarmulke graced head towering five foot nothin' above his feet, I was roped in. I coyly asked, "Sir, you're a gentleman of advanced age…" He interrupted, "Nicely put young man."

"In your lifetime, as long as you've been politically aware, do you ever recall a time when the people of this country were ever so divided?"

He gently, and sadly, shook his head.

"Trump is dividing us, not united us.", he said. Further, as if to end our pleasant give and take said, "I'm 93 years old. For the first time in my life, I feel that I can die now. I really don't want to witness any more of this!"

I let that hang in the air as I shoved more AARP flyers into boxes.

Other than the essence of the hard work itself, I finished the very long day without too many issues. There's no "Phoning in" this job. You've got to get up and gear up or else you're going to have a problem with performing.

Yet another example of events that add to my wealth of feelings of disorganization was that, after I'd gotten back to the office, I was sent back out for a sort of emergency pick up at a CVS pharmacy. I'm guessing that it was medication for a time sensitive delivery. I was very tired but, the only way that it's going to get done is to get it done. Back out on the road. Before I left, I was told that it was a CVS on Hillsborough Ave., out by Powerline Road. I was now familiar enough with the area that I knew of where this intersection was and, I at least could head in the right direction out of the gate. I was told that I'd be texted the exact mailing address.

This was around 5:30pm and the traffic was bad and I just wanted to get home at that point. But, whenever you're in a rush, that's when everything slows down. Every red light. Every slow or turning or oncoming car gets in the way. I get the text message with the mailing address and felt that I didn't really need it. All I had to do was drive west on Hillsborough and as I approached Powerline, I'd look around for a CVS. How many can there be?

I drove west, past the intersection of Hillsborough and Powerline and no CVS was in sight. I kept driving until I reach the edge of town and knew not to go any further. I wonder if it was on Powerline? I checked the address; no, it says Hillsborough. Tick-tock…

I figured that I'd swallow my self-proclaimed geographical expert pride and pump the address into the map app, just to get this done. I head east and get to the intersection of Hillsborough and Powerline and it says that I've arrived.

I don't see no damn CVS. I mean, they're not that hard to miss, after all. Maybe I was too close to the destination and I didn't get an accurate reading on the map. I kept going east on Hillsborough and then u-turned. Back and forth, back and forth. I reengaged the map search and I followed it. Again, it took me to the corner of the intersection where there was a gas station. I pulled in and stopped to try to figure out what the hell was going on. I got out of the LLV to look around and I didn't see any CVS. I had to call the office.

This, at the end of a long day. It's what exhausts a person beyond reason. I called in and Enzo answered and I said that I had been driving back and forth around that address and that I couldn't find any CVS.

He said, "Oh, behind the gas station is a Target. The CVS is inside the Target. I should've told you that!"

Pins and needles, needles and pins…

I picked up the medication thinking, I sure hope this person REALLY needs this stuff, because, I'm gonna be on meds doing this shit pretty soon!

At home, I looked at a calendar and tried to determine when my last day would be and came up with July 17 as I figured I should give two weeks' notice. That was still three weeks away and I had a week to get all things in order before giving my notice. And, still, it was three weeks away. That's a long time in this business. It reminded me of when I had run the New York City Marathon and, after almost twenty six miles, I turned into Central Park at Columbus Circle and, I could see the finish line and, I still wasn't sure if I'd make it or not!

There are few better feelings when you are comfortable with a decision, such as leaving a job, and you've targeting an exact stepping off point. Problems sort of roll off your back when in that situation. Not that one should slack at that point, you're still being paid to do a job and this job is not something that can be accomplished by slacking off. But, you know the end is near and it makes all the annoyances somewhat palatable.

I actually wasn't sure about if I was even obliged to give two weeks' notice but, it's the right thing to do, I thought. And, it's an odd thing about giving notice within an organization such as this as, you don't really know if you can say anything to anyone. If I open the can of worms too soon, will I be relegated to the shit of the shit duty? I don't want that. You can't approach the union rep about it as, you don't know how people will react. So, I did the best I could by gleaning any information on the subject from the Postal Employee website. I couldn't find anything that said anything about how much notice to give but, it did say that there was a form that needed to be filled out. I was able to find it online, print it and filled it out by hand and have it ready for when the time came.

The week trickled by, one day after the next, and I felt a little guilty not at least confiding with some friends as to my intentions, not only in leaving but, what the whole reason was for my existence at the USPS to begin with. But, I still felt that keeping things close to the chest was the lesser of the evils.

I was scheduled to be off on the day that I was to give notice, even though actually having the day off that was written on the schedule was a rarity, so, I figured that I might as well give notice the day before that, just in case.

And, of course, on the morning that I needed to have an actual talk with a supervisor, and mind you, this eats heavily into one's completion time, we had "special visitors" coming in that wanted to address the carriers. "Special visitors" means upper management. District or Division or, some other type of nomenclature used to describe management upstream from the local office. This was rare so, you knew it was big.

Chapter 24

I was a little annoyed, I have to say. I'd been gearing up for the moment for over a week and now, I have to wait and hear whatever it is they had to say (eating up time) before I could have my audience?

At that point, COVID-19 was bulldozing its way across the country, and world. Businesses were closing, people hurting from lack of work. At workplaces across the country, "Furlough" had replaced "Layoff" when advising that the employee should go home and, perhaps, be later recalled, should there be the need of their services, perhaps as a means of not stinging so much. People were dying at an alarming rate with hospitals being overwhelmed and overrun. And there were a few carriers within the very office in which I stood that have been diagnosed with Covid 19 and are on medical leave.

The talk was basically a speech to quell any panic or uprising that might be brewing amongst the carriers who were left. They had some sort of nurse walk around and talk to each individual and answer any personal question they might have. They tried to make sense of which could not be made much sense of at that particular time. They said that, yes, while there were three confirmed cases within the office that, we had nothing to be concerned about.

Odd that, if you were exposed to someone at home, you were to quarantine yourself for two weeks but, if you were exposed to someone at the workplace, you're ok, just keep plugging away. Their explanation was that, you're only at risk if you have a face-to-face conversation with someone for fifteen minutes or more.

There was some pushback from the carriers expressing concern over the fact that, this is not what we were hearing from the scientific community. Who is to be believed? I thought, I'm getting outta here just in the nick of time.

The speech made everyone feel uncomfortable and antsy and left them whispering to each other, and themselves. And, like a guitar player that was billed after Hendrix, I thought, "I've got to follow THAT guy? Well, there was no getting around it. I couldn't kill any more time as their speech had already eaten up a lot of delivery time and who knew how long my talk was going to take.

I approached Nick at the desk and asked if I could talk with him for a minute. He said, "Uh oh! Ok, give me a minute and I'll meet you in the office".

We enter the office and Nick starts with, "Don't tell me you've got COVID cause, that would just kill us!".

I said, "Well, the good news is, no, I don't have it. The bad news is that, I'm going to have to resign."

Nick held his head for a moment and processed the information. "Ohhhh mannn….."

He appeared to have had to deal with this on many occasions and, after a beat, shifted into a professional way of going about processing an exit so that, the machine can keep moving. There's no time for a long, drawn out discussion. After some chit chat, he said, "This job isn't what it used to be. I'm going to need you to fill out a form."

I whipped it out and I think he was a little surprised. We shook hands and he wished me the best. I returned the well wishes and, got out of the office as fast as I could.

In the following two weeks, I was put on a variety of routes and I waited to see how the rumor mill would process the news of my departure. I didn't say a word about anything and just kept my head down and tried to do the job that was expected of me.

During those two weeks I was assigned to both the west and east side and that was fine, as it gave me a good overall look at what I had just endured at various levels of success. I'm not sure how most handle themselves during the final two weeks of a lame duck situation but, as I've said, with this job, you just can't "dog it". You're either full on or don't even bother. Honestly, it's the day-in, day-out of that, which wears on a person. Even as a dishwasher in a Chinese restaurant in High School, there were lulls in the waves of dirty dishes containing poked through remains of food where I had a moment to have a drink and stare out of the window and think, for a second, what teenagers think about.

Not so with this gig! And frankly, I'm too old for it. Staring into space has not only become a favorite pass-time but, a necessity to my survival.

However, I am a short-timer. I'm a one digit midget! The end was very near and, it does make the remaining work to be done just a little more palatable and gave me the opportunity to start processing how to put this experience to words. I had kept thorough notes from the very beginning and consulted my notebook, tucked away in my backpack, whenever I had something I thought should be remembered. It's going to take me while to review the mass of these notes and compile them into some sort of descriptive. But, I'm not undaunted.

Rather than name names of those who had something to say to me during the last days of my time with the USPS, I thought I'd just list them in no particular order. And I must say that these words are not contained in any notes, rather, in my memories which I hope will endure.

- "I hear you're leaving us. That's a shame."
- "Couldn't take it, huh?
- "Great, now I've gotta do this 2-ton shit all by myself?"
- You've had enough huh? I'll tell you, if I didn't start when I did fifteen years ago, there's no way that I could do this job now!"
- "You're fucking me!"
- "The good one's leave and the shit one's stay!"
- "This job isn't what it used to be. You're going to gain back all the weight you lost!"

And my favorite; with a soft handshake and genuine well wishes from a young lady I always found entertaining and made me smile, "Spallone, it was a pleasure working with you. You were one of the best. I wish you luck. Congratulations, you did something the rest of us couldn't do; you got the hell out of here!"

On my last day, there were no morning speeches. No, "It's Tom's last day, there're bagels and donuts in the break room.", no words at all. I returned from yet another long hot day of delivering, to an almost vacant office. No one was around except for a clerk going back and forth, doing what they do.

I sorted the returned mail, placed the vehicle key on its hook, put the scanner back into its recharging station, turned-in my arrow key and swiped out at the time clock after entering the appropriate code:

ET (End Tour).

Chapter 25 – Post Postal

As irony seems to be the order of business lately, on my first day as a "civilian", a Postal vehicle pulled up to the house and delivered a large box. I sympathetically thanked the carrier and as they drove off, I began opening the package. The box contained all the uniform items I had ordered with my uniform voucher, including the Pith helmet.

I needed some time to digest what I'd just experienced in the previous months and I didn't begin to try to make sense of it all until about a month later. I got to experience a little bit of what the rest of the country had been going through due to the pandemic by not intermingling with much of society. For me, it was therapeutic, while for those who had been enduring the isolation and frustration of not being able to move about or, at least operate on anything resembling a normal way of life they'd gotten used to, proved in some cases to be life altering.

The Covid-19 virus was still going strong and cutting families down by either death or, by not being able to at least be with, or normally process the death of, a loved one. As of this writing, I'd lost four relatives myself. And there doesn't seem to be any relief in sight in the near future. The world, as we used to know it, is on hold with maniacal elevator music playing in the background.

And yet, the mail doesn't stop. It never stops.

Chapter 25

"Neither snow nor rain nor heat nor gloom of night stays these couriers from the swift completion of their appointed rounds."

Fuckin'-A right! However, be it known that this saying is not an official motto of the United States Postal Service. That it is generally known as one, is a testament to the mettle of the American postal worker. You're going to get your mail. Make no mistake about that. All you need is a little bit of reasonable patience at times but, whether you want it or not, you're going to get it.

As Seinfeld's "Newman" said to Kramer;

"Calm down everyone, no one's cancelling any mail!"

Kramer: "Oh yes I am!"

Newman: "But what about your bills?"

Kramer: "The bank can pay them."

Newman: "The bank.... What about your cards and letters?"

Kramer: "Email! Telephone, fax machine, FedEx, Telex, Telegram...Holograms..."

Newman: "Alright, it's true! Of course no one NEEDS mail! Whatya think you're so clever figuring that one out!? But you don't know the half of what goes on here!... So just walk away Kramer. I beg of you!"

I sit at the computer and write with my Pith Helmut on for inspiration and looking like an idiot. Maria walks in and said, "Is that the hat you made such a big deal about getting? You look like an idiot!"

Three months later I'm at a Wawa and pumping my own gas, successfully mind you. I see the 2-ton truck on the side of the building and then I see Tim rushing out from inside. I finish with what I was doing and head over to the truck. Tim was nowhere in sight. I stuck my head through the open passenger side window where I had greeted the police during a BLM protest only months earlier. "Hey, what the hell is goin' on in there?

Tim appeared from the depts of the truck with sandwich crumbs around his mouth and still chewing. "Oh Hey! They got me on three different routes today and one that I have never been on. I'm trying to choke down this sandwich so I can get to the first round of pickups in time but, with these routes they got me on, there's no way I'm going to be finished in time in order to get back to do the afternoon pickups! There's no way! It's so fucked up!!"

"How are you Timothy?"

Tim slows himself. "Ugh, sorry. They got me so wound up I don't know if I'm coming or going. But you know me, I can't complain. How are you?"

We chatted and I cut the conversation shorter than I would have like because, I didn't want to keep him. We promised to grab a beer sometime and we parted but, I knew the truth. There's no time for that. The man gets one day off a week and he's not going to spend it telling war stories over warm beer with the likes of me. And I don't blame him.

He's been on the job (as I would have been by that time) for eight months and he's still chasing his ass. He's still unsure of the day. That can't be right. Especially if looked at it from the uneducated point of view of, assuming that all that is needed is to go door-to-door and bring the necessity items to that location. Perhaps that IS was it's really all about but, it's just not that simple to execute. There's just something wrong with the way things are done at the Postal Service.

And how can, after all these years, it continue to operate this way? Surely they're aware of their own pitfalls and shortcomings. But I believe that part of it can be attributed to the same malady that a lot of long term relationships tend to fall under where, as time goes by, day to day existence becomes insular where it's hard to look at objectively from the outside anymore. And therefore, it's difficult to identify the problems at hand, and certainly almost impossible to correct without shaking the relationship to its very foundation. It's hard to fix a car when it's travelling at 70mph. You need to take it off the road and put it up on jacks and take a breath to gather the proper tools and replacement parts, or else, you're just duct taping things and hoping for the best.

In my humble opinion, perhaps it's trying to kill a fly with a shotgun when thinking that the United States Postal Service should be dismantled and services replaced by private delivery companies. But, no doubt, there's work that needs to be done. And it's change that probably wouldn't sit well with the masses within, as well as outside the service. Something has to fall. I don't personally feel that there needs to be a Saturday delivery, or Amazon Sunday delivery, in an effort to create a less abrasive work environment for the carrier where they can work a semi relatively standard 9-5, M-F schedule on a salary vs hourly pay scale, toward the preservation of a more healthy home/office working environment. I had heard that, since my resignation, Larry, (from the Dark Side) was incapacitated by some sort of heart issues and was in the hospital. I'm not surprised. This might also help with being able to retain temporary "part-time" help as CCAs/RCAs would then be able to be scheduled on a more regular and consistent basis and thereby, dare I say, be able to have more of a life?

Perhaps the USPS should take the next step in becoming its own entity and being financially independent from the U.S. Government and run itself like a true private company. But that's going to mean a massive rate hike and, part and parcel, massive salary increases with incentives for employee retention. Or, perhaps a look could be taken at the abolishment of the prefunded pension in favor of a more standard 401K plan. And, even more radical, revert back to how the Post Office ran in its early years; do completely away with the last mile delivery. Reconstruct each Post Office in each town to be a multi-level storage facility of sorts (they're there anyway) where each address has a Post Office box where mail can be picked up by each owner at will at any time day or night.

Of course, someone's going to have to figure out how to employ the majority of the 600,000 Postal employees who would have to take the fall under that plan.

On June 17, 2020, Louis DeJoy was appointed to the office of U.S. Postmaster General by the Board of Governors of the United States Postal Service. Upon taking office, he implemented a series of cost-cutting measures within the Postal Service such as banning overtime, cancelling late or extra trips to deliver mail, removing and dismantling hundreds of high-speed sorting machines, and removing some under-used collection boxes from streets. That confirms, once again, the answer to my Son of Sam question. And I loved the suggestion of cancelling late or extra trips to deliver the mail. Wasn't that MY original suggestion of, "If we can't get it done today, what harm will it do if it gets delivered tomorrow?" Perhaps I should have shot higher and applied for the position of Postmaster General.

The initial implementation of his changes caused significant delays in mail delivery and it resulted in an investigation by Congressional committees and the USPS Inspector General.

DeJoy was an outsider. He came to the Postal Service from the private sector, never having any prior experience in the trenches of the mail delivery game. Prior to his appointment, he was CEO of a North Carolina-based firm with interests in real estate, private equity, consulting and project management.

But, there lies evidence that someone from the outside with fresh eyes can assess a given situation and come in and do a hatchet job on a perceived broken business model and claim to be trying to breathe new life into the Service. The result of which was met with opposition and he was accused of "deliberate sabotage" of the Postal Service.

In August of 2020, DeJoy announced that the changes that he implemented would be suspended and in October, the USPS agreed to reverse all the changes that he made.

The USPS Board of Governors, who appointed DeJoy as Postmaster General, were all selected by President Donald Trump and confirmed by the Senate despite concerns about conflicts of interest as, prior to his appointment, DeJoy was a Republican Party fundraiser and donated $1.2 million to Donald Trump's campaign in both 2016 and 2020.

The chess moves by President Trump were impressive in an apparent attempt to manipulate the situation for his ultimate goal of USPS abolishment.

But even with that, the drastic changes needed were extremely hard to implement. How can these needed changes be made without causing a major blood bath with either the employment pool or for the citizens in which they serve? Baby-stepping won't seem to do the job and there just may have to be a drastic occurrence where the Postal Service's claims of running out of money and shutting down, may need to occur in order for meaningful changes to take effect. If not, I'm afraid the Postal Service is just rearranging the deck chairs on the Titanic.

As for the allegations of voter fraud with relation to the Postal Service misplacing or not delivering or flat out, disposing of mail-in ballots; I'll say this, I'm certainly no fan of how the process of voting for elected "leaders" of this country have been bogarted and turned into a three ring circus. I have no doubt that there are misadventures in this, and every election. It all depends on your interpretation. For me, that the will of the people may be overturned by a group of appointed individuals is indicative of a tainted process. However, the process is allowed to continue due to the wording of the Constitution. But, like the person who references the Constitution as a fallback position on why they should not be required to wear a mask during a pandemic because it infringes on their freedoms, the entire Constitution becomes rife with controversy and interpretation.

Are election ballots somehow compromised by the USPS? I can report that, if they are, it is not done at the local level. From the beginning of early voting in the State of Florida, every ballot went to each addressee. Are addresses incorrect? That's someone else's issue. When the ballots are filled out and properly returned in the vessel to which they're supposed to be, rest assured that they are retrieved by a USPS carrier and taken safely back to the office and gathered and put on a tractor trailer at the end of each and every day with the intention that they reach their destination properly.

If ballots go missing, they go missing upstream of the local Post Office.

And even if they do, I fail to see that the number of missing ballots can actually make an impactful difference in the outcome of an election. From the view of an internal ballot processor, I just don't see it happening.

If the issue is a timing one, a suggestion for improvement can be that all mail-in ballots should be postmarked no later than October 1st of an election year. Even during a pandemic, I would think that all ballots would be able to reach Washington, D.C. within five weeks and be at the ready to be counted by Election day.

I can armchair quarterback with the best of them and I know that serious problems exist within the United States Postal Service that extend far beyond the Board of Elections and I have no delusions that my little journal might actually have a positive impact. I'm just calling them as I see them.

A career within the Postal Service is a noble and good one. However, it's my suggestion that, if you're over thirty five years old, don't even think about it. It's not for the faint of heart, or body, or mind, or family.

Start young, grind it out, tuff it out and, after a seemingly long period of years, you'll be in good standing. The problem is, after putting in a great amount of time, you'd be hard pressed to find a better deal of employment after putting in that much time and effort. You might as well stay the course and retire at the job. As we used to say in the Navy at sea for a long time, "The days go slow, but the years go fast!"

In the months since leaving the service, I was able to put some distance between my experience and the now more everyman perspective of the USPS and, I'd sometimes retrace a mail delivery route while driving my car. I was on the east side recently and I was retracing the route in with I had so many problems with juggling the DPS, the Flats, the SPRs, the sweat soaked advos that I had to peel from my arm to deliver, the dog spray at the ready, the unbearable heat…and as I drove along the quiet, manicured homes of Deerfield Beach, Fl, I pictured myself as the mailman there, walking door to door, delivering anticipated and important messages to the residences, and I thought, "Hmph, this looks like it could be a pretty good job for someone!"

Acknowledgments

My views contained within these writings are just that, my interpretations of the events and information presented to me at any given time. And because of that, one must acknowledge that, they can simply be off the mark. Some people see aqua as blue, some see it as more green. I have trouble with both (I'm told).

This was a work of creative non-fiction. No incidents described in these pages were fictionalized, although embellishments have been made in certain circumstances in the interest of creative license. Every name mentioned are creations of my own and therefore, don't implicate any one individual for culpability in any situation.

I would like to thank the USPS for providing the materials conveyed to me so that I may absorb, interpret and reword the information, so as to attempt to create an interesting and creative journal of events in fair representation. And of course, the gratitude in providing me the opportunity to experience working as a City Carrier Assistant in order that I may try to convey the demands of the job in literature.

My sincere gratitude and apologies to Maria, my life partner, who had to endure the many days of my frustration, anger, stories-of-the-road, and exhaustion. "Wait'll you hear what happened today!"

One year later, Tim is still on the job. He kept me abreast of his endurance during the holiday season reporting that, he had something like forty hours of overtime during the busiest pay period. Those are 60 hour work weeks during a time when people like to spend it with their families. From what I understand, he plans on sticking with it, although, one year after hire, the USPS fires the employee, for a week. And then, the situation is reevaluated and the employee may or may not be asked to return. I still don't understand why this occurs. Yet another grandfathered USPS peculiarity.

To the carriers of the United States Postal Service as a whole, and more specifically, the Deerfield Beach, Fl annex and east side offices; to the superhuman magicians who, day in and day out, turn mountains of …shit… into satisfied smiles of completed anticipation, I bow in awe at your perseverance and endurance. Frankly, I don't know how you do it!

As of this writing, Carl Higgins has refrained from fully "Going Postal".

Tom Spallone
January 2021

References

The following are works I used as sources as well as guidance in this endeavor and are highly suggested as further reading on the subjects of immersive writing, the history of the USPS, intelligence, and, of course, SoS.

Ted Conover, *Immersion: A Writer's Guide to Going Deep*, (2016), The University of Chicago Press, Chicago, Il, 60637

Maury Terry, *The Ultimate Evil: An Investigation into America's Most Dangerous Satanic Cult,* (1987). A Dolphin Book, Doubleday & Company, Inc. Garden City, New York, ISBO-385-23452-X

U.S. Government Publication 100, (2020), *The United States Postal Service: An American History*, The United States Postal Service

Douglas Hofstadter, *Gödel, Escher, Back: An eternal Golden Braid*, (1979), Basic Books, ISBN 978-0-465-02656-2

References

CPSIA information can be obtained
at www.ICGtesting.com
Printed in the USA
LVHW051600210221
679588LV00013B/185

9 781736 291894